LEFT FIELD

GRAEME LE SAUX

Left Field

HarperSport

An Imprint of HarperCollins*Publishers*

HarperCollins*Publishers*
77–85 Fulham Palace Road,
Hammersmith, London W6 8JB

www.harpercollins.co.uk

First published in 2007 by HarperSport
an Imprint of HarperCollins London
1

A CIP catalogue record for this book
is available from the British Library

ISBN 13 978-0-00-722581-1
ISBN 10 0-00-722581-4

Printed and bound in Great Britain by
Clays Ltd, St Ives plc

All photographs supplied courtesy of Graeme Le Saux with the
exception of the following: Action Images 4 (top), 10 (top left),
12 (middle and bottom); Alpha 10 (bottom); Colorsport 3, 5 (top),
6 (top), 9 (top), 10 (top right), 11 (middle), 13 (bottom);
Express Syndication 5 (bottom left), 7 (bottom); Getty 11 (top);
ITV 15 (top right); Luckhurst 13 (middle); Mirrorpix 16 (top left);
Offside 4 (bottom), 15 (bottom); PA/Empics 6 (bottom), 7 (top), 8,
9 (bottom), 12 (top), 14 (top), 15 (top left); Reuters 11 (bottom);
Solo 5 (bottom right), 13 (top), 14 (bottom); Wire (top right).

For Mariana, Georgina and Lucas.
I'm proud of my professional achievements,
but nothing could make me more proud
than our family

Contents

Introduction

I am a lucky man. I've got a wife I adore and two children I dote on. I have a loving father and two sisters of whom I'm very proud. Once, I had a mother who doted on me. I've got a good life and a lovely house and I know I have an awful lot to be thankful for. I owe my material possessions to my career in football. The opportunities that are coming my way in the media and in business now also stem from the fact that I was a high-profile sportsman. And I'm proud of the links I still have with Chelsea and the ambassadorial role I have been asked to fulfil for them. I have every reason to be grateful to the game for the things it has brought me, but it hasn't come easy. I was a man apart for much of my career. I came out of left field and, for a long time, I stayed there.

I was regarded as an irritating curiosity when I first signed as a professional footballer with Chelsea in late 1987. I was ridiculed for reading *The Guardian* rather than staring at the half-naked women on page 3 or raging at the stories on the back pages of the tabloids that the players reading them swore were lies. But they kept reading them. Partly because of me, partly because of them, I didn't fit in. Partly because of an experience that had affected me in Jersey when I was thirteen, there was an urge to succeed inside me that made me more sensitive than I might otherwise have been. I was coming out of left field, a callow kid raised in the Channel Islands who knew nothing of the wider world, and most people didn't know quite what to make of me.

Because I had different interests to the rest of my team-mates, because I didn't feel comfortable in the pre-*Loaded* laddish drinking culture that was prevalent in English football in the late Eighties, it was generally assumed by my team-mates that there was something wrong with me. It followed from that, naturally, that I must be gay. For fourteen years, I had to listen to that suggestion repeated in vivid and forthright terms from thousands of voices in the stands. I seemed to be everybody's favourite whipping boy.

My colleague at Stamford Bridge, Graham Stuart, who had a fine career with Chelsea, Everton and Charlton, says now that I was ahead of my time when we played for Bobby Campbell in the late Eighties. Off the pitch, he meant, obviously – a renaissance footballer in a dark age. Well, I was certainly in a minority. He was right about that. I just liked different things, ironically the kind of things footballers like now: a nice meal, an afternoon's shopping, a trip to the cinema or a gig at The Fridge in Brixton, getting ready for the next game, feeling the intensity of a life in sport. Now, the traditional English approach I grew up with, where men were men and only women wore sarongs and used moisturizer, has been completely shattered. The pendulum has swung. It's more acceptable for players to talk about the clothes they wear, the restaurants they frequent, the bars they go to. And, yes, the latest game for their PlayStation or the latest innovation on their iPod.

It would have been easier for me back in the early days if I could have found it inside me to subordinate my personality to the group and do what it took to blend in. But I was taking care of my diet when the team coach was still stopping at the fish and chip shop on the way back from away matches. I was hanging out at an Armenian café called Jakob's in Gloucester Road in west London while 'The Lads' were organizing pub crawls. Again, it wasn't that one was better than the other. Jakob's wouldn't be everyone's idea of fun; I know that. But I liked it. It was just that I fell out of their 'norm'. As far as the culture off the pitch was concerned, I pitched up ten years too early.

My Chelsea career spanned different worlds. I started it playing with Kerry Dixon, Steve Wicks and John McNaught. I ended it alongside Marcel Desailly, Gianfranco Zola and Jimmy Floyd Hasselbaink. I gravitated towards the couple of foreign lads at the club in my first spell and people called me a homosexual. I gravitated towards the mass of foreign lads at the club in my second spell and people called me cosmopolitan.

That was the funny thing about my life in football, the theme that runs through it. Football began to move towards me; events conspired to help me. In 1995, when I was winning the Premiership title with Blackburn Rovers, the Bosman ruling came into force and changed the face of the game in this country. Bosman swept away the quota system that had limited the number of foreigners allowed to play in each team and, flooded by players from all over Europe, our game entered an age of enlightenment.

I wasn't an outsider any more; I wasn't perceived as being different. Football old-schoolers like former Chelsea captains Peter Nicholas and Graham Roberts, who had regarded me as a dork, a swot and a pretentious weirdo, didn't hold sway any more. Traditional bastions of English football clubs – men who ruled by intimidation and bullying – began to be marginalized, and a culture that rewarded professionalism, instead of pouring scorn on it, took hold.

There were more changes in the three decades in which I played football in England than there have been in any other era of the game. The horrors of Heysel and Hillsborough were washed away by Gazza's tears in the 1990 World Cup and the football boom that England's run to the semi-finals in Italy engendered. The *Fever Pitch* generation rose up in the Nineties and suddenly it was trendy to be a football obsessive. There was the Britpop influence, too. A lot of the successful bands of the Nineties were made up of football fans who were always making reference to the sport they loved. I was friends with one of the lads in the Inspiral Carpets who was an Oldham fan, Noel and Liam Gallagher were Man City fans and Tim Booth from James was a Leeds fan. Together, they crossed the music–student–football divide and broadened the appeal of the game. The Lightning Seeds did the theme tune for Euro 96 and the separation between footballers and pop stars became more and more blurred. The Taylor Report forced football stadia into a brave new world, too, and when the Premier League was formed in

Introduction

1992 and soon flooded with money from Sky TV, it made players into millionaires pretty much overnight.

I was part of that; I rode the wave. I went from an era when people like Ken Bates, David Moores and Doug Ellis owned football clubs to the age of Roman Abramovich and the invasion of the international oligarchs. I played for the only team apart from Manchester United, Arsenal and Chelsea who has ever won the Premiership. I played thirty-six times for England. I didn't get carried away with it. I never lost my obsession with winning and my hunger to keep moving forward as a player. I was relentless about it. I never looked back. I didn't like looking back – not after what had happened to my mum.

It wasn't as if I had it easy, either. For a start, I had people chanting 'Le Saux takes it up the arse' at me wherever I played. What an incentive that was never to make a mistake. Even in the winter of my career, playing for Southampton in a reserve game against West Ham at Upton Park, this young kid in the West Ham side started yelling abuse at me, spitting 'faggot' and 'queer' at me. I told him that when he'd achieved what I'd achieved in the game, he could come back and talk to me. At half-time, I heard him getting a bollocking from West Ham's reserve team boss.

I enjoyed highs and I saw lows. I heard the snap of Robbie di Matteo's leg breaking in Chelsea's UEFA Cup match against St Gallen. When Pierluigi Casiraghi's career came to a terrible end at West Ham, I ran off the pitch and grabbed the stretcher from the St John's Ambulance men who were standing in the tunnel while he was in agony on the floor with terrible injuries to his leg. I saw the grief and the pain that football can bring as well as the riches and the glamour. I saw the last snapshot of Chelsea before the revolution: its extravagance cheek by jowl with its miserliness, and the fantastic idiosyncrasies of the Ken Bates era. I was man of the match in the game that took Chelsea into the Champions League and made it viable for Abramovich to buy them.

I went to Buckingham Palace to meet the Queen. That was in the summer of 1998 after the World Cup in France when we had been knocked out in the second round. The squads from the Commonwealth countries involved in the tournament – England, Scotland and Jamaica – were invited to the palace and being driven into the courtyard behind the railings felt to me as if the gates of Willy Wonka's Chocolate Factory were swinging open and I was being ushered into a secret world that I had long imagined but never glimpsed.

Once we were inside, we were led up to one of the reception rooms and we all stood around in small groups, chattering away nervously until Her Majesty arrived. Soon enough, a door opened and the Queen walked in and made straight for the group that I was part of. She came up to me and asked the first of what I am sure are her standard questions. She asked me who I played for and when I said Chelsea, she seemed quite pleased. 'Oh,' she said, 'local.'

On the other side of the room, Sol Campbell was being introduced to Prince Phillip.

'What part of Jamaica are you from?' the Duke of Edinburgh enquired.

'Walthamstow,' Sol said.

At the other end of the scale, I remember the simple, visceral thrill of wrapping the white tape around my socks when I was preparing for games, just like one of my heroes, John Robertson, had once done. I loved Robertson as a player. He was left-footed like me and he was part of Brian Clough's great Nottingham Forest side that carried all before it when I was growing up.

I chipped Peter Schmeichel once, too. I played my first stand-out game for Chelsea against Spurs in 1991 and rushed home to catch the highlights on the television but the Gulf War had broken out and the programme had been cancelled. I scored my only England goal against Brazil; it wasn't a bad one, either. I played against some great opponents; if I had to pick my most difficult one, I'd say Brian Laudrup.

I did have my own share of injuries. I missed Euro 96 and Euro 2000 but at least I made it to the World Cup in France in 1998. Apart from the moment when I broke my ankle in 1995, that World Cup gave me my worst moment in football – when I was blamed for the late Dan Petrescu goal that gave Romania a 2–1 win over England in our second group game. Generally, though, I felt I over-achieved in football. I gave it everything and it gave back to me a lot more than I ever dared hope for.

In the end, I even learned the gift of being able to laugh at myself. I wish I'd been able to do that earlier. I wish I'd been able to ignore it back in 1991 when people started sniggering about how they thought I must be gay. In my second spell at Chelsea, I was at the core of the dressing room. I was secure in myself. People even laughed at my jokes and I laughed at theirs.

I used to take the mickey out of Gianfranco Zola, who was a particular friend of mine during my second spell at

Chelsea. I used to tease him about his image of being the White Knight of Stamford Bridge, adored by all for his ready smile and his sublime skill. People had such a fantastic image of Franco, they could not imagine him being anything other than honest and truthful and the epitome of good sportsmanship, but I knew different.

One day in training, we were all square in a five-a-side game and Franco and I were running for a ball that was heading out of play. It went out so I turned around to shout something to one of my team-mates. When I looked back around, Franco had retrieved the ball and was in the act of curling a beautiful shot around our goalkeeper for the winner. He was adamant that the ball hadn't gone out and when I disputed it, the other guys looked at me as if I was disputing the word of a saint.

'Franco,' I said, 'you're a cheating, low-down Sardinian git. When I write my book, I'm going to tell the truth about you and let everyone know what a sneaky, low-down, horrible little man you are.'

'That's fine,' Franco said. 'And when I write my book, I'm going to say that you look at me in the showers.'

ONE

Camping with Ken

A sad and ugly irony lay at the heart of my career as a professional footballer. I represented my country thirty-six times, won a Premiership title with Blackburn Rovers and the Cup Winners' Cup and Super Cup with Chelsea, played in an FA Cup Final and won the League Cup, and all of it was accompanied by the soundtrack of a lie. Even though I have never been gay, for a fourteen-year stretch of my eighteen seasons in the game, I became the leading victim of English football's last taboo.

It started in the summer of 1991 soon after we reported back for pre-season training. I was in my first spell at Chelsea. We had what is known as 'a strong dressing room' – which is usually a euphemism for a group of players who were very good at dishing out a lot of stick. It was not a place for shrinking violets. The banter was flying around more than ever in those first few days back at our Harlington training ground. There was a lot of talk about where people had been for their holidays.

1

I'd had a good summer. I was twenty-two and had just broken into the first team. Over the previous eighteen months, I'd got matey with two of the forerunners of Chelsea's foreign legion: Ken Monkou and Erland Johnsen. Ken, who was originally from Surinam, had signed from Feyenoord in the spring of 1989 and we made our first-team debuts within a fortnight of each other that May. Erland, who was Norwegian, arrived from Bayern Munich the following December. During that season and the next one, the three of us became good pals.

Erland invited Ken and me to go and visit him in Norway once the 1990/91 campaign was over. He wanted us to go and put on a few coaching sessions for some kids in a town on the border with Russia. So when the season finished, I took Ken down to Jersey, where I'd grown up. We spent a couple of days there and then we drove up through France, Belgium and Holland. Then we flew up to Norway. We had a good time. When the trip was over, Ken headed back to London, Erland went on his honeymoon around the Caribbean and I went off on holiday with my girlfriend.

When I got back to Chelsea and the boys asked me where I'd been, I told them. Somebody – I can't remember who – said 'Oh, so you went camping with Ken'. There was a bit of chortling and sniggering. It got to me straight away. I was sensitive about it immediately. I bit on it. I told them we hadn't gone camping. I told them we'd been staying in hotels. But it stuck. It became a bit of a running gag. And soon, to my horror, it was out there on the grapevine that Ken and I were an item.

I was insecure enough as it was. I had come over from Jersey a couple of years earlier when I was eighteen and signed a professional contract. I felt isolated from the start. I didn't belong to any of the groups or cliques I found at Chelsea. I didn't do an apprenticeship so there was no group of lads that I'd come through the ranks with. And just because I had signed a professional contract didn't really make me a professional footballer or part of the established group.

There were a lot of old-school footballers there when I arrived: men like Steve Wicks, Joe McLaughlin, Colin Pates and John Bumstead. They were soon joined by lads like Vinnie Jones, who arrived at the start of that 1991/92 season from Sheffield United, Andy Townsend, John Spencer and Dennis Wise. Some of them were good guys but I never got to know them during that time. They were footballers and I was this kid fresh out of Jersey. They would go back to their homes in Hemel Hempstead or wherever it was and I would get the tube back to my digs in Burnt Oak.

The club had stuck me in there. It was one stop away from the northern end of the Northern Line, about as far away from Harlington as you could get. It took me an hour and a half and two trains and two buses to get into training each day. It was ridiculous. It was one of these situations where the assistant manager, Gwyn Williams, knew a friend of a friend who had a spare room and was doing him a favour. But he wasn't doing me any favours at all.

Everybody regarded me as an outsider. I was an easy target because I didn't fit in. The only couple of people I knew in London were students so I turned up at training with my student look. I had my jeans rolled up and my Pringle socks on and my rucksack with *The Guardian* in it.

For much of my career, reading *The Guardian* was used as one of the most powerful symbols of how I was supposed to be weirdly different. It was pathetic really. It was used to give substance to the gossip that I was homosexual: *Guardian* reader equals gay boy. Some people really thought that added up. Most of the rest of them read *The Sun* and *The Mirror* and complained about how they were being stitched up all the time by those papers.

Andy Townsend got on the bus to an away game once and saw me reading *The Guardian*. He picked it up and said he wanted to look at the sport. He threw it back down a couple of seconds later. 'There's no fucking sport in here,' he said. The rest of the lads laughed. I tried to laugh, too, but I felt a bit embarrassed – not embarrassed enough to stop reading it and conform to what they wanted but embarrassed nonetheless. I don't know, maybe they were just trying to help me fit in.

By the time I broke into the first team at the end of that 1988/89 season, the other players had pigeonholed me as a bit of a loner. I wasn't a loner. In fact, away from football I was pretty sociable. It was just that because of my background, I wasn't what footballers regarded as typical. I got the impression they hadn't really come across anyone like me before and that was the basis of a fair amount of stick I used to get.

Everything that led up to the spread of the rumours that I was gay stemmed from the fact that I didn't fit in. Team-mates looked at me and thought I was a bit different, a bit odd. So I became the target of day-to-day ribbing which just got worse and worse. I'd never had any problem with bully-ing at school. I never had any sort of problems of that type. I wasn't the main kid but I wasn't unpopular. Being a pariah was new to me.

I was sensitive and pretty naive and my greatest fault was that I stuck up for myself and took things a bit more seriously than I should have done. I reacted to jibes when I can see now that I should have just laughed them off or come back with a decent riposte. But I didn't do that. And by the time I started to try and laugh them off, it was too late.

Going into training became an ordeal. I was trying to get used to London, trying to get used to living away from the tight-knit community in Jersey. And I was trying to persuade myself that I really could make it as a professional footballer. All the people I was competing against seemed so much older than me. So I lived in my own world with my Walkman and my newspaper and spent my spare time discovering London, like anyone new to a big city.

Ken and Erland used to get plenty of stick, too. This was partly because they were doing their own thing; they didn't fit the stereotype. Foreign players had a better attitude to diet even back then. The British lads used to take the mickey out of Erland and pretend he was from a different planet just because he had a Scandinavian accent. But I had more in common with Erland and Ken, and so when the three of us went on this trip, it was manna from heaven for the piss-takers.

I think Ken probably got some ribbing about the gay stuff. He was a good-looking guy, single, did his own thing. In the programme that season, he listed his hobbies as 'swimming, reading and meditation'. He probably ticked some of the boxes the bigots look at; but I don't think it ever got to the same level that it reached with me. He was guilty by association with me but that was it. The more successful I got, the more it became an issue. The focus was more on me than Ken because I gradually became more newsworthy. I was also a lot easier to rile.

Once all the taunts about homosexuality started, Ken and I drifted apart. We stopped being friends, really. You succumb to the pressure, I think. When I left Chelsea, he went his way and I went mine. It's not anything we ever spoke about which is quite strange in a way. None of the other players ever sympathized with me about it. I suppose they were just glad none of it was aimed at them; or perhaps the people who had initiated it felt embarrassed about it.

I took the homosexuality stuff very seriously very quickly. In those days, if anyone thought you had the slightest hint of the effeminate about you, you were in trouble. It was such a delicate stage of my life anyway. I already felt like the odds were stacked against me without being pitched into a world of double entendres and nudging and winking about being gay. I didn't feel comfortable in my environment unless I was playing football. But the more my supposed homosexuality became a topic of humour, the more upset about it I became. I started confronting people about it all the time. It felt like everyone else in the dressing room was in on it. It even extended to people like Gwyn who would wander up to me before training and say 'Come on poof, get your boots on'. It chipped away at me.

Bobby Campbell had succeeded John Hollins as manager by then but neither he nor anyone else in authority said 'Lads, look, this is getting a bit silly'. By now the rumours were out of control. The piss-taking about camping with Ken started some time around the beginning of July and eight weeks later, my worst fears were realized.

On 7 September, we went to play a league game against West Ham at Upton Park. I got the ball on the left flank some time in the first half and played it upfield. Then the chant started. It came from the hard-core fans in the North Bank and was set to the tune of the Village People's 'Go West': 'Le Saux takes it up the arse, Le Saux takes it up the arse,' they yelled – again and again and again. I stood there in shock. 'Oh my God, that's it,' I thought. 'It's reached the terraces.' I knew fans everywhere were going to try and make my life a misery.

Justin Fashanu had 'come out' in the *News of the World* a year earlier and even though his career was practically over, he was ridiculed and scorned for his admission. A few years later, he committed suicide. There also had been rumours about Trevor Morley and Ian Bishop, two West Ham players. They probably had about as much foundation as the rumours about me and Ken. I didn't think I could afford for people to think there was the slightest hint of me being gay. Everything I was worried about, my preoccupation with being isolated and ostracized, was now turning into reality. Suddenly, I had something else to cope with as I tried to make it as a footballer, something else I had to fight against.

That afternoon at West Ham really scared me. I felt it had the potential to ruin everything. I didn't know how to deal with it. It left me feeling isolated on the pitch. It left me feeling apart from the team, even on the pitch which had been my last refuge. I didn't know who to be angry with, because it was my own team-mates who had started it.

It made me even more sensitive and my life at Chelsea even more complicated. It was the start of a series of problems for me at the club that ended with me hurling my shirt to the floor when Campbell's successor, Ian Porterfield, substituted me and my departure from Stamford Bridge soon afterwards. I was very insecure, very nervous. I kept myself to myself because I didn't feel I could trust anyone.

At Upton Park, no one mentioned the chanting when we got back to the dressing room at half-time, or at full-time. No one spoke about it at all. Maybe it didn't register with some of them. It was never discussed and I didn't make a point of saying to any of them 'Thanks a lot for that boys'. But after that game, the chanting about me grew more and more regular. The pressure I was under when the taunts about being homosexual took hold was immense. I would go out onto the pitch knowing that I was going to get a torrent of abuse before I had even kicked a ball. Normally, as a player, you want to stand out but you want to stand out for the right reasons. If you get stick from the away supporters because you have done something well, you can live with that. It's actually quite satisfying. But what started happening to me was that if there was some sort of lull in the game, I was the first fall-back option and the taunting would start. If the home fans got bored, they'd start singing about me.

I often wonder whether I could have prevented it. I tried damned hard to prevent it. I stood up for myself and got physically angry with people who pushed it too far, but I also withdrew more and more into my own little world to try and protect myself from the abuse so I wouldn't have to confront it.

Once the thing about me and Ken spread beyond the dressing room, it went crazy. It became an urban myth. Wisey's friends from Wimbledon would ask him about it; other players would talk to their mates at their former clubs. Soon, everyone was talking about it as if it was a fact. People said there was no smoke without fire. It was generally accepted – in football and in the media – that Ken and I were in some sort of closet relationship.

It never got to the point where I would go in the showers and someone would say 'Watch out boys, Graeme's around, backs to the wall'. But it was enough to give me a sense of isolation and paranoia. Once it really gained momentum, everything I did was used as evidence I was gay. The way I dressed, the music I listened to, the fact that I went to art galleries and read *The Guardian* all turned into more clues about my sexuality.

The sheer number of people that would ask me about the situation between me and Ken was bewildering. I got bits and pieces of abuse in the street: the odd shout of 'poof' or 'shirtlifter' from the other side of the road, mainly from lads trying to get a laugh from their mates. No one said it directly to my face unless they were in a crowd at a game but the variety of insults aimed at gay people became my specialist subject. The worst thing was when you'd go to get the ball for a corner or a throw and there would be some-body a couple of feet away from you in the front row. Their faces would be contorted with aggression and they'd be screaming this homophobic abuse at me that was often really vicious stuff. When it was that close and one-on-one, it was shocking.

Pretty soon, opposition players were winding me up about it on the pitch. It didn't happen that often but there were a couple of occasions when I responded or retaliated and all hell broke loose. When I made it an issue, the lack of action taken against the people responsible said a lot about the reluctance of the authorities to confront the problem, a reluctance that still exists today.

The media hounded me about it, too, particularly the tabloid newspapers. When I first started going out with Mariana while I was playing for Blackburn, she was a press officer for Camelot. The lottery was very high-profile back then and gradually people began to find out that we were seeing each other. A couple of papers started harassing her at work. They phoned up on the pretext of asking something about the lottery but pretty soon they dropped the pretence and started asking her about me.

The *Daily Star* was particularly persistent. Their reporter kept going on about how there were all these rumours about my sexuality and how the paper wasn't convinced we were actually seeing each other. Mariana could have lost her job because she was spending so much time fielding these crackpot calls. She had to go and see her boss about it. In the end, this guy from the *Star* rang again and blurted out 'Is he gay?' She just said 'Of course he isn't' and he said 'Thanks' and put the phone down. The following Friday, they ran a front page that said 'Homo Le Saux? Not my Graeme'. On the inside page, it had the rest of the story and there was a picture of me. Underneath the picture, they ran the caption 'Le Saux: all man'. It's funny now but at the time I was fuming. It was the day before a game and we were travelling. All the players were getting on the Blackburn team bus and Tim Sherwood asked me if I had seen the paper. The guys were upset for me. It felt like I had some support from them. In contrast to the way it had been at Chelsea.

I think they were genuinely mortified that I was having to go through all that kind of stuff. I wondered whether it was defamatory: being called gay if you weren't. In the context of football, I think it is, because, sadly, it could cost you your career. No manager would want to buy you, in those days, anyway. It's a terrible indictment of the game but I'm afraid it's true.

I was in my second spell at Chelsea when the real problems on the pitch began. Ironically, the atmosphere at the club had changed radically in the time I had been away. It was much less threatening, much less intimidating. Most of all, it was much more cosmopolitan. Ruud Gullit was the manager when they brought me back and they had recruited players like Gianluca Vialli, Roberto di Matteo, Gianfranco Zola and Frank Leboeuf. It could hardly have been more different from the dressing room I had left behind. From feeling like an alien in my first spell at the club, I fitted in easily second time around. Unfortunately, the age of enlightenment hadn't yet spread to some of my rivals at other clubs.

I had had four years at Blackburn Rovers by then, four years of an increasingly high profile and four years of taunts from opposition supporters. Everyone assumed that the fight between me and my Blackburn team-mate, David Batty, during an away game against Spartak Moscow in November 1995 had been over a gay insult he'd aimed at me but it wasn't, not really.

From the time the rumours about me being gay first surfaced that afternoon at West Ham, I got plenty of comments from other players about me being 'a faggot' or 'a queer'. It happened all the time. Robbie Savage was one of the players who seemed to get a particular thrill out of it. I guess that won't really surprise anyone. I told him he should say it all again to me at the end of the game when I'd tackled him a few times. I told him we could sort it out in a football way and then see if he still wanted to call me a poof. It was irrational really, schoolboy behaviour.

There weren't many players who went out of their way to keep going on about it. Most of the time, I let it go. But when Chelsea played Liverpool at Anfield in October 1997, Paul Ince started winding me up about it repeatedly and in the end, I gave him a taste of his own medicine.

Paul and I had always got on really, really well. We were England team-mates and I respected him a great deal. The game against Liverpool was a Sunday afternoon match and afterwards we were due to travel down to Burnham Beeches to meet up with the rest of Glenn Hoddle's England squad and start the preparations for the make-or-break World Cup qualifying game against Italy in Rome, which was the following Saturday.

Paul was really wound up during the game. He'd get so frantic in matches sometimes that his eyes would change – they'd kind of glaze over. There was a frenetic atmosphere at Anfield and it was an all-action game. They ended up winning it 4–2. I'd been clattered a few times already when Paul launched himself at me with a tackle, took my legs away and left me on the deck.

When I was on the ground, he started jabbering away at me. 'Come on you fucking poof,' he said, 'get up, there's nothing wrong with you.' He said it a few times. I let it go. People get called 'a poof' all the time in football. It's a generic term of abuse. But it was loaded when people aimed it at me. A few minutes later, he clattered me again and started yelling the same stuff. I snapped.

I said something that I knew would hurt him. I insulted his wife.

Paul went absolutely ballistic. He was livid. He spent the rest of the match desperately trying to kick lumps out of me. He was in a towering rage. When the final whistle went, I was going down the tunnel when I caught sight of him out of the corner of my eye about to try and land a punch on me. I ducked out of the way and scarpered back out onto the pitch. The guy had lost it completely: he wanted to kill me.

Paul was a prime example of a guy who could dish it out but couldn't take it. He had been calling me all the names under the sun, personal stuff that he must have known would hurt me, stuff that I found offensive. And yet as soon as I retaliated in kind, he couldn't cope. I didn't feel proud of what I'd said, and it was out of order. I knew his wife, Claire, and I liked her. It wasn't about her, though; it was about letting him know what it was like to try to have put up with that kind of abuse.

Paul quickly turned it round in his own mind so that I was the villain. I knew it was going to be very awkward when we got to Burnham Beeches to meet up with the rest of the England squad that night. I got there before him and there was plenty of banter among the lads sitting in the restaurant about what he was going to do to me when he arrived. I laughed nervously. I didn't want a punch-up with him – he was a lot stronger than me.

I decided I needed to be the adult about it. When it was obvious he had arrived, I phoned him in his room and asked if I could go up and talk to him about it. He was reluctant but he agreed. I got up there and he got into me straight away. 'You're out of order talking about my wife like that,' he said. 'You know her, and anyway no one talks about my family like that.'

I told him that I hadn't really known what I was saying but I asked him how he thought it made me feel when he was calling me 'a fucking poof'. I explained to him that I hadn't done it to insult his wife. Just to get back at him. But he wouldn't accept it; it was an honour thing for him. It's a shame, but ever since then my relationship with him has been very cold.

By then, the gay slurs had become a big part of my career. But the homophobia that surrounded me put me in a desperately difficult situation. It was difficult for me to keep denying I was gay and reacting angrily to any suggestion that I might be homosexual without being disrespectful to the homosexual community. Talking about something that isn't actually true makes it impossibly difficult to confront. That's why I didn't brave the issue in the newspapers.

I have gay friends and I don't judge them. I am not homophobic. If there was a gay player and he was part of a team I was playing for, that wouldn't be an issue for me at all. Someone's private life is entirely up to them. But when supporters and other players accused me of being gay, it got to me. It was complicated. I never believed there was anything wrong with being gay but I felt that if it came to be accepted that I was gay, I would be unable to continue as a professional footballer. That's how deep-seated the prejudice in the game is. That's why I fought back as strongly as I did.

Homosexuality really is football's last taboo. We've got past pretty much everything else. The problems with racism that disfigured football for much of the Seventies, Eighties and Nineties are not over but they are on the wane. An awful lot of good work has been done and attitudes have changed. You don't get people making monkey noises at English football grounds any more. You don't get supporters throwing bananas on the pitch as they used to do when John Barnes and Ces Podd were playing.

But there is still terrible prejudice within football. That is part of the culture. People try and pick on other people's weaknesses. You have to deal with constant mickey-taking and being derided for the most trivial matters: the trainers you have just bought, the haircut you have just had, the piece about you in the newspaper. It is endless and it can be draining. It is part of the competitive nature of the dressing room. Your team-mates are digging away all the time, trying to get one up on each other. If you can make someone else look stupid, that's the ideal.

Given that kind of peer pressure, I don't think a modern footballer could ever come out as a gay man. I don't think anyone could think of any positive reason to do it. It would immediately isolate you from the rest of the team. The group would be too hostile for you to survive. The situation would be too daunting.

Football has not had to deal with a group of gay footballers standing there and saying 'How are you going to deal
with us?' They haven't had to confront homophobia yet
because the gay footballers that are probably playing in our
leagues are understandably too frightened to declare their
homosexuality and cope with the backlash they would face.
Until there is a powerful voice for a minority group, football
will never make provision for it.

The abuse I had to suffer would be multiplied by 100 for a
player who was openly gay. The burden would be too much.
I think of the stick I had from the fans and it made me feel
anxious and nervous even before I got out on the pitch.
Sometimes, you go out there not feeling 100 per cent confident anyway and that apprehension is compounded by the
fact that you are going to be targeted in the warm-up.

Every time you run to the side of the pitch, there is going
to be a little group of people giving you abuse. Suddenly, all
the anger and prejudice hidden away under the surface of
someone's everyday life starts spewing out. You start to get a
sense of the mentality of the mob and to anticipate the way
the collective mind of a hostile crowd works. You know that
if the game starts badly for the team you are playing against,
then within ten minutes they will turn their anger and their
frustration on you. And then a whole stadium of 40,000 or
50,000 people will start singing about how you take it up the
arse.

Most of the time, you try and blot that out but sometimes
you can't. On another occasion at Anfield, I went over to the
touchline to get the ball when it had gone out for a throw. A
kid in the crowd was holding it. He was nine or ten and his

dad was next to him. 'You fucking poof, you take it up the arse,' he screamed at me. His dad was joining in as well. I got the ball and then I stopped and looked at him.

'Who do you think you are talking to like that?' I asked him. I pointed at him and then, of course, everyone else starting piling in. I was all for hauling that kid out of the crowd and putting him on the side of the pitch with me. Sometimes you have just got to draw the line and say 'That is wrong, you don't treat people like that'.

That has happened a few times: where I have confronted people and made eye contact with them. It never worked because there were always so many people around them. They are usually the kind of so-called fans that will scream personal abuse at a player for ninety minutes and then report them to the police if they look at them the wrong way.

There was another time when I stood up for myself, too, a time when I refused to look the other way. I had a family by then and my wife, Mariana, brought our new-born eldest child, Georgina, to her first game at the end of February 1999. It was Liverpool again but this time it wasn't Paul Ince who was the problem. This time, it was Robbie Fowler.

I had admired Robbie when he was a young player. He was a magnificent finisher, one of the best natural strikers you would ever see. But as people, he and I are probably about as far apart as it's possible to be. His trademark was his sarcastic, put-down humour. That's fine, that's great; if that's how you play the game – fine. He had an irreverent, caustic attitude. I didn't mind that but the thing with Robbie was that he didn't know when to stop. When things became unacceptable, it felt as if he was ignorant of his social responsibilities and the consequences of his actions.

That Chelsea–Liverpool match at Stamford Bridge was a high-tempo game like all the clashes between the two teams seemed to be and there were a few incidents. Early in the second half, I moved to clear the ball from left-back and as I did so, Robbie tried to block it but ended up coming across me and fouling me. I went down and the referee, Paul Durkin, booked him.

Robbie looked down at me. 'Get up, you poof,' he said. I stayed on the turf while the physio was treating me and then got up. By then, Robbie was standing ten yards away. The ball was in front of me, ready for the free-kick. I looked at Robbie. He started bending over and pointing his backside in my direction. He looked over his shoulder and started yelling at me. He was smirking. 'Come and give me one up the arse,' he said, 'come and give me one up the arse.'

He said it three or four times. The Chelsea fans, in the benches where the new West Stand is now, were going berserk. The linesman was standing right next to me. He could see what Robbie was doing but he didn't take any action. He didn't call Durkin over. Everyone knew exactly what Robbie's gesture meant. There wasn't a lot of room for interpretation. I asked the linesman what he was going to do about it. He just stood there with a look of suppressed panic on his face.

So I stood there with the ball, waiting. Robbie could see he was winding me up and I suppose that gave him a great sense of gratification. So he carried on doing it. I told the linesman I wasn't going to take the free-kick until he stopped. It was a

Mexican stand-off. I wish Paul Durkin had found it in him to decide what was going on and then send Robbie off for ungentlemanly conduct.

It was a big moment. What Robbie did provided a chance for people to confront a serious issue. Some people compared it to sledging in cricket but sledging is still essentially private – an exchange or series of exchanges that stay between the players on the pitch. Only the people on the pitch are aware of the insults that are being hurled. That's where I believe Robbie crossed the line and betrayed the game. When a fellow professional does something like that to you, when he mocks you for public consumption, it adds credibility to unfounded rumours. That is why it upset me so much. I just cannot accept that that is just part of the game. In my football career, I never saw anyone do something like that to another player.

Whatever happens on the pitch should stay on the pitch. There is a huge amount of pressure not to break that omertà. I don't know where it comes from but it surrounds you. It is self-protecting. If you're a player and you talk about things that should be kept private because they happened on the field, you risk losing the trust of team-mates and opponents. As soon as you step out of the circle and expose what actually happens, it's very difficult to get back in.

I felt that what Fowler did – because it was so blatant – allowed me to step out of the circle and hit back at him in whatever way I needed to. He had betrayed me on the pitch. He had broken the code first. I have felt that conflict of interest on a few occasions and until then I had always taken the stick that came my way and laid low until the fuss blew over.

Black players have had plenty of foul abuse aimed at them over the years but no fellow player has ever made a public gesture like that at any one of them. Robbie wouldn't dream of making gestures to a black player so why did he feel it was acceptable to incite me by sticking out his backside?

I think football had a chance to make a stand there and then against this kind of thing. The game could have made a strong statement that such blatant homophobia would not be tolerated. Durkin would have been feted for that if he had taken a stand and I believe that maybe it would have taken some of the stigma away for gay footballers who are still petrified of being found out. It could have been a turning point.

But football didn't make a stand. Durkin ran over and booked me for time-wasting. I was dumbfounded. I asked him if he was just going to let Robbie get away with it. He didn't say anything. He said later that he hadn't seen what Robbie was doing but I wonder if it was just that he didn't want to deal with it. No one wanted to deal with it.

My head filled up with anger. I still didn't want to take the free-kick. Perhaps I should have taken even more of a stand. Perhaps I should just have refused to take the kick and been sent off. That would at least have forced the issue but it would probably have made me a martyr for the cause and I didn't want that. In that kind of situation, the pressure to play on is overwhelming. The crowd is screaming and baying, the rest of the players are looking at you expectantly, waiting for play to restart. I looked at Robbie again and he had stopped bending over. So I took the free-kick.

I was consumed with the idea of retribution. I wanted vengeance. I kicked the ball as hard as I could. It was like smacking a punchball. I tried to calm down but I couldn't. There was no way I could get rid of my anger. I ran up to the halfway line and tried to confront Robbie. I told him my family was in the stand. 'Bollocks to your family,' he said.

Robbie revealed a slightly different version of the episode in his autobiography – and a different attitude to it. He wrote that after all his insinuations about me being gay, I had run up to him on the pitch and shouted 'But I'm married' and that he had replied 'So was Elton John, mate'. It's a nice line and it makes Robbie look funny, which is the most important thing to him. But I'm afraid it's what's called dramatic licence – he didn't say it.

I waited for my opportunity. I should have come off really. My head was gone. I wasn't even concentrating on the game. I felt humiliated. It was an age until the ball came near us again but I was possessed with the idea of getting my own back. In the cold light of day, it sounds inexcusable but I felt as if the anger of so many years of being taunted was welling up inside me.

Eventually, the ball was played down their left-hand side and Robbie made a run towards our box. I came across and ran straight into him with a swing of the elbow. I clattered him as hard as I could but thankfully I'm not very good at that kind of thing. In fact, it was pathetic. Durkin didn't see it so I didn't get punished. Thankfully, it didn't do Robbie any lasting damage. We had a couple more kicking matches and in the end he caught me on the calf and I had to come off. About eight minutes from the end, Vialli brought Eddie

Newton on to replace me and the most traumatic match of my career was over.

I was still incredibly angry after the game. I went to see Durkin. I had already heard that the *Match of the Day* cameras had captured my elbow on Robbie and I wanted to outline to him exactly why I had done it. Dermot Gallagher was the fourth official and he said he'd seen the whole thing with Robbie jutting out his backside. He started talking about the amount of stick he'd had over the years for being Irish.

I had ten minutes with them, talking about the whole thing. I asked Durkin about the booking. I asked him why I'd be time wasting when we were playing at home and the score was 1–1. He didn't have an answer. I asked the linesman again why he hadn't done anything and he didn't want to engage. He didn't know what his response should have been: a guy sticking out his backside to taunt another player – it's not in the rule book is it?

The aftermath was awful. I got buried by television and the newspapers because I had tried to take him out off the ball. That was fair enough. But it seemed bizarre that they were focusing on that rather than the extreme provocation I had been subjected to. Because I had reacted, a lot of people seemed to want to excuse Robbie for what he had done. Three days after the game, the FA charged us both with misconduct.

I sent him a letter of apology for thwacking him over the head. I got a letter from him, too. It was a non-committal explanation of what he had done. It wasn't an apology as such. It was an attempt to save face, couched in legal niceties, drafted by a lawyer or an agent, and designed to appease the FA tribunal before they sat in judgment on us. It was a sad excuse of a letter really. It was an insult to everyone's intelligence:

Dear Graeme,
I am in receipt of your without prejudice letter about what occurred on Saturday, February 27 at Stamford Bridge.
   I am sorry if you misinterpreted my actions during the game, which were not meant to cause any offence to yourself or anyone else. Hopefully this unhappy incident can now be brought to an end.
   I am sure you share my hope that when we play together again either on opposite sides or on international duty, people have no reason to judge us other than on our footballing abilities.
   Best wishes,
   R. Fowler

It was supposed to be a private letter but Robbie released it to the press. He did make one serious point about the incident in his autobiography, though. 'Football's a tough sport,' he wrote, 'and to get to the top, you have to be incredibly thick-skinned. A bit of name-calling never hurt anyone and the truth is that I wasn't being homophobic, I was merely trying to exploit a known weakness in an opponent who had done me a number of times.'
   It's an interesting line of defence. According to Robbie's rationale, then, it's okay to call a black man a 'nigger' on the

pitch and pretend it's all in the line of duty. I don't think so. I don't think even Robbie would try and argue that. Maybe he just didn't think about his argument. It's more likely he didn't really have any defence and that that was the best he could come up with. It wasn't a very good effort.

The television and radio presenter Nicky Campbell produced an article about what Fowler had written: 'I bet what Fowler did that day at Chelsea made thousands of youngsters feel pretty crappy about themselves,' he wrote. 'Imagine if he had performed a craven Uncle Tom shuffle of subordination to a black player. A bit of name calling never hurt anyone?

'But it is unfair to blame Fowler. The insular and impenetrable culture of football is the fundamental problem. There, difference is frowned upon and intelligence scorned. This is the world of the institutionally incurious.'

A month after Robbie offered me his backside, we both found ourselves in another England squad. There was another awkward reunion at Burnham Beeches. By now, Kevin Keegan was the manager and we were preparing for his first match in charge, a home European Championship qualifying tie against Poland. Kevin summoned us both to his room. He wanted us to stage a public reconciliation for the press. Robbie didn't have quite as much bravado in that situation. He looked like a naughty little boy. He seemed shy and tongue-tied. Kevin wanted us to do a photo-call for the media but I said immediately that unless Robbie apologized to me first, that wasn't going to happen. Otherwise, there was no way I was going to go out there and pretend we had resolved the situation – no chance.

I made it clear that I didn't want a public apology from Robbie; just a private word would do. But he refused. He said he had done nothing wrong, that it was just a bit of a laugh. Keegan started to back off at that point. He wasn't qualified to deal with it but I felt more confident about it. By now, I felt bolstered by the debate the incident had caused, and in a strange kind of way I felt relieved that the issue was totally out in the open. Now, at least, everyone knew the kind of taunting I had to put up with from the fans every week. Now, they could guess at the routine abuse I had to deal with on the pitch. From that moment on, there seemed to be less animosity about the chants that were directed at me. The debate about the incident with Fowler took some of the mystery out of it all and exposed it for the puerile cruelty it was.

I don't feel any animosity towards Robbie now but you cannot do that to people. Because of the kind of stuff that he sought to justify, sometimes during my career it felt as if the whole world was against me. It was hard to deal with. It's starting to sound like a sob story now, I know, and that's not my intention. But this was like bullying, out and out bullying.

I was determined to stand up for myself. I confronted Robbie about it while we were in Keegan's room. I pointed out to him that if he'd taken the piss out of someone like that in the middle of Soho where all the gay clubs are, he would have got chased down the street and beaten up. Even then, Robbie couldn't resist it. When I mentioned the gay clubs in Soho, he muttered: 'You'd know where they are.' I laughed, I admit it. He can be a funny guy. I told him I'd be professional with him on the training pitch but that there was no way I was going to shake his hand.

On 9 April, six weeks after the original incident and six days after Robbie had got himself in more trouble by pretending to snort the white lines on the pitch at Goodison Park during a goal celebration in a Merseyside derby, we were both told to attend our separate FA disciplinary hearings at Birmingham City's St Andrews ground. I took a barrister called Jim Sturman with me to act in my defence and the Chelsea managing director, Colin Hutchinson, came along to support me. Jim had put a dossier together to show the disciplinary committee which detailed the homophobic abuse I had suffered from crowds over the years. We had video footage of some of the more extreme incidents and Jim also brought some of the hundreds of letters of support I received from members of the public.

Jim presented my case very eloquently and the panel seemed surprised by our approach. It wasn't so much punishing Robbie that I was after. I didn't want to get him into more trouble. He seemed to be doing pretty well by himself without any extra help from me. It was more about illustrating to them the problem with homosexual abuse that still existed in English football and the extent of what I had had to deal with.

If they had given me a punishment based on what I did, I would not have accepted it. I felt it was important to make a stand. I also saw it as an opportunity to get the whole thing off my chest. I had put up with it for so long and this was like a chance to exorcize a demon. In my mind, it wasn't about Robbie Fowler. It was all about me. It didn't matter who had done it to me. It wasn't personal. It was about the victimisation and the lies.

I expected a token punishment for the fact that I had done something wrong on the pitch. If they had tried to make an example out of me, though, I would have taken it further. I would have made the FA accountable for what had happened. In the end, they banned me for a game and gave me a £5,000 fine.

They hammered Robbie. He was suddenly dealing with the fall-out from his mock-cocaine-snorting antics as well as what he did to me. In a way, it got the FA off the hook over confronting the issue of homophobia in football. But in another way, it was a fascinating glimpse of the governing body's moral code. They gave Robbie a much harsher punishment for making what was clearly a joke about snorting cocaine than they did for his attempt to humiliate me and encourage homophobia everywhere – both serious issues.

I wonder if Robbie appreciated the irony of that. He did something as a retort to malicious rumours that had been spread about him and yet he had been happy to exploit a malicious rumour that had been spread about me.

Robbie got a two-game ban for taunting me and a four-game ban for his goal celebrations at Goodison. So a joke about cocaine was twice as reprehensible as a gay taunt. I wasn't angry about that, but it was interesting. It was indicative of the continuing ambivalence that exists about homophobia in sport. The American sports agent Leigh Steinberg once said it was easier to get an advertising deal for a player who was a convicted felon than a player who was gay. Nothing's changed.

But I felt that the debate about what Robbie had done and the FA hearing gave me a form of closure on the whole thing. It was a watershed for me. After that, I still got the taunts from the crowd but some of the venom seemed to have gone out of them. Some of the seriousness had gone because what Robbie had done had underlined the absurdity of what was happening to me.

It didn't completely get rid of it – I had people singing at me and abusing me for the rest of my career – but it did get it out in the open. It did change something. Perhaps it was because what Robbie had done had actually always been my worst fear. It represented my dread of the most extreme humiliation anyone could visit on me. Now it was over, I knew nothing could be worse than that ordeal. So no one could offend me any more. It was a necessary evil. After the hearing, the distress I had always felt about the taunts I had to endure began to ebb away.

The episode still causes me some problems, particularly over the way I reacted to Robbie's provocation. When Zinedine Zidane head-butted Marco Materazzi during the 2006 World Cup Final, I was asked to talk about it many times because people drew comparisons with what had been said to him and what Robbie had done to me. I found that very difficult because I felt Zidane was totally wrong to do what he did and that he set a poor example. I can understand there is part of his psyche that is weak because he has suffered abuse all his life and that is why he snapped. Whatever was said that night in Berlin was between him and Materazzi, not between him, Materazzi and every supporter in the stadium. So it was a different affair entirely to what happened between me and Fowler. Zidane had just missed a header that he would have thought he should have scored. It was his last game for France and emotionally he was probably in a bad place.

The first time we played at Anfield after the incident with Robbie, the Chelsea boss Gianluca Vialli put me on the bench. On that day of all days, he put me on the bench. Robbie was God at Anfield and there I was having to run up and down the touchline in front of the Main Stand. I was scared stiff. I thought the fans were going to kill me.

In the second half, Luca told me to go and warm up. Because the linesman was running the line in the half to our right, we had to warm up at the Kop end. So when I ran down the touchline towards the Kop, the entire Kop started singing 'Le Saux takes it up the arse'. I think it was the loudest I'd ever heard it. Then the wolf whistles started. But something really had changed. For the first time ever, it didn't upset me. For the first time, I felt I had the confidence to see it as the wind-up it was and take the sting out of it without getting upset.

During my stretching, I was in the corner near the Kop and I turned my back to them. I did a hamstring stretch where you open both your legs out wide and you get really low and touch your elbows on the floor. As I did it, I looked between my legs at the supporters and winked and smiled. And they all started applauding me. There was nothing pre-meditated about it. It's funny, but it made me feel as though the pressure was lifting a bit. It took the edge off everything. It was a catharsis.

In the end, I got there. But it didn't wipe out what I'd been through. It didn't wash it away. Let's be blunt: it was awful;

it nearly drove me out of the game. The homophobic taunting and the bullying made me feel left out and misunder-
stood. People have read me wrong because they thought I
wasn't a team player just because I was different, just
because I didn't conform to the stereotype of a laddish footballer.

In my first spell at Chelsea, I was so close to walking away
from football. I went through times that were like depres-
sion. I didn't know where I was going with it. I would get up
in the morning and I wouldn't feel good and by the time I got
into training I would be so nervous that I felt sick. I dreaded
going in. I was like a bullied kid on his way into school to
face his tormentors.

Sometimes, when I look back at what I went through,
I don't know why I carried on – other than this single-
mindedness and some sort of belief that I had a destiny to
make it as a professional footballer. I can't work out why I
didn't pack it all in but it was like I was on a path and despite
all the baggage I was carrying, I never let myself stray from
that path.

It's an indictment of our game and the prejudice it allows,
but I felt a great surge of relief when I retired. Playing was
such an emotional drain. I had to get myself up for the game
and then I had to prepare myself for being singled out by
opposition supporters. That's another notch altogether.

Abuse is abuse, whatever it is. I never understood why, if
you could be kicked out of a football ground and prosecuted
for racism, why not for other forms of prejudice? Early in
2007, the FA finally said that homophobic abuse should be
treated in the same way as racial abuse inside football

grounds. Given the abuse that I, and others, suffered, it feels like it was about twenty years too late. Perhaps that's their idea of a rapid response unit. Still, better late than never.

The result of football's strange tolerance of the homophobic victimization is that for somebody in the game to admit they are gay just couldn't happen. If somebody came to me and said they were a gay footballer and asked my advice about whether they should be open about it, I would find it difficult to give them an honest answer.

I would find it difficult to say to a gay man that he ought to be true to himself and to the community he is representing. That's what I'd want to tell him but the reality is that if you are a footballer and you want to do well, keep your mouth shut about being gay. That's a terrible indictment of the English game but football is a society within a society. It's another country.

TWO

A Secret

The thing is, I did have a secret; a secret I kept all through my playing career. I thought of it as a guilty secret. I was ashamed of my part in it and sometimes the guilt ate me up. Sometimes, it still does. Maybe that's why I haven't spoken publicly about it until now. Maybe that's why I've never really even spoken to my dad, Pierre, about it, why I've tried to blank it out for so long. It had a big effect on me as a man and as a player. I was always concerned that it might be used as a reason for why I was so sensitive and quick to anger when I was on the pitch. For a long time, my secret went to the very heart of me.

My secret is this: when I was thirteen, my mother, Daphne, died. I know now that she had developed breast cancer a couple of years earlier and had a mastectomy. I know now that she thought she had beaten it but that it came back more deadly than ever. I know now that when I went away on a school football trip to northern France, my dad knew that my mum might have died by the time I got back to our home in Jersey. I know now that he had agreed with the doctors that it would be better for my mum if it was kept a secret from her. He was told that it might benefit her if she didn't know how seriously ill she was. And obviously, if he wasn't allowed to tell her, he couldn't tell me or my two sisters.

So I didn't even really realize my mum was ill. I was full of life and energy and busy chasing all my football dreams, haring to matches and training sessions all over the island. As a youngster, you don't think about life or death. Anyway, mums and dads are always there. The thought of mum being ill never really crossed my mind. Perhaps I blinded myself to how poorly she was. Perhaps I shrugged off the signs I saw and I suppose everyone else helped me with my denial. It was only twenty-five years ago but people weren't as open about cancer back then as they are now. It was still talked about in hushed tones.

My mum didn't have chemotherapy so she didn't lose her hair. She didn't show too many outward signs of being ill. There were a couple of occasions when I walked into the room and found her crying but I just put it down to Mum being emotional. Even when an ambulance came to pick her up from our house in St Ouen, I failed to appreciate the seriousness of what was happening. I thought it was a bit of an adventure and my best mate, Jason, and I cycled furiously down to the parish hall and waited on the steps so we could see the ambulance driving past on its way to the hospital in St Helier. That was the last time I saw her. She was forty-one.

My poor dad: what a burden it must have been for him to carry. On the day he was in the hospital being told that my mum's cancer had come back and that she had approximately nine months to live, I climbed onto the flat roof of the garage next to our house to retrieve a football. When I was getting down, I slipped and fell and gashed my shin so badly on a breeze block that it needed fifty stitches. It was a pretty dramatic injury and I was taken to hospital, too, without knowing of the terrible events that were unfolding there. Jason's mum took me and bumped into my dad on the hospital steps. He thought she had come to inquire after my mum. When she told him what had happened and that the doctors were saying it might impede the use of my leg, the combination of it all was almost too much for him to bear. He says now it was the worst day of his life.

My mum was in and out of hospital in the weeks before her death. Then, that ambulance took her away and I went off on a football exchange trip to Caen for a long weekend. It was Easter and I was incredibly excited about it. I had an amazing time in France. We won the tournament we were playing in and some scouts from Caen, who were then in the French first division, were talking about me going over there for trials for their youth team.

When I got back to Jersey, I was euphoric. I'd bought some Easter chocolates for everyone and I couldn't wait to give them to Mum and tell her all about my trip. We got the boat back to Jersey and I ran off it with my friend James Robinson, who was one of my close mates from school, when it docked. I spent a lot of time round at his house so I thought it was a bit weird when his dad looked straight through me on the quayside.

Soon, I caught sight of my dad. I was full of myself. I showed him the trophy I'd won and I gabbled out all the stuff about the trip. I was yakking away and we got in the car. We got about five minutes down the coast road from St Helier heading towards St Aubin. Out there in the bay was Elizabeth Castle on its rock. I suddenly thought 'Oh Mum, how's Mum?' I asked Dad and he drew the car slowly into one of the lay-bys overlooking the beach.

He muttered something like 'Just a second' while he was stopping the car.

So I said 'How's Mum' again.

'Mum died whilst you were away,' he said.

I couldn't comprehend it. I said: 'What?'

'Mum's died,' Dad said. 'She's not with us any more.'

I couldn't believe what I was hearing. It all seemed horribly unreal. As much as I tried to comprehend it, I just couldn't accept it. I burst into tears while Dad tried to comfort me. As we drove home, fear gripped me. What was I going to say to my sisters? Who would I turn to now that Mum wasn't ever going to be home again? Arriving at the house we walked into the lounge and there were all these cards of condolence – bizarrely it reminded me of Christmas. Mum was a very popular lady. She was a great netball player. She had loads of friends. And I just felt so lost. I looked around and I thought: 'Everyone knows and I don't. I'm their son and I'm the last one to know.' Both my sisters were there – Jeanette is two years older than me and Alison is six years younger – and I felt that I hadn't even been there for them. I can't really express how difficult it was or how desperate I felt. I suppose you just spend time trying to come to terms with it.

I couldn't even go to my own mother's funeral – I was too embarrassed. I felt guilty because I suddenly saw it with such clarity after the event. It was like when someone throws a surprise party for you and you genuinely don't know about it until you walk in. It's that instant when you realize what has happened and suddenly all these pieces fit together.

Suddenly I knew why James Robinson's dad couldn't look me in the eye. I knew why we had been asked to go to church in France on the school trip the previous Sunday when we weren't even a religious school. The teacher knew mum was seriously ill so he was desperate for us all to go to church and say a prayer for our loved ones. I didn't realize any of that at the time. I was distracted because I had a game of tennis organized for that Sunday morning and I didn't want to go to the church. So the teacher let me off church and allowed me to play tennis. I thought that was unusually generous. I thought I'd got the best of the deal because everyone else was going to church while I was hurtling round a tennis court.

On reflection, all these pieces came together and I just couldn't deal with it. I regret not going to the funeral more than anything now because it stopped me coming to terms with my mum's death. On the day of the funeral, I went down to a hotel in St Brelade's Bay with Jason, where his father worked, and just sat by the side of the swimming pool, staring into the water. I grieved and I went through a lot of emotions but I never had any support in those early years. I'm not blaming anyone – it wasn't anybody's fault. We just didn't speak about it and it wasn't until later in my life, when I met Mariana, that I felt I could open up about it. I did grieve at the time. I cried – a lot. It was more shock than anything. I found it really difficult to let go of her. I tried to remember her and relive things that happened before she died as part of trying to preserve her memory. But that made me even more upset. I'd transport myself back to a time when she was there and then, when I was forced to come out of it, it just accentuated the loss. I was a thirteen-year-old kid having to deal with that kind of emotional baggage. It added a complicated layer to my psychology.

It certainly wasn't my dad's fault. He didn't have anyone to tell him the best way of dealing with the situation. It all happened a generation ago and cancer was still a bit of a taboo subject back then. You were supposed to deal with tragedies like that with a stiff upper lip and just get on with it.

I went back to school after the Easter holidays. I can still see the look in people's faces now: their sympathy. When people said how sorry they were it used to annoy me. I wanted to say to them 'Why are you sorry; it wasn't anything to do with you; you're not to blame'. Emotionally, I became a lot more sensitive. Add the sensitivity from my mum's death to the alienation I felt at Chelsea when I first arrived there in my late teens and it made me particularly vulnerable.

My mum had been so supportive of me as a child. One of the things that upset me most about not having her around was that I could no longer share my experiences and achievements with her. She was the one who picked us up from school. She took so much interest in us. Some of the things I did, I felt I was doing for her. We couldn't wait to tell her what we'd done at school when she was there waiting for us at the school gates. She was so interested in our lives. After she died, I felt this huge hole because she was no longer there. From the age of seven upwards, I always played football on the school pitches during lunch hour. Because I was left-footed, every day I used to come home with eight inches of mud down my right trouser leg, a crusty, muddy mark that mapped out the trajectory of a slide tackle and invariably ended with a hole in the trouser knee. Mum used to wash them and mend them patiently. She had a rota with my school trousers because I got them muddy every day. I often think now 'Thank God she let me carry on ruining my trousers'. I wish I could communicate that to her but I can't.

That was one of the saddest aspects of it. Through all the various milestones of my life and my career, I always had a moment when I wished she could see it. It would have made all the sacrifices and the hardships that she had endured for me worthwhile. And I know, just like any mother, she would be proud of me and my sisters.

My mum's death changed me. It strengthened my drive and my outlook. I was always single minded anyway. I was always feisty and ambitious but when she died it made me want to leave Jersey. It is such a small island and it was such a traumatic experience that it turned parts of Jersey into unhappy places for me for a few years. Whenever I went down certain roads or visited certain beauty spots or beaches or shops, it brought back memories of my mum. It just used to upset me. Now, I can look back on them as happy memories and happy associations but for a long time those memories just upset me deeply.

I love my island. It's only nine miles wide and five miles north to south but I loved growing up there. My identity is Jersey. Even though my dad wanted to call me Jean-Pierre (he was overruled by my mum), I feel more English than French – but more Jersey than English. Life seemed uncomplicated and happy there in the years before Mum died. I would cycle down the hill from my house to St Ouen's Bay, with its dramatic dunes and its miles of beach and the warren of underground tunnels the Germans built after they invaded Jersey at the start of the Second World War. I'd play football for hours on the firm sand. Then, for a real challenge, I'd cycle back up the steep hill past Stinky Bay, where the smell of seaweed wafted up from the rocks below, and past the trees bent over by the sea breeze and the signs advertising Jersey Royal Potatoes back to my house on the hill.

It's such a beautiful place, such a stark contrast to what I had to confront in London. No wonder I felt the culture shock so badly when I swapped Jersey for Burnt Oak. Often, in the evening, when I was seventeen or eighteen, I would drive my car to the headland at Grosnez, the most north-westerly point of the island, and park it by the ruins of the fourteenth-century arch there. I'd get out, stare over the water to Sark and then lie on the bonnet, listening to the waves and staring up at the stars. Sometimes, going to those places still makes me melancholy but back then it would bring tears to my eyes. I suppose it was part of coming to terms with letting go of my mum. I never said goodbye to her. I never had that raw sort of emotion. I kept it all within me.

People can psychoanalyse me as much as they want and it would be very easy to pin all my emotional baggage onto this one massive event. It would be easy to say I reacted to Robbie Fowler because my mum died or I hit David Batty because my mum died. But I might have been like that anyway. I don't know. One of the reasons I believe I kept it from everyone at Chelsea and was glad that no one knew about it was because I had this fear that if people knew about my mum, then at some point someone would have made reference to it to try to use it against me. And I knew that that would have made me uncontrollably furious.

That would have been worse than anything I experienced, worse than any of the homophobic taunts. That's one of the reasons I have never spoken about it. I never told anyone at Chelsea about it. In that way, I used football as a valid reason not to talk about her death. It was part of my process of denial. I told myself I couldn't talk about it because people would use it against me and that meant I didn't have to talk about it.

At various points during my playing career, I might get a casual question about what my parents did. I'd say my dad was a chartered quantity surveyor and my mum was a house-wife. I just never talked about it publicly because I wanted to protect what I had. Some people would probably say it was a classic case of denial but it wasn't that. I shared my thoughts with my friends in Jersey, friends like Jason and Susie, and now that I have moved away from football, I don't feel as uncomfortable talking about it with people outside the game.

It's strange. I have a close relationship with my dad and my sisters. We're a loving family but we don't talk about that time much. There are times when I think we ought to talk about it. My younger sister was only seven, just a bit younger than my own daughter is now, when Mum died. She never knew her mum. She deserves to know more.

When I became a footballer, it was my decision not to say anything about my mum so it's always been my responsibility to deal with people that don't know about her death and therefore say something inappropriate. But with any problem I've ever had, the easiest thing for me to do would have been to blame it on the fact that my mum died when I was a kid. I have never used her death as an excuse. That's one thing I find hard to accept about some people: there is a type of person that uses things that have happened to them as an excuse to fail. Some circumstances cause people to implode. Equally, you can try and be determined to cope with adversity and get over it. I went through a stage of just feeling utterly lost. I questioned everything. I questioned the fundamentals of my life and there probably was a time when I could have made some bad decisions that derailed me.

However, I avoided that. It is a huge credit to my dad and my two sisters, and to my school and friends, that things happened that way. Football was always a huge release for me, too. It was just there. That was my time – I was never distracted. It allowed me to block out all the stuff about my mum. It helped me focus. I was desperate to win anyway but this made me even more absorbed in my football. And my mum's death had another effect: I've been through bad times in my career and I've been able to cope because none of it was as traumatic as my mum dying.

I also owe a huge debt of gratitude to the woman who became my dad's partner in the years after Mum died. Her name was Alice and she became a mother figure to me and my sisters. There was no sense of resentment towards her because she had taken our mum's place or anything like that.

I only feel a deep and lasting appreciation towards her. In many ways, she kept our family together. She and my dad never lived together but we always went round to her house for Sunday lunch and she became a steadying, stabilising influence in all our lives. She was a lovely, loving, caring, gentle and kind lady.

Alice knew my mum and dad when they were younger but after Mum died, Dad was working on a building contract at Jersey Potteries and he bumped into Alice again while she was working in the gift shop there. She was like a saint to us. She had a massive role in a lot of people's lives: she gave her life to other people. Her sister and her own mother completely and utterly relied on her. She had met my dad again when he was a widower with three children. Why on earth did she take us on when she already had so many responsibilities?

Sadly, Alice has now gone as well. One Tuesday in August 2002, I was in London having lunch with Gianfranco Zola when Mariana rang me and told me I had to come straight home. I asked her what the matter was. Had something happened to the kids? Was she alright? She kept telling me to come home and that there was something she had to tell me. When I got back, she told me Dad had called and that Alice had died. She had gone to bed the night before and she hadn't woken up. It seems her heart had just given out and they never discovered what caused it. A partnership of twenty years with my dad came to an end with shuddering suddenness.

I spoke at her funeral which was at St Martin's Methodist Church. It was the hardest thing I have ever done. But I had to do it: I had to do it for her; I had to do it for me; and I had to do it for my mum. After what I had been through with my mum, I would never have forgiven myself if I hadn't done that last thing for Alice. All the emotion that I went through on that day counted for double and in a way, it gave me some closure about my failure to attend my mum's own funeral. I told myself that day that I had to stop taking small things so seriously. I told myself I had to remember what was important in life. I told myself I had to enjoy every moment because life can be so fleeting and brutal. We have all these constant reminders of our mortality and yet we still get so upset and stressed about the most ridiculous things. All great thoughts and then the next day you have a row about whose fault it is you've run out of milk.

I don't know what my dad must have gone through. After Alice died, he said he felt lucky to have known both her and my mum but he must sometimes think 'What did I do to deserve this'. But he never let his commitment to me and my sisters drop. He and my mum used to spend a lot of what is known now as 'quality time' with the three of us. After she died, Dad worked hard but he was always there for us. My mum was a good netball player and Dad had played football to a decent amateur standard so we were all encouraged to be sporty.

Dad was ambitious for me when I was a child. He would drive me here and there. He was a taxi service. But his way of connecting with me was through football. He would get a football out when I was two or three and he felt pretty quickly that I had an eye for it. As I got older, he became much more serious about my football. It helped that I was an outdoor kid. I wouldn't think twice about going on a two-hour bike ride and I took cross country very seriously. Football, however, soon became all-consuming. I played for my school, St Saviour's, and for the Island Primary Schools and the Island Cubs. That was the first time I ever came up against Matt Le Tissier, who was from Guernsey. He was right-sided, I was left-sided, so we were always rivals.

I came up against him time and again and it often seemed our careers shadowed each other's. We were the first players from the Channel Islands to represent England. He made his debut sixty-six minutes after I made mine. There seemed to be something linking us. He was born on 14 October 1968. I was born on 17 October 1968 – weird. Every time I played against him when we were kids, I used to get that nervous feeling you have when you're up against someone who you think is better than you. I can't remember him showing me up too badly but that may just be because I have erased it from my memory. I do remember, though, that when he signed professional forms for Southampton when he was sixteen, it felt like someone had finally burst the dam as far as Channel Islands football was concerned. He was the first from the islands of my generation to get a professional contract. He showed it could be done.

There was some good schools football in Jersey. At a younger age, there was an Easter primary schools tournament which is still an annual event now and has become very prestigious. Deeside Schools always came down and they were one of the best sides in the country: Ian Rush, Gary Speed and Michael Owen all played for them at different times. So I was exposed to a good standard of football. Later,

I went to a secondary school called Hautlieu and continued to play football while I studied. What went against me in terms of the bigger picture and getting a shot at a trial with a professional club was the fact that I lived on the island. For a club to invite me for a trial was a big commitment because they would have to pay for the cost of the flight and put me up in digs. The expense was prohibitive.

When I was thirteen, my dad paid for me to go to a soccer camp put on by Southampton. I had the accident when I fell off the garage roof a few weeks before the camp was due to start but even though I had all those stitches in my shin, there was no way I was going to miss it. I loved it. I spent a week there. They asked me to stay for a second week and said they would keep an eye on me. My dad had high hopes for what that camp might achieve for me but when I went back the next year, they said I had not developed as much as they had hoped.

I endured some of the rites of passage many aspiring foot-ballers go through – such as the careers meeting with the sceptical teacher. She had a computer with a fairly basic careers programme. She asked what I wanted to do. I told her I wanted to be a footballer. She keyed it in and it was reminiscent of *Little Britain* – the computer said no. 'Nothing's come up,' she said. So she put 'sportsman' in and again nothing came up. In the end, she said 'What else would you like to do?' I shrugged. She gave me a printout of how to become a bank manager, just so she could tick her box. When I signed for Chelsea a couple of years later, they took me down to the Lloyd's Bank at Fulham Broadway. I looked up at the bank manager as I was writing 'professional footballer' on the form. I thought of my careers meeting. 'I could have been you,' I said.

Anyway, I kept plugging away. I had had a trial at Notts County when I was thirteen or fourteen and got my picture taken with Howard Wilkinson and Jimmy Sirrell. I played for Southampton in a testimonial with people like Kevin Bond when Chris Nicholl was the manager. But nothing materialized and I began to think nothing ever would. However, when I got to seventeen, I won a soccer scholarship to the Florida Institute of Technology, which is on the Atlantic coast, well north of Miami and not far from Orlando. I still had this determination to put some distance between me and Jersey and all the melancholic memories of the loss of my mum that used to flood over me now and again. Moving to the States for a couple of years, studying marine biology and playing football, seemed like the perfect opportunity to do that. Everything was ready to go. I had a big farewell party and then I went up to London to stay with my aunt the night before I was due to catch the plane to Miami. That night, my dad phoned. There was a last-minute hitch. Florida Tech had been on. There was a problem with my visa at their end – it was something to do with them having miscalculated their numbers of foreign students. Anyway, it was all off. I felt devastated.

I dealt with it like I'd dealt with a lot of other setbacks: I threw myself into football. I played morning, noon and night, training and playing, training and playing, squeezing in a Saturday morning job on a fruit and veg stall and my A-level homework when I could. And I had a stellar season that year. By then, I was playing for a team called St Paul's who I thought were the best team in Jersey. I played for their juniors and their seniors and that year both sides won the Jersey league and qualified to play for a Cup called the Upton against the winners of the junior and senior leagues in Guernsey. I won the junior and the senior Upton that year and I also represented the island at junior and senior level against Guernsey in a competition called the Muratti. We won both of those, too. So I won six major trophies. From the outside, it might sound a bit like Channel Islands small fry but for us it was a big deal and it formed an important part of the Channel Islands sporting calendar. It made me a bit of a schoolboy phenomenon in Jersey because nobody before had ever accomplished what I had that season.

Some time that summer, the Chelsea manager, John Hollins, came down to Jersey to present the end of season prizes for the island's football clubs. I wasn't eligible for the Player of the Year award for the senior team because I was under age so I wasn't even at the ceremony. However, people kept going up to John and telling him about me and all these records I'd set in Jersey football. 'If he's as good as you're telling me,' he said, 'I better get him over and have a look at him.' He wrote my name down on the back of a match box next to the phone number of an official of St Paul's. When he got back to Chelsea, he made the call and in July 1987, they contacted my dad.

I went over for a week's trial and at the end of it, they offered me a professional contract. There was still one more hurdle to overcome, though. I'd failed my biology A-level and my dad asked John Hollins if he would mind if I re-sat it that November and postponed joining Chelsea until

48

December. That was pretty ballsy of my dad and my heart was in my mouth because I thought Chelsea might be offended. But John Hollins didn't seem to mind and it was all agreed.

So, eventually, I left Jersey. I didn't feel I had to be on the island any more. I still loved it but my mum's death gave me a real determination to get away and fulfil my ambitions. A lot of people who grow up in Jersey feel they would miss the island if they moved to the mainland but emotionally, I was out of there. I couldn't change what had happened. If only I had known then what I know now. But then we can all look back and regret things. It's how we deal with them that is important. Perhaps it will help me be an ear for someone who has been through a similar thing. Perhaps it's already making me value my children with an extra keenness. My mum's death changed many things in my life but back then, it made me feel as though I had to carve out a life for myself away from Jersey. I felt like I was on a mission.

THREE

First-time Blues

In theory Chelsea's training ground at Harlington should have felt as though it was at the centre of the modern world. It was a few hundred yards south of the M4. You could hear the hum of the traffic streaming in and out of the capital when you walked from your car to the changing rooms. On the other side, it was bounded by the runways at Heathrow. You could see the planes queuing up to land as they glided in over the west London suburbs, and the roar from Concorde as it took off sometimes stopped training in its tracks. Harlington and being part of Chelsea Football Club should have felt like a launch pad. It should have felt like a hub. But to me, it was a desolate place. It was no man's land.

I saw it first in the summer of 1987 when John Hollins, who was a manager heading into a storm, invited me over for a week's trial. I arrived so full of energy and enthusiasm and determination. It makes me smile now to think of how naive and raw I was. I ran myself into the ground that week. I was determined to seize my opportunity – I thought I might never get another. So I hurtled around like a madman in training and the first teamers loved it. They probably recognized that wide-eyed enthusiasm from the time they had it, the time before the routine of being a professional footballer gripped them.

One of the most popular training drills was for the first team to form a big circle and stick one of the trialists in the middle of it. We had to try and get the ball off them and they had immense amounts of fun with that. They were like matadors with a young bull. I charged around and flew at them. They knew they had a live one. They were doing olés every time they touched it and kept the ball away from me. There were cheers and whoops. Roy Wegerle, who also played for Blackburn, QPR, Luton and the USA and was one of the most skilful players I've ever seen, did this trick where he received the ball on his right foot, dragged it behind his left foot and then flicked it out the other side all in one movement. I couldn't get anywhere near the ball. Every day that week, I was utterly exhausted at the end of training. I gave it absolutely everything.

After seven days, I went back to Jersey. When I got home, there was a letter waiting for me saying that I had failed one of my A-levels. The amount of football I had been playing that year, it was a miracle I could even read. A few days later, John Hollins phoned my dad and said they wanted to offer me a contract. I couldn't believe it. But my priorities were slightly different to a lot of footballers even then: my dad told John that I wanted to resit my biology A-level that November and that I'd like to postpone joining the club until then. John was relaxed about it. It wasn't as if he was planning to rush me into the first team. So he said that was fine. I re-took biology and passed it and at the beginning of December I became a Chelsea player. I had just turned nineteen.

The club was going through a difficult period and its future was uncertain. Ken Bates, the chairman, was fighting to buy Stamford Bridge and save it from the developers. John Hollins was a good manager but I soon realized that he was a gentle man in charge of a very strong dressing room and that that was not a good combination. There was nothing sophisticated about Chelsea in those days, certainly not among the players. It was staffed by tough, unyielding men some of whom played hard and drank hard and then came to training. These men did not eat pasta salads and florets of broccoli.

These men were not King's Road dandies like Alan Hudson and Peter Osgood and the playboys of a previous Chelsea generation. I was scared witless of some of them. There was a bloke called John McNaught, a really rough, tough, Scottish central defender who was literally hard-nosed. He was terrifying. He only played thirteen times for the first team but I played plenty of reserve football with him. Pat Nevin, who I respected, liked McNaught for his honesty but he just scared me rigid.

Some of my team-mates in club football in Jersey had played their football in Scotland and Wales and Ireland so it wasn't as if people like McNaught and Peter Nicholas, when he arrived later, were aliens to me. Nonetheless it amazed me that people like them were professional players. I was expecting professional footballers to be professional in every sense of the word but there were players there for whom football was all about the lifestyle off the pitch. Their work had to fit into their lifestyle rather than the other way around. McNaught would arrive in the morning a bit hungover and ragged. You could tell he had been out. He would turn up late for reserve games. He was a good centre-half, tough as old boots, but I was taken aback by his approach. I thought that if you were professional, you needed to be in top condition. Back then, before the influx of foreign players made English football much more driven and professional, you could just about disguise the fact that you lived your social life to the full. Some of these guys could get away with it.

The minute I signed my contract, I really appreciated what I was doing; I felt so fortunate. But with some of these players it was a way of life. They had grown up with it. They had always gone out and they had still made it. I didn't feel the two were compatible for me. I knew that if I did that, I'd be shot to pieces; I knew I couldn't afford to do it. To be honest, I didn't want to do it, anyway: it wasn't me.

I found it hard to make good friends at Chelsea. I was caught between the apprentices and the battle-hardened professionals. That's what I mean about the no man's land. I hadn't come up through the ranks at the club with good apprentices like Jason Cundy, David Lee, Damian Matthew and Graham Stuart; and I was regarded as an over-earnest young swot by blokes like Nicholas, Steve Wicks, Kerry Dixon, David Speedie and Andy Townsend, the men who called the shots at the club and ran the dressing room.

I don't know how much of my alienation at the club was about class. I have always shied away from class issues and I have never judged anyone on class. But I think I was judged. Some of the lads told me I was a bit posh. In England, unlike in Europe, I've always noticed that there seems to be an issue with young players who have been educated academically, purely because they are so much in the minority. Those players find it hardest to fit in, particularly when they are trying to fit in with a group of young lads. It has changed a lot now and improved but some footballers still have a very insular mentality.

Class wasn't obvious in Jersey. I didn't consider my family privileged in any particular way. I didn't consider myself middle class. I wasn't privately educated, for instance, but apart from the fact that my parents couldn't have afforded it, there wasn't really any need for private education in Jersey: there were no problems with lack of books or facilities. The class boundaries weren't defined there. We all played rugby and football. I played football with some really street-wise guys in Jersey: builders, plumbers, electricians and other labourers. I grew up in a team that had quite a solid base of Scottish and northern English players and rather than scorning me, they took me under their wing.

But when I arrived at Chelsea, everything felt very closed off. There was a lot of intimidation. Suddenly I was involved constantly with people who were alien to me. In Jersey, most of my routine was about school and I only saw the lads now and again. Now, the main part of my life was about mixing with players at Chelsea with whom I had nothing in common. I wasn't a poor little rich boy but I think some of them regarded me like that. Also, there was no respite from it: the micky-taking seemed absolutely relentless and it gets hard when you're always the target.

It was a tough environment. By the time I got back there in December, the club was sliding towards relegation and John Hollins was in trouble. People look after themselves, particularly when a club is in trouble, and the lads ran the show. Anything went. The management did not solve the problems I had, they didn't tackle my isolation – in fact, they helped to perpetuate it. Once, in training, we were sitting round in a big circle talking something through as a team and I said something that Bobby Campbell, who succeeded Hollins, took exception, too. 'I don't know what you're talking about,' he joked. 'You're just the product of a German rape.'

He didn't know that my mother had died, of course, so he couldn't know quite how deeply that comment hurt me, but I was still astonished he could say something like that. He was clearly aware that the Channel Islands had been invaded by the Germans during the Second World War and I suppose that was his idea of humour. Comedy was different then: he was mates with Jimmy Tarbuck, and people like Freddie Starr were considered funny at the time. But Campbell didn't make anyone laugh. Even the other lads looked surprised by what he said; most of them just looked at the floor. I raged inside. I didn't say anything but I never forgot what he had said. It was part of the wider problem I felt I had at the club: no one ever stood up for me. You expect to feel nurtured when you go to a club like that but I wasn't. I felt alone most of the time.

If you have not come through the ranks from fourteen or fifteen, it becomes more and more difficult to integrate.

You're an outsider to the players who have been there together for a few years. You're a threat to them and you're a threat to their mates. No one could put me into a definite category which also made them suspicious of me. That created mistrust. I didn't relate or conform to fit into a group. I didn't compromise enough. I challenged a lot of stereotypes and I didn't have any allies. I couldn't compete in a talk-off with the smarter guys because I wasn't quick enough or confident enough to take them on verbally. I certainly couldn't challenge them physically. If you have got a little group of players you are friendly with, you are safe within that group. I never had that. I had been at school with my friends and protected within that environment. There were confrontations as at any other school but I was popular and confident when I was in Jersey. However, as soon as I came into football, I was getting stick from all angles. Over a period of time, it wore me down.

Of course, there were happy moments within it all. I was there for more than five years in my first spell. I couldn't have survived if there was no respite at all. There is always laughter at football clubs. There are incidents every day. Once, at the end of a five-a-side game on one of Harlington's muddy pitches, David Lee slid in to prod home a goal. He opened his mouth to shout 'Yeah' as his momentum carried him into the goal and then suddenly he started clutching his face. One of his teeth had got hooked by the net as he shouted; it had twisted the tooth and flicked it clean out. I was doubled up with laughter like the rest of the lads. For some reason, we spent several minutes scrambling around in the mud trying to find it. What were we going to do with it?

Give it to the tooth fairy? I don't know if we thought they could screw it back in if we got it. But we never did.

The same thing happened to Craig Burley when he was an apprentice. He had two front teeth missing most of his career. Know how he did it? A ball came to him chest high and he got caught in two minds about whether to stoop to head it or do a falling volley. In the end, he did neither. In the end, he tried to knee it and he just kneed himself in the face and knocked out his two front teeth. Cue more scrabbling around in the mud. It was funny at the time.

I'm not saying I felt I had a lot of enemies at Chelsea, either. I liked lads like Graham Stuart and Damian Matthew and Jason Cundy. Graham and Jason used to pick me up from the bus stop at Hampton Court, near the digs in Kingston I'd moved into after I left Burnt Oak, and drive me into training. We got on fine and they used to laugh about what Indie band I'd been to see the night before. Some of the lads gave me a nickname, Berge, after the television detective Bergerac, who gave the impression that my beautiful island was riddled with violent crime.

Mostly, however, I struggled. Perhaps I was a bit homesick as well but I found many of the aspects of my new life intimidating and hostile. At Harlington there were separate dressing rooms and groups of players were separated off into their own little space. That made integration even harder. It was like a little passport control system. If you did well, you moved into the next dressing room and up the food chain as it were. The young lads were down at the far end, furthest away from the entrance. The first teamers were just inside the door. There was another one for the also-rans.

There was scope for moving onwards and upwards within that strange little hierarchy but places in the coveted dressing rooms didn't come up until a player left. So if you wanted to be in a dressing room with The Lads, you needed to wait for someone else to be sold and then jump in before the replacement came. If you knew someone when you signed for Chelsea, you might get fast-tracked. That kind of separation meant I never really got to know a lot of my team-mates in the first team. I might train with them occasionally but when you are training you are focusing on that. It was really disruptive.

In the early years, I never really thought I was going to be good enough to make it at Chelsea and if I analyse it, a lot of my success was based on insecurity. A lot of ambition is based on fear of failure. I have seen so many players get dispirited, walk away and give up before they should have done. I've wanted to say to some of them: 'You are too good to give up.' But the one thing you can't do is change that desire in someone. You have either got the will to succeed or you haven't. It's not going to happen unless you make it happen

For a long time at Chelsea, I felt I was way behind people like Graham and Damian because, when I first arrived, they had been playing football at that level for two or three years as apprentices. I felt like an outsider looking in. There were plenty of moments when it would have been easier for me to jack it in. That's why I never signed a long-term contract at Chelsea. I always gave myself targets. I signed for two years and got through that. Then I signed for three years and got through that. I had a little bit of security but not too much.

I'm such a safety first guy normally but I took a risk by signing short-term contracts because I wanted to play football on
my terms. I didn't want to be tied into something that I
couldn't get out of if it wasn't working.

I played the first six months in the reserves under Gwyn
Williams, one of Chelsea's great survivors, a Bates man who
only bit the dust when Roman Abramovich took over. Gwyn
held plenty of positions at Chelsea down the years – mainly
because he was a good coach and because he was always
upbeat and lively. At different times, he ran the academy, the
reserves, he was assistant manager, he did the travel, and he
was chief scout. When I was there, he was really hard on the
players – he used to hammer us. His idea was to try and
prepare everyone for the profession. In some ways, I liked
him but he destroyed a few people.

He was always very hard on the black lads but I know he
didn't see it as racist – he was hard on everyone and didn't
single them out in particular. It was very much a product of
its time. It seems harsh and brutal now but even then, less
than 20 years ago, it was seen as acceptable. Racism in the
game was more of a problem then and I suppose Gwyn could
argue that he was just trying to steel the Afro-Caribbean
guys for the stick they would receive from their fellow
professionals and from sections of the crowd at away games.
Thankfully, racial abuse has dwindled in English football
now to the point where Gwyn's kind of education isn't
acceptable any more.

Frank Sinclair and Eddie Newton still liked Gwyn despite
all the insults he levelled at them but there were others like
Nathan Blake who found it more difficult. That brings us

back to the Robbie Fowler dictum: football is a tough business and if anyone has a weakness, it gets picked on.

Some players can handle it and others can't. I could take it – at least most of the time. But it changed me. I found it very hard when I was younger. The atmosphere was so intimidating. People would play on your weaknesses and really get stuck into you – more psychologically, but also as a player. At Chelsea in the late Eighties, there was a tradition that if you were judged to have been the worst player at a training session, you were awarded a yellow bib at the end and you would have to wear it at the start of the next one. Once I had the bib, even if I had a brilliant training session the next time, I tended to get it again – because that amused The Lads. That got demoralising and it was quite isolating – it made you feel like an outcast. I noticed that Dennis Wise introduced that ritual at Swindon when he was manager there. I saw a newspaper article about how Paul Ince had had to wear the yellow bib once or twice when he played there for a spell. I bet he took that well.

When the accusations about my sexuality started and I took it seriously, that snowballed. But even apart from that, the taunting and the mickey-taking and the picking on people was relentless. Some of the lads had this routine they thought was hilarious. We'd be on the mini bus to a reserve game and we'd be driving through Parliament Square, say, and past Big Ben. Nobody would mention Big Ben but then one of the boys would say to me, 'What's the time, Graeme?' I'd say, 'Quarter to seven,' and they'd fall about laughing and go on about Big Ben being right there. Or we'd get onto the forecourt at Old Trafford and one of the lads would say innocently 'Are we nearly there yet?' I'd say 'Of course we bloody are, look there's the ground' and the laughing would start again. I suppose I was pretty gullible. If somebody wanted to know what the time was, I'd tell them the time. I never recognized it as a prank.

There were cheap shots like that constantly. I felt I came in for quite a bit of stick. I must have seemed very different and so I was an easy target. I had my rucksack and my Walkman; I had jeans with a hole in the knee. I used to get hammered. Now that I've stopped playing, I look at the younger players and the ones that stood out were the ones who got the grief. It wasn't the kind of life I had imagined it would be. There were times when I was very unhappy. It had almost got to the point where I had separated my football life from my life away from the game in order to stay sane.

I had a few run-ins with people. I had a go at Kerry Dixon about being lazy in training and we both threw punches. I had a ding-dong with Peter Nicholas, too. But those things happened every week. John McNaught and a striker called Billy Dodds were having a massive argument about something and John called him a 'thick Scottish prick'. When Billy pointed out John was Scottish, too, that kind of short-circuited John's brain and they had a punch-up. Fights in training still occasionally happen now but it was a much tougher environment back then.

Maybe it was partly because Chelsea were going through a tough spell fighting relegation but sometimes training just felt like anarchy. Some of the guys just didn't care. In the reserves, we used to do shooting practice and the lads would boot the ball over the bar on purpose so that it flew into the field behind the goal. They'd climb over the gate into the field and have a kick-about over there while the coach was trying to put on a shooting session on the pitch. The reserves was a sub-culture. There were players in the reserves who only ever seemed to play for the reserves. For some of them, the idea that it was supposed to be a stepping stone into the first team had ceased to exist – they had gone missing in action. Quite a lot of them had dodgy attitudes. They didn't want to be at the club. It's very easy for a young player to get influenced by that and think that's the way to behave. You've got to be single-minded to avoid that trap.

I earned £120 a week when I first signed. The first thing I bought was a Sony Walkman for £100. It had wind-in headphones and it was my pride and joy. It got me through the journey to and from my digs in Burnt Oak every day. It was nearly a week's wages for me so it was like Michael Ballack spending £100,000 on something. My second contract, which I signed in 1990, took me up to £400 a week. That allowed me to have a mortgage of £75,000 at a time when the interest rate was 15 per cent. I wanted to get a fancy car and live the life a bit but prudence got the better of me and I decided to invest everything in a flat.

My thinking was that whatever happened in my football career, if I could come out of it with a property and no mortgage then that was a worthwhile ambition. So I climbed onto the property ladder and bought a flat and then, later, a four-bedroomed Victorian house in Thames Ditton, Surrey. We were in a recession at the time. When I sold the flat eighteen months later, I only got what I paid for it. I was only twenty-three and I suppose I bought it for the family that I didn't have. I thought that if I bought this house I could live there if I had a wife and family, too. I wasn't planning to get married imminently but I was always thinking ahead and planning stuff. I thought I could live there okay if I did find someone.

So I paid £225,000 for it and I never got my flash car. I imported a Suzuki jeep from Jersey instead. The rest of the lads were driving XR3is and Renault 5 turbos and I had a Suzuki jeep. It had a maximum speed of about 50mph. I drove it to Wales once on the motorway and I had to take a run up of about two miles if I wanted to overtake anything.

At least the football side of things went okay. I made my debut for the reserves against Portsmouth at a half-frozen Fratton Park and I was awestruck because the former England forward Paul Mariner was in the Portsmouth team. I played left-back that day but on other occasions Gwyn had me playing all over the place. I played at centre-back for three or four months and at one point, I said to Gwyn that I couldn't play centre-back any more. He said that in that case, he wouldn't bother picking me – so I played at centre-back. I think that was part of my problem in my first spell at Chelsea: they felt I was so versatile that I never got settled in one position. When the players who played in a set position regularly were fit, I'd find myself out of the team. You become easy to drop: I hadn't cost them anything and I was part of the furniture so it was easier to drop someone like me than someone they had paid a lot of money for.

But they were a good group of young players in that Chelsea reserve side. Jason Cundy was sold to Spurs for £800,000 in 1992 and his career was marred first by back problems and then by a struggle with cancer. Dave Lee was a really good player but he broke his leg badly and never really recovered from it. And Graham Stuart, who was a clever, creative player, had a good career at Everton, where he won an FA Cup Winners' medal, and at Charlton Athletic where he was part of the Alan Curbishley success story. It was a good bunch but sadly most of us had to leave in order to realize our potential.

The reserve team did okay but the first team was struggling. A couple of months after I arrived, John Hollins began to come under serious pressure. He had fallen out with players like Speedie and Nigel Spackman and team spirit had disintegrated. One day in February 1988, Bobby Campbell suddenly turned up at training. I hadn't been aware of speculation linking him with the job and he hadn't been officially given it: he just loitered around a bit at Harlington, watching from the sidelines, that sort of thing. It was very odd. He was supposed to be John's new assistant but it was obvious he was the manager-in-waiting. After a few days of that, John told him to get lost and that while he was still manager, Campbell wasn't welcome. In March, John got the sack and Campbell took over.

Campbell was a Scouser. He was flash, flash a bit like Ron-Manager. He wore a lot of gold. He had a Rolex that didn't lock properly, which was something that he seemed to like. He used it as a kind of gimmick. Every time he clapped his hands, the strap would come undone and the watch would rattle and it would all draw attention to the fact that he was wearing a Rolex. He was a bit tougher than John and he brought in players like Graham Roberts, Peter Nicholas, Dennis Wise and Dave Beasant and they became powerful people within the club. The club was going through a stage where things were going to have to get worse before they got better and, at the end of the season, we were relegated from the top flight after losing a two-leg relegation play-off against Middlesbrough. To make things worse, there was crowd trouble after the game and an attempted pitch invasion. Chelsea were forced to close the terraces for six matches the following season as a punishment.

It wasn't a happy time to be involved at Stamford Bridge but the next season, Campbell did a great job. We were promoted at a canter with ninety-nine points, seventeen clear of our nearest rivals Manchester City, and when the Second Division championship was already won, I finally got my chance in the first team. I'd travelled with the first team a couple of times before that but I hadn't made it to the bench. On the last day of the 1988/89 season, we were away to Portsmouth at Fratton Park, just like we had been for my reserve debut.

When Campbell told me to warm up, I did about twenty sprints up and down the touchline. I was hyperactive; I was petrified; I was desperate to get on – all at the same time. I was so nervous, I kept checking to make sure I had my shirt on. Campbell beckoned me over with about fifteen minutes to go and sent me on for Steve Clarke. Tony Dorigo was in the team at left-back and Clive Wilson was playing left-midfield. Dorigo was an England left-back and Wilson should have been – not much competition there then.

The line-up that day, just to give an idea of the time warp between then and when I played my last game for Chelsea alongside men like Marcel Desailly and Jimmy Floyd

Hasselbaink, went like this: Dave Beasant; Steve Clarke, Joe McLaughlin, Graham Roberts (capt.), Tony Dorigo; Gareth Hall, Peter Nicholas, Kevin McAllister, Clive Wilson; Kevin Wilson, Kerry Dixon (Monkou).

When I ran onto the pitch, I felt like I was starring in a movie about me. Everything had been building up to this point and now that I was living it, part of me wondered whether it was real. But I felt so alert, hypersensitive. It was as if everything around me had a different perspective. I was so wired that I was absorbing everything around me. I felt quicker than I had ever felt – I had so much energy I felt I could run past anybody. On an entirely different level, I also knew that if we beat Portsmouth, I'd get a win bonus that would pretty much double my salary for the month. It seemed like a vast amount of money to me at the time. We won 3–2 and I felt like I'd hit the jackpot. It was the only league game I ever played outside the top flight.

I had moved from Burnt Oak by then. I was renting a room from a friend's parents in Kingston-upon-Thames. John and Carole Denvir were antique clock dealers and they were wonderful people to stay with. Being with them gave me back my perspective when I got home from training and I felt they were a very positive part of my life, so when I had some spare time, I used to go up to Portobello Road and go to antiques fairs. I loved hearing about the history of something – where it had been made and who had owned it and the character of the carver or the manufacturer. I collected antique tins and old football boots. For a while, funded by the Professional Footballers Association, I even took an evening class in antiques in Oxford Street. Most of the people there had double-barrelled surnames and wanted to open their own antiques shop. I was the footballer at the back of the room. I'd also started a part-time degree in sociology and environmental studies at Kingston Poly, which took up another two nights a week, but I didn't finish it. When I broke into the first team, I didn't have the time any more.

In 1989/90, I trained with the first team before the season began and then played in the reserves until Christmas. I got back into the first team for a game against Crystal Palace. Andy Gray, Palace's midfielder, spat at me – which was nice. I shoved him and regretted it immediately. He was a scary guy. I spent the rest of the game thinking my life was probably in danger. We both got booked. Then, in the last minute, when we were 1–0 down, I scored an equalizer. For the first time, I felt like I really belonged with The Lads. They were so pleased in the dressing room afterwards and I had never seen that before. I suddenly felt ... not popular, but part of it, and accepted more, because I had done something that had had an effect on them.

It didn't really last. There were still plenty of times when I felt like jacking it in. I felt intimidated by my own peers. Peter Nicholas was one. He was the club captain and he could be really sarcastic. Then there was Graham Roberts, the former Tottenham player, who would throw his weight around.

I remember my full first-team debut in a Full Members Cup third-round tie against West Ham three days before Christmas 1989. There were 8,418 hardy souls there to see it. It was auspicious for me, but probably not for them, although we did win 4–3. But it was overshadowed by the behaviour of Roberts, who was captain at the time. As captain, it was his job to hand out the players' complimentary tickets before each match. The rule was that each player got five tickets for a game he was playing in to hand out to friends and relatives. He only gave me two so I asked him where the rest were and he said he was taking those. I told him I had people coming to watch because it was my debut so I needed all of them. He kept saying he needed a couple of extras for himself and I kept telling him I needed my full allocation.

So he beckoned me towards him and ushered me into the boot room at Stamford Bridge. He said he was going to knock my block off if I didn't give him my tickets. I said he could knock my block off if he wanted to but I was still having my tickets. He gave them to me very begrudgingly and then the next few days he kicked lumps out of me in training.

Roberts was somebody I had admired when he was at Spurs. But I had lost all respect for him. Perhaps it was something to do with the fact that he was coming towards the end of his career by then. Sometimes, when people are in that situation you see the worst of them. But I never forgave him for what he did over the tickets.

There's a funny story about Roberts on the pitch. We played Bristol City in the fourth round of the FA Cup in January 1990 and the night before, we had a discussion about the system we were playing and one of the coaches brought out a Subbuteo mat with players to illustrate what we were talking about. Bobby Campbell wanted to play

3–5–2 to accommodate Roberts because his legs were going. Ken Monkou and Erland Johnsen were supposed to play alongside him but they weren't happy about it because they knew they couldn't rely on Roberts to hold the line. Campbell told Erland and Ken what the plan was and asked Erland if he was okay with it. 'Not really,' Erland said. He picked up the Subbuteo player that represented Roberts and moved it up into midfield. 'At least that way, we know where he is,' Erland said. We lost 3–1 the next day at Ashton Gate.

We finished fifth in our first season back in the top flight. That didn't bring European qualification in those days, just after the ban on English clubs in European football had been lifted, but we won the Full Members Cup again with a 1–0 victory over Middlesbrough at Wembley. Campbell resigned the following season and Ian Porterfield, who had been a very popular coach, took over. The idea that the players were running the show increased when people like Wisey, Vinnie and Andy Townsend established themselves and Porterfield took over.

It had been easy for Porterfield when he was Campbell's assistant. He was always a players' man, but when he became manager, the players were too strong for him. He was never in control: the influential players used to get in his ears. He used to go and ask Andy Townsend who he should pick and inevitably the whole atmosphere became very unhealthy. Wisey was having a big effect on the dressing room by then, too, because he is a very strong character. He was a real handful, but not in a bad way. I got on with him a lot better the second time I was at Chelsea when we had both grown up a bit.

I was very competitive, as he was. We were both good runners and we trained hard together. We respected each other on the pitch but he always had an edge to him. A lot of those guys did. Socially, they were inseparable – they would spend a lot of time together and they were the main part of the group. I never felt part of that. I didn't want to do the things they were doing. They'd go to the pub or the bookies after training. They had a lot more money than me, for a start, so I couldn't really have joined in with them even if I'd wanted to.

I had my own thing going on. I didn't live where they lived. I had my own flat in Surbiton while they lived towards Gerrard's Cross in Buckinghamshire. I always planned things: I preferred to do that rather than pretend I was enjoying going to the pub. Pat Nevin took me under his wing and I looked up to him. I hung around with Jason Cundy and Dave Lee a bit, but I enjoyed my own space. I used to go and meet up with some people I had made friends with in London. I used to go to record shops and hang out in Covent Garden quite a lot. I would go to the odd museum. I did stuff you would do when you had time on your hands. I went to gigs. I had a girlfriend who was a student in Roehampton so I socialized with her friends. I was into my Indie music, too – Prefab Sprout, Waterboys, James Taylor Quartet, Gil Scott-Heron. While the lads were at the pub or the nightclub, I'd be at Brixton Academy, the Fridge and, maybe a bit later on, the Jazz Cafe.

I never had any problems with people like Vinnie or Mick Harford, who was almost as terrifying as John McNaught had been. I wasn't any sort of threat to them. I just didn't get involved with them but I still felt like a bit of a whipping boy, even when I had been at the club for a few years and was beginning to hold down my place in the first team. If I used to try to be funny by being sarcastic, they just wouldn't understand. 'Did you hear what he just said,' they'd say. I'd say I was joking but they wouldn't have it. I felt like I couldn't win. I couldn't really be myself.

I felt like the whole thing was quite demeaning. However well I did on the pitch, I wasn't getting the support off the pitch. In 1991/92 under Porterfield, I thought I had cracked it. When I had first arrived at the club, I didn't think I had any chance of making it at all particularly as Dorigo and Wilson, two brilliant left-backs, were both on the playing staff. But they had both left by the summer of 1991 and I was the man in possession. I played more games than any other player that season. At last, I was playing regularly. Then the following season, Porterfield's troubles began to mount up. The situation got worse and worse. Tensions at the club began to rise.

Porterfield began to use me as a scapegoat – or at least that's how it appeared to me. In the first half of the 1992/93 season, I only started three times. I was coming on as sub most of the time, mainly for Graham Stuart, and it was starting to wear me down. Porterfield gave me the impression that he didn't trust me to play in defence because he thought I was too impetuous so even when I did get a chance, it was usually as a left-winger. The thing was, he didn't have the bottle to drop any of his mates among The Lads so he used me as a default option. I was so unhappy at the club in other ways that when I started to feel as if I had stopped making progress on the pitch as well, it was the final straw. I was the easy option for Porterfield to leave out and it just kept happening and happening and happening.

The truth is that I didn't feel part of the team on the pitch or off it. I was fighting against everyone – not literally, obviously, but I never got in the main dressing room and even though it sounds pathetic, that felt like quite a powerful symbol of defeat. Maybe the other players thought I didn't want to have any interest in them; perhaps they were reacting to my obvious unhappiness. I could be pretty chippy myself and they probably thought I didn't want to know – but I did want to be part of it and I never felt I was. I wanted to be part of the team; I wanted to be successful. The last six months, I was being treated like a whipping boy and I didn't want that. The constant drip-drip-drip of piss-taking was really starting to wear me down and when all the gay stuff came out in the autumn of 1991, I blamed The Lads for that, too. I had had enough of Chelsea.

In particular, I'd had enough of Porterfield. He was just someone I didn't respect. The players didn't respect him and he didn't respect himself. He wasn't very coherent about what he wanted and he was too easily influenced by his senior players. Basically, he was one of those guys who just wanted to be liked – he wanted to be close to the players. All the older players could still talk their way into the team because of who they were rather than their contribution. Porterfield was one of those men who was a weak manager.

I wasn't getting a fair crack of the whip and by midway through the 1992/93 season, my patience was ready to snap. Porterfield had included me in the starting line-up for the

Boxing Day game against Southampton at the Bridge and I got myself fired up about how I was going to seize my opportunity and prove him wrong. But ten minutes from the end, we were still losing and I saw the board go up with my number on it and Craig Burley with that gap in his front teeth standing there waiting to replace me.

I was over on the far side of the pitch in front of the West Stand when play stopped. It was a long jog over to the bench and the tunnel and by the time I got across to where Porterfield was standing, something just overcame me. I had started untucking my shirt and as I was coming off, I looked over at Porterfield and he couldn't even meet my gaze because he was so embarrassed. I worked myself up into a rage. I felt my shirt in my hand and I just ripped it off and hurled it at him. I still don't know whether it actually hit him.

The instant I did it, I could sense the atmosphere change in the crowd. Throwing the shirt was sacrilege to the supporters. I now understand that. I was sad that some of them thought I was disrespecting the badge – that was the last thing I meant to do. If I could have taken my boot off and thrown that at Porterfield instead, I would have done. But I was so upset with everything that was happening that the pressure of it all got to me. As soon as I disappeared down the tunnel, I burst into tears.

At the end of the game, the rest of the players filed into the dressing room. No one said anything to me. Porterfield didn't even say anything to me. I got hammered in the papers for having let down the club. I was left out of the next game as a punishment but Porterfield did play me again when he brought me on as a sub against Crystal Palace and then gave me a rare 90 minutes against Manchester City. Ken Bates was okay about what I'd done. He said I needed to apologize but I'd done that already. He probably felt the same as me: he sacked Porterfield a few weeks later. It wasn't much of a reprieve for me, though. David Webb was the next man in and I didn't last long with him.

I had a couple of chats with Webb. He said the usual stuff about this being a new chapter and he backed it up by picking me to start in his first game, away at Blackburn Rovers on 21 February 1993. The supporters were okay with me, just about, and even though by now I was keen to get away from Chelsea, I felt like I was on trial again. I thought I had a chance to prove myself to the new manager and that maybe this might just be a new beginning.

It didn't quite go according to plan at Blackburn, though. Frank Sinclair got himself sent off in the first half for hand-balling a certain goal and we were under the cosh. We came in at half-time and Webb was already talking about changing the formation. Nine minutes after half-time, the board went up and my number was on it again. I was replaced by Mal Donaghy. Fair enough, he had to make a tactical change. It was unfortunate but I didn't take it personally. Then, when I was at Harlington the next day, Webb came up to me in the medical room and started talking to me in front of everyone else who was there.

He was honest, I'll give him that. He said that having seen me play at Ewood Park he was happy to let me go. 'There are a few clubs interested in you,' he said, 'and my job is to weigh up whether you will go on and do all right for yourself or if we will never hear of Graeme Le Saux again. The reason I'm letting you go is that I don't think we'll ever hear of Graeme Le Saux again.' And that was it. Thank you and goodnight. Rejected after fifty-four minutes of one game. I obviously made a big impression on Dave Webb.

And that was it for me at Chelsea the first time round. That was the end. I came back in the summer to buy Batesy lunch and say thank you to him for everything he had done for me. He's an amazing man in many ways, a driven, stubborn man who saved the club. The year before I left, he had finally outmanoeuvred the property developers who wanted to build on Stamford Bridge and reunited the free-hold with the football club. He had done a lot for me, too. He had given me my foot up and I owed him. I took him out to his favourite fish restaurant on the Brompton Road, feeling pretty nervous about the price of the wine he was ordering. Part of me thought he wouldn't let me pay – but he did.

I came to love Chelsea later in my career and got to know the likes of Dennis Wise a lot better second time round. But when I left in 1993, it was a relief. I felt like I had escaped. I felt like I was suddenly at liberty. My relationship with the supporters had got awkward and my progress in the first team had come to a dead end. Blackburn was my way out. It was the best thing that ever happened to me in terms of my advancement as a player. It gave me the opportunity to prove to myself I was a better player than Chelsea thought I was. And I suppose they admitted as much when they brought me back four years later.

A few months after I left, Webb was sacked and Glenn Hoddle became Chelsea manager. A revolution started at the club that led to the arrival of Ruud Gullit and Gianluca Vialli and a whole new era of glamour and success on the King's Road. I'm sad I missed out on Hoddle at club level. He would have been good for me. But not as good as the men who took me to the peak of my career and to the summit of the Premiership with Blackburn Rovers.

FOUR

Glory in the North

I didn't know where Blackburn was when I heard Kenny Dalglish was interested in signing me – not exactly, anyway. The northern mill towns had always merged into one in my mind before then and Blackburn had disappeared off the football map for a few years. I had to have a look at a road atlas to check just how far north of Manchester I might be living in my prospective new home. Six months after I signed, I bought a little cottage in a beautiful village called Waddington near Clitheroe. It was a quaint and picturesque place: a little stream ran through the back garden. Chris Sutton gave me a lift back from training once with a couple of his kids and I invited them all in. 'No thanks,' he said, deadpan as usual, 'I don't let my kids in houses that cost less than a hundred grand.'

That was Chris – and that was Blackburn Rovers. I loved it there. People might compare Jack Walker, the club's owner, to Chelsea's benefactor, Roman Abramovich, but I bet Michael Ballack has never bet money with Abramovich over a game where you bounce a penny against a wall and the person who gets the penny to stay closest to the wall wins. Jack was unbelievable at that game. He used to play it with all the lads and he always won. He took money off everyone. Because he lived in Jersey, he and I had quite a close connection. Sometimes, he used to invite my dad to fly up to the games on his private jet. My dad loved that.

Things turned sour for me at Blackburn in the end. I had a fight on the pitch with my own team-mate, David Batty, during a Champions League game in Moscow and then I got an injury that nearly ended my career and turned a few people's stomachs because it was so horrific. Almost all the players from the club came to visit me while I was recovering in hospital but none of the officials. But none of that spoiled what I had already achieved at Ewood Park. None of it altered the fact that at Blackburn I won back my love of the game.

At Blackburn, I became part of a great adventure. I was part of the only team aside from Manchester United, Arsenal and Chelsea that has won the Premiership. It was the only title I won but what an achievement it was to win it for Blackburn Rovers, a club who had emerged from the shadows of a proud past to challenge the giants of the present game. When we won the title in 1994/95, it was the first time the club had done it for eighty-one years. Jack Walker said it was a miracle.

People talked about how Blackburn bought the title with Jack's money but that was wrong. A lot of the signings were cheap: Jason Wilcox didn't cost anything; I was £750,000; Colin Hendry wasn't expensive; Stuart Ripley was £1.3 million. Anyway, there are plenty of clubs who throw money at success and get nowhere. Look at Newcastle United's troubles over the years.

In four years at Blackburn, Kenny led the team to promotion from the First Division, fourth in the first year of the Premiership and then won the Premiership two seasons later. Of course he spent big money on players – he had broken the British transfer record for Alan Shearer and Chris Sutton. In Kenny's four years at the club, they spent £28 million. He used the money wisely, and didn't buy players that ended up in the reserves. When the team broke up, they made a £30 million profit on the players Kenny had bought. Compare that to the £190 million Chelsea spent on players in the first year after Roman Abramovich's arrival.

Look at what we had to beat, too: probably the best United team of them all – certainly the one that most United fans rate most highly. This was the United side that won the Double in 1993/94, the powerhouse team of Peter Schmeichel, Gary Pallister, Andrei Kanchelskis, Paul Ince, Mark Hughes, Ryan Giggs and Eric Cantona. They were an awesome side. Most people felt they were an immovable object – but somehow we shifted them.

I felt liberated just being away from Chelsea and the negativity of that dressing room for a start. For some reason, I felt I fitted in okay at Ewood Park; I never had a problem. That was an incredible relief. It made me realize that perhaps I hadn't been solely to blame for the general sense of alienation that had infused everything I did at Chelsea, on and off the pitch.

There I was, a young guy who came from about as far south as you could possibly get in the British Isles, playing in

one of football's northern outposts and yet I was as happy as
Larry up there in Lancashire. I didn't feel any of the alienation I felt at Chelsea. I still wasn't really one of The Lads
but nor was I an outsider any more and I wasn't picked on or
victimized. This gave me the confidence to be happy on and
off the pitch. I was holding down a regular place in a team
that was on the rise. I grew up as a footballer at Blackburn.
At Chelsea, I was someone who had potential. At Blackburn,
I began to realize my potential.

The move to Blackburn in March of 1993 nearly didn't
happen. It nearly got derailed at the last minute. I was on a
train travelling north with John Hollins, who was effectively
acting as my agent, and Eric Hall, who had managed to put
himself in the middle of the deal somehow. Then the train
broke down at Warrington. It was transfer deadline day and
the deadline was approaching fast.

We didn't notice there was a problem for a little while
because Eric had been telling anecdotes for two hours solid.
There was one that caused everyone particular amusement.
It was a story about an Italian guy Eric had met who worked
as a waiter in one of the swanky Park Lane hotels. In his
thick accent, he'd told Eric about this gala reception they had
held for John Hollins and all the film stars and celebrities
who had attended and how much champagne had been
drunk. 'For John Hollins?' Eric had said in amazement. 'No,
not John Hollins,' the guy said, making a tremendous effort
with pronunciation, 'Joan Collins.'

Eventually, we got off the train and jumped into a taxi.
Even though I was just about to make a big move, I felt a bit
nervous about how much that particular cab was going to

cost. Everyone was starting to panic a bit by then. There were a few frantic phone calls assuring Blackburn we were on the way and updating them about our progress. We got there in the end. I've got no idea what Eric got out of the deal but I'm sure he wasn't going up there for charity. I didn't pay him but it was him who had contacted me to say Blackburn were interested in the first place. Perhaps he got the equivalent of a finder's fee. I don't know – I didn't ask any questions. The official fee was £750,000. It broke down into £400,000 plus a Blackburn forward called Steve Livingstone, who didn't have a great time at Chelsea.

Since I'd first heard about Blackburn's intention to sign me, I'd been taking a closer interest in their games and what was going on at the club. They were flying – going places very fast. A lot of it was down to Jack Walker, the local steel magnate who was ploughing chunks of his fortune into the club he had supported from when he was a boy. He'd sold WalkerSteel to British Steel for £330 million and in the summer of 1991, he'd bought 62 per cent of Rovers. He wanted to get the best and he was happy to pay for it. The key was getting Kenny on board as manager. He did that; then everything else started to fall into place.

They were still in the old Second Division back then. Kenny bought Colin Hendry, Mike Newell and Alan Wright to propel them towards the top flight. They blew automatic promotion but then a goal from David Speedie in the play-off final against Leicester City took them up. In the summer of 1992, Kenny snatched Alan Shearer from the under the noses of Manchester United and paid a British record transfer fee of £3.6 million to Southampton for him.

When I became aware of their interest in me, they were on their way to finishing fourth in their first season in the top tier. Stuart Ripley, Tim Sherwood and Henning Berg had also signed by then. I knew that Crystal Palace, Ipswich, Villa and Manchester City were also interested in me but because of the presence of Kenny, who had always been one of my footballing idols, and because of the challenge they were mounting, Blackburn was the possibility that interested me most.

I watched them on the telly a few times. I looked at their left-back who was a guy called Tony Dobson. He was a centre-half really and I was hopeful I would be able to force my way into the side. But I wanted to make sure Kenny wasn't just signing me as a stop-gap for Alan Wright, who was injured at the time. I spoke to him about it briefly when I finally arrived at Ewood Park on deadline day. Kenny said he was buying me as a left-back but that that didn't mean he wouldn't play me in another position.

He didn't make any promises he couldn't keep and he didn't give me any guarantees about having a first-team place. I don't really understand how any manager can sensibly do that in the modern era of big squads and fierce competition for places. How can you guarantee a player a first-team place even if it becomes obvious at some point that someone else deserves it more than him? What Kenny did say was that if they played me in a different position, he would take responsibility for it. He might play me at right-wing, he said, and if the experiment failed, he would make sure he took the flak for it, not me. I thought that was a great answer, not that I needed much convincing and anyway there was no time for arguing. I signed a four-year deal.

I never regretted it – not even when I realized how bad the training facilities were. It was worse than Harlington – and being worse than Harlington took some doing. But the situation at Blackburn was like some sort of throwback to parks football. It was so bizarre it was almost funny. In fact, it was funny. We trained at a place called Pleasington Playing Fields which was a public park so we got changed at Ewood Park, jumped in our cars and drove the few miles down there. There wasn't any chance of a coach or a mini-bus to take us down there – that would have been far too sophisticated.

So we played on these pitches at Pleasington, though it wasn't very pleasant at all. I used to say they were going to get done under the Trades Descriptions Act. There was a road running between them and it led to the local cemetery and crematorium. At regular intervals, a funeral cortège would wind its way slowly down that road with its cast of sombre mourners. It seemed disrespectful to carry on booting a ball around in those circumstances so sometimes we would stand and wait as the cortège passed by to show our respect. They would always arrive looking very melancholy but on the way back down the road, the mood had often lifted a little. By then, the mourners would be yelling out encouragement or wishing us good luck for the following Saturday. Often, they'd try and get players' autographs.

That was what it was like – running around trying not to step in dog pooh and stopping now and then for funerals. After training, filthy and tired, we jumped in our cars again and drove back to Ewood Park for a shower. That wasn't the end of it either. It's hard to believe now in the era of the totally pampered professional, but at Blackburn we still had to wash our own kit. Nobody ever questioned it or complained about it: Kenny took his kit home; so did Alan Shearer. No one got special treatment.

Not that anyone could really have complained if Alan had got special treatment. He was phenomenal. He was coming into his prime when I arrived at Blackburn and he was a scoring machine. He was in amazing form. When he got the ball in certain areas, I learned that I didn't really have to dash up to support him because I knew what he was going to do. He just didn't miss. Sometimes, I'd see him bearing down on goal and I'd start to turn around to walk back to the halfway line because I knew he was going to score. I'm not exaggerating. I had that level of confidence in Alan.

Sometimes when certain players take penalties, you know they are not going to miss. Well, Alan was like that from outfield play. He was hitting goals from thirty-five yards out as if they were a matter of routine. He and I developed an incredible relationship on the pitch. We started to connect and I was able to anticipate the kind of runs he made. He made brilliant runs, too, and I had a hand in a lot of his goals, swinging in my crosses from the left or sliding the ball into the channels for him.

I loved playing in the same team as Alan. It was a real privilege. He was a tough guy to play with in some ways. He demanded a standard. If he had made a run and your cross didn't clear the first defender, he'd scream at you. He'd make his displeasure known. I didn't like that particularly but it had the desired effect. It wasn't the kind of disrespectful moaning some players go in for. You knew there were going to be consequences if you didn't get it just right. It made me work even harder to make sure I didn't screw it up.

Right from the start, Alan always came across as a person who had ambition, desire and focus. He was going to get to where he needed to be in his career and it wouldn't have done to get in his way. He had a very obvious path he was following. He used to say time and again that it wasn't about him, it was about the team. But when you're a goalscorer through and through like he was, it has to be about you, really. I don't think he needed to make any apology about that – that's just the kind of person he was.

Sometimes, a team benefits from a striker's individuality and when it came to our title challenge in my second full season at the club, Alan carried it with his goals. He was the difference and we were built around him. That's why him and Mike Newell got on so well – because Mike sacrificed himself for Alan and was willing and happy to do it. Newelly dragged people away and created a lot of space for Alan. Newelly scored plenty himself, by the way.

Alan was very, very driven but he was uncomplicated, too. After we won the title in 1994/95, he went home and, according to his book, he celebrated by creosoting his fence – not the sort of thing to admit. He never made a big fuss or stood out. There was a group of the lads who played golf in Southport a lot and when we went out on club days to the races, he was always the luckiest man alive. Any sort of gambling, Alan was always a winner. Maybe it's what they say about money coming to money.

Things changed for him a little bit at Blackburn when Chris Sutton arrived in the summer of 1994. His arrival created a lot of fuss because Kenny paid £5.5 million for him and broke the British transfer record again. It wasn't as if Alan was overshadowed because nobody could do that to him when he was in that kind of form, but it disrupted the cosy relationship he had with Mike Newell. Suddenly, he was being asked to play with a guy who wanted to score as many goals as him and who was a stubborn man.

That was when I saw a side of Alan that I wasn't as keen on because Chris had a hard time. It wasn't part of Alan's script that someone else should be scoring as many goals as him. He had always had the luxury of having the team built around him so he could score the goals – him, not someone else. Alan knew his relationship with Mike Newell revolved around himself and neither he nor Mike reacted well when Chris broke up their partnership. There was never any camaraderie between Alan and Chris, they were never close.

Nevertheless, they made a great partnership on the pitch. They were both tremendous goalscorers but they created chances for each other, too. If Alan was phenomenal, Chris wasn't far behind – Chris scored plenty of goals, too. We weren't quite as reliant on Alan after Chris Sutton arrived and for all the understated antipathy between them, the team was better for both of them being in it.

I thrived, right from the start – both on and off the pitch. It was such a relief for me to get on with the core of the dressing room. I still wasn't really part of any of the cliques – I still did my own thing. I didn't become what I'd hated so much at Chelsea. I was never really one of The Lads but that was partly because there weren't really any cliques at Blackburn – not in the first couple of years anyway.

Everything was inclusive, rather than exclusive. At last, I felt I was on the same wavelength as the other players.

I enjoyed the banter at Blackburn where I'd hated it at Chelsea. I suppose if I'm honest it was partly because I wasn't really the target any more. No one in particular was the target, which is why it seemed so much less malicious than what had happened at Chelsea. My nickname changed from Berge to Rag: I had a soft-top car which is called a 'rag-top' in America and the number plate involved RAG somehow. Kenny started it, I think, and it stuck. I got my fair share of practical jokes played on me but I didn't feel like I was being picked on. In fact, I liked the sense of humour the Blackburn lads had. They made me laugh. I even joined in some of the time which was a quantum leap from my experience at Chelsea when joining in was never an option.

There was a game some of the lads played which was a kind of high-stakes brinksmanship involving the huge windows in the team coach. We drove down to Selhurst Park for a game against Crystal Palace and we'd only just got onto the M6 heading south when Mike Newell, Alan, David Batty, Tim Sherwood and Paul Warhurst started playing at the back of the bus. The game involved the small hammer they often have in coaches to break the glass in an emergency. The crux of the game was that each player took a turn hitting the window. You had to hit it as hard as you could without breaking it and each player had to hit it harder than the last one. You can guess the outcome of that particular game.

Eventually, of course, the glass broke and the bus had to pull over onto the hard shoulder somewhere near Knutsford services. We had to kick the rest of the window out because there were shards of glass everywhere. Our bus driver was a bloke called Stoney who was the butt of a lot of the boys' tricks and japes. He had a very high-pitched voice and the lads loved doing impersonations of him. He went mad when he realized what had happened. 'What the fucking hell have you done to my coach, you bastards,' he said. The perpetrators said a stone must have flown up off the motorway and smashed the window. 'Lying bastards,' he said.

Stoney said he was going to tell the chairman. He said we needed to learn a bit more respect. In the end, Kenny had to come to the back of the bus, calm him down and persuade him it wouldn't be a good idea to tell the chairman. Kenny came up with a different explanation. He said the microwave oven that we had at the back of the coach must have heated the window to the point where it cracked. Begrudgingly, Stoney went back to the driver's seat and we continued with our journey. A few minutes later, I looked around and Mike Newell was sitting by the open window with no shirt on. It was obviously him who had dealt the window the fatal blow and this was his forfeit. He had to sit there for half an hour, the curtains flapping around his head while he shivered and the rest of the guys laughed at him.

Stoney used to get more grief when we got to our hotel on away trips, too. The boys would have a whip-round for him and everybody would put a fiver in. He had to earn it, though. They would make a foul concoction of milk, eggs, tobasco and salt and pepper – basically anything they could get hold of – mix it up in a pint glass and tell him he could have the money if he drank it down in one. He always drank

90

it. His face would start going red and he would look like he was about to throw up but he usually managed to keep it down.

The thing was, Stoney wanted to be one of the boys, and £100 was a lot of money to him, probably double his money for the trip. So, even though he was the victim of these challenges, he put up with it. Another time, during some slightly stuffy candlelit dinner we were having at a hotel, Mike Newell and Tim Sherwood were messing about playing the game where you breathe on the end of a spoon and then see how long you can hang it off the end of your nose. Then they asked Stoney to do it, too. I could tell they were up to some sort of mischief. I think Alan Shearer had been heating the spoon while no one was watching. Stoney grabbed the spoon and put it on the end of his nose and then started screaming. He ran off and dunked his head in a bowl of water. He had a scar on his nose for about three months.

There was a phase where the practical jokes all got a bit out of control. At one hotel, I left the window open in my room and suddenly a balloon full of water exploded on the floor. Another favourite was unscrewing the eye-piece in the room door from the outside and then squirting a jet from a fire extinguisher through the hole. Those extinguishers are so powerful that the jet would spurt right across the room and soak the curtains on the far side.

But there was no harm in any of it. It was just the product of boredom, really, and no one got picked on more than anyone else. No one got picked on at all, in fact. It wasn't the kind of malicious humour it was at Chelsea. You might think the jokes on Stoney were a bit out of order but they were more like slapstick than anything else – and Stoney was a willing participant. Getting him to drink his cocktail for the whip-round we'd had for him was pretty puerile, I suppose, but he enjoyed the camaraderie of it all. He was part of the gang, really. Sometimes, footballers are like kids on a school trip.

I learned to relax a bit more at Blackburn. I chilled out – to an extent anyway. We were all in it together to win. I learned to laugh at jokes and understand maybe that sometimes people could make fun of you without meaning to offend you or humiliate you. Perhaps the lads at Chelsea had done their job – they'd toughened me up. Maybe that's part of the reason why I was more at ease in the North-West than I'd ever been at Stamford Bridge.

Mainly, though, it was because of the standard of the football at Blackburn. I was swept along by the success we were having. We all were. The playing side of the club was brilliantly run by Kenny and his coach, Ray Harford. It was through them that I came to appreciate just how much good training sessions contributed to a positive result on a Saturday afternoon. That was the first thing I noticed at Blackburn: the intensity of the training that Kenny and Ray organized. The inadequacies of the facilities didn't matter when you had Kenny and Ray orchestrating the sessions.

I got on well with Kenny but he could be difficult. He might have presented a dour image to the media but he did have a very dry sense of humour and he got emotional in private. If he was displeased with something someone had done during a game, he hammered them. If you were injured, he didn't want to know you. Bill Shankly was like that, too, apparently. I was carried off on a stretcher during the first half of a pre-season game at Bramall Lane one August. My shinpad had been snapped in half by the force of the tackle and I thought I had broken my leg. I was lying on a treatment table in our dressing room when the half-time whistle went and the team starting filing back in. Kenny glared over at me. I thought he was about to express his concern but he started bollocking the physio. 'Can't you take him somewhere else to do that?' he snapped. 'I've got a team talk to give.' I had to haul myself off the table and hop into the Sheffield United dressing room to get stitched up in there. There was nothing compassionate about that but it was practical – and that was the way he was.

Kenny was passionate; he was determined; and he could get angry. Even when he played in practice matches, he would lose his rag. He was viciously competitive. Alan Shearer learned so much from him. You couldn't do anything but look up to him and admire him but as a forward Alan was in a particularly good position to eke everything he could out of listening to Kenny and watching him in training.

Whatever Kenny said, I always admired him. He was always very down to earth. He never played the big star or abused the power he had. He made you feel equal. He never patronized any of us or looked down on us. In training, he was still incredible: the way he used his body to shield the ball was amazing. Gianfranco Zola was the only other person I saw who could do it like Kenny. As the ball was coming to them, they had a gift for judging the weight of the pass and the position of their marker and using those two variables to dictate what they did. They could let the ball roll on for an extra yard or they could take a touch but their appreciation of time and space was everything.

Most of all, Kenny was a players' man. Some managers side with the club; Kenny always sided with the players. Gordon Strachan was like that, too. Kenny always defended us, always backed us. I liked his humour even though I couldn't understand him half the time. I said 'Pardon?' and 'What?' a lot, or I just laughed and hoped he'd been making a joke. Kenny and Ray were a great foil for each other. It was a bit like good cop, bad cop: Kenny could be hard but Ray was an unfailingly lovely bloke.

Ray was like a father to us all. He was the one who would put his arm around you. Kenny was more volatile. What really wound him up was if you kept making the same mistakes. He was very keen on the basics, too. He criticized me in the dressing room once for two throw-ins that he said had put the team in trouble. Kenny didn't get in your face – it wasn't like Sir Alex Ferguson's hairdryer – but I never wanted to court his anger. When he got angry, his face changed; he looked at you as if he hated you. If anyone ever answered him back, he got very personal with them very quickly. If I hadn't played well, I knew I was going to be in for it when I got back to the changing room. If I made a mistake, I knew he would have noticed. It made me accountable and kept my standards up.

Ray was different. For a start, he sounded a bit like Tommy Cooper and even reminded us generally of that comedian. The lads loved him. He was the organizer. Kenny would come in like a whirlwind and change things around or make new demands and Ray would sweep it up and fix it again. Kenny got emotionally involved while Ray was like an older statesman who saw the bigger picture. The balance between them was excellent. Both of them played in this great five-a-side we used to have on Friday afternoons: Kenny and Ray with Colin Hendry, Alan and Newelly against me, Tim Sherwood, Jason Wilcox, Kevin Gallacher and Stuart Ripley. It was the Southport Serious Boys against the Wannabes. It was always feisty. Ray wasn't very mobile so he was the butt of a lot of jokes but he could still play. There was no love lost even though it was the day before the game. It was like walking into a Friday derby match between long-standing rivals.

We worked very hard on the basics in training. Often, we did the same thing over and over again. Kenny and Ray created mental pictures for us for every situation and it worked like clockwork. We concentrated a lot on pattern of play which is basically an unopposed game situation. We lined up in our formation and worked through different scenarios that might unfold. A lot of our play went through the full-backs and that's one of the reasons why my development progressed so quickly at Ewood Park. That's why I went from being a mixed bag of tricks at Chelsea to the finished article at Blackburn. Kenny and Ray felt full-back was one of the few positions where you could often find yourself with a bit of time and therefore the opportunity to start a move well. That gave me and David May, who was usually right-back at that time, a huge amount of responsibility. The point was clear: if we didn't start it all off properly, an attack would break down.

Typically, when I got the ball at left-back, my first option was Jason Wilcox. If he came short, then Alan or Newelly would drop into the space that Jason had created. Then the support came from there. When you got the ball in a certain position, it set off a chain reaction. We were very well organized but we had plenty of flair, too. People accused us of playing long-ball football because we used to get forward early, but that was unfair. We were direct but once we got into good areas, we were as creative as any team. We had some wonderfully creative players.

I learned a lot from the players around me, particularly Kevin Moran. Kevin had had a great career at Manchester United, and won the FA Cup with them in 1985. He was a veteran when I arrived at Blackburn, a veteran who struggled with his knees, but what a great professional he was. Kevin was happy to pass on his experience to me. He was a very generous team-mate and he taught me a great deal. He was a huge influence on me. He made me tackle properly and made me defend properly.

Kevin never got in my face but he kept me motivated on the pitch. He led by example in everything he did. He always helped people out because he read the game so well. He'd yell at me when he knew I needed to be woken up. He made me brave because he was brave. If I went into a tackle with a bit of fear, he really dug me out for it – not in a horrible way but in a manner that made me feel accountable. Colin Hendry was the other centre-half when I first arrived and he was brave as well. I knew that if either of those two asked me to do something, I couldn't accuse them of not being willing to do it themselves.

I was given my chance straight away when I arrived. Kenny threw me into the team for the next home game against Liverpool and we won 3–1. Kevin Gallacher had joined at the same time as me and he scored a couple of goals. I won man of the match – you got a brass carriage clock for that at Blackburn – so it was the perfect start for both of us. I never let my place go. When Alan Wright came back from injury, I kept him out of the team. In a way, I felt bad about that because he was such a lovely guy, such a popular bloke, and I knew I was affecting his career. But he never held it against me and that says a lot about him. He and Jason Wilcox were close mates and I wondered whether maybe Jason might feel some awkwardness towards me because I had usurped his friend. I wondered if that might be an issue but Jason was fine about it, too. The relationship I formed on the pitch with him was the best I had in my career to that point. We really clicked. We complemented each other's games. The other thing about Jason was that he was great at doing impressions and if you're good at impressions you've got it cracked in football – you're in with the in-crowd straight away. I really missed a trick there.

We were water-tight as a defence, first with Bobby Mimms in goal and then Tim Flowers. A couple of months after I arrived, we finished fourth in the first season of the Premiership. We played Manchester United at Old Trafford in the spring of 1993 the night after they had been confirmed as champions for the first time since 1967. That was a weird atmosphere for us. We wanted to gatecrash their party and spoil it but even though most of them were hung-over, they still beat us.

The next season, we were up to second even though United ran away with it and won their first Double.

Finishing runners-up to them felt like a big achievement but we had the hunger to try and go one better the following season. Because we were such a young side, we were always positive and optimistic. We played away games with the same approach as home games – we went for it. Everybody began to treat us as if we were genuine title contenders.

We signed Chris Sutton that summer and we led from the front the following season. We lost 2–0 to United in the Charity Shield and everybody predicted immediately that United were going to canter to a hat-trick of titles. We drew our first game against Southampton but then won five of the next six. Over Christmas and New Year, we went on another great run. We won eleven out of twelve games this time and by the end of January, we were six points ahead of United. Even I scored a couple over the festive period. I was particularly pleased with a free-kick over the wall against Manchester City.

Sutton and Shearer were quickly christened the SAS and for a while Chris overshadowed Alan. That didn't please Alan and it got difficult for Chris for a while. I always liked Chris but he found it hard to forge close relationships within the club and Alan had such a power base at Blackburn that sometimes it felt as though Chris was always going to be condemned to being an outsider. You wouldn't have known that from the way they played together on the pitch, though. They were superb, both good professionals.

My time at Blackburn is really the only period when I've played football and actually felt sorry for the opposition. Even when things had started to go wrong in the 1995/96 season, we were capable of flashes of brilliance. We scored seven against Nottingham Forest at Ewood Park that season, including a 25-yard screamer from me that blasted in off the underside of the bar. We absolutely battered them. For half an hour, they couldn't get out of their half. It was just wave after wave of Blackburn attacks. I spent most of my time standing on the halfway line, admiring the display but knowing how miserable the Forest players must be feeling.

We were great in 1994/95 but we nearly blew it. At the start of the run-in, Alex Ferguson said the only way United could possibly win the title now was if Blackburn 'did a Devon Loch', a reference to the Queen Mother's horse that threw away the Grand National in 1956 when it slipped within sight of the finishing line. He'd learned that trick from the former Celtic boss, Jock Stein, who had said the same thing about a Rangers' championship lead back in the Sixties when Ferguson was the centre-forward at Ibrox. Rangers collapsed and Celtic won the title. Ferguson's a clever man. He knew that nerves would begin to grip us. He knew that none of us at Blackburn had ever won anything and that we would start to tighten up. United began to reel us in.

We began to bottle it. We stopped playing. We lost to West Ham at Upton Park over Easter. Then we lost 3–2 at home to Manchester City. We started listening to United games on the radio. We became obsessive about how they were playing and what results they were getting. We started hoping they would drop points. I listened to one match while I was driving back up the M6 in my car. United's opponents took the lead and I went mad. My car must have veered across three lanes. I was ecstatic. But United came back and won it.

Every game in that run-in was unbelievably tense. Our last home game was against Kevin Keegan's Newcastle at Ewood

Park and both sides had chances. Near the end, there was a goalmouth scramble and the ball squirted out towards the byline off Darren Peacock, the Newcastle central defender. I got to it first and dinked a cross to the back post where, inevitably, Alan was waiting. He climbed all over John Beresford and powered his header in from point-blank range. I ran across to the supporters with him and it felt like being in Roy of the Rovers. We survived a couple of late scares. Tim Flowers made two brilliant saves from Ruel Fox and Beresford. We won 1–0.

I was still so ecstatic after the game that I got one of my friends, Susie, out onto the pitch in the empty stadium and we copied Fantasy Football and did a Phoenix from the Flames re-enactment of it. She pretended to be me and I pretended to be Alan heading it in. We were in semi-darkness and I didn't think anyone was watching. Then I heard some cheering high in the stands and realized that the people who were still enjoying the hospitality in the executive boxes had seen it all.

The win over Newcastle put us five points clear for one night. Then United beat Southampton with their game in hand so our advantage was two points going into the final match of the season. United were at West Ham. We were at Liverpool. We had better goal difference so we only needed a draw if United won at West Ham. Ferguson sneered and said we were safe because there was no way Liverpool would beat us and run the risk of handing the title to their most bitter rivals. He was playing psychological games again and, again, he was getting it right.

Kenny and Ray didn't appear to know how to control the situation. They tried to play it very calm and positive but I was more nervous before that game at Liverpool than for any game before or since. So much was hanging on it. And I wasn't the only nervous one. The atmosphere in the dressing room at Anfield was tense: it was quiet; it was uncomfortable – very different to how it normally was. Jason Wilcox was normally funny and bubbly and a bundle of energy, but now he was quiet. Stuart Ripley was even more pale than normal. We were like rabbits trapped in the headlights. Still, we got a couple of good breaks. The crowd wanted us to win for a start; and then Alan ran onto a pass from Stuart after twenty minutes and scored to give us the lead. That bought us a bit of security but we wasted it by playing some of the worst football in the history of the game. We seemed to be working purely on the principle that if the ball wasn't near our goal, they couldn't score. It was panic defending and Liverpool were a good side, too. It was only a matter of time until they took advantage of our discomfort.

Stuart Ripley, amongst others, was appalling in that game; it was the worst I had ever seen him play. He came in at half-time and sank down on his seat. 'My bloody legs won't work,' he said, 'I'm so nervous I can't make them work.' I knew what he meant. I think we all felt a bit like that. We knew how close we were. We knew that United were all over West Ham at Upton Park and that they looked like they were going to win there. But in the second half, we didn't play any better.

It was more of the same. We just kept giving the ball away. Liverpool were also a good team, a good passing side. They had Jamie Redknapp in the centre and Steve McManaman out wide. I'd say he was one of my most difficult opponents. He was very hard to play against. He was clever and he was two-footed and it was hard to pick which way he was going to go. He enjoyed himself that day at Anfield but it was John Barnes who got their equalizer with a clipped shot from the edge of the box.

We hung on and hung on until the last couple of minutes of the game. Then they got a free-kick on the edge of the box when David Batty chopped down McManaman. McManaman got up limping and grimacing. I lined up the wall for Tim Flowers and stood there on the left-hand side of the wall. Redknapp stood over the ball and then took it quickly. As soon as he struck it, even though I had my back to goal, I knew we were in trouble. It went over my head at just the right height. I heard it fizzing over me and I turned round to see Tim scrambling to the right across his goal to try and reach it. He couldn't get to it and we were 2–1 down. I looked round. Everyone had their hands on their heads. I did, too. It was a sickening feeling.

They didn't celebrate that much. There was the prospect of them handing the title to United for a start; and Jamie and Kenny were close. We were all absolutely devastated. As far as we were concerned, the title had just been ripped away from us by that goal. We had been able to tell throughout the second half that the Blackburn fans were agitated about what was going on at Upton Park. They were all listening to their radios and they were quiet and fitful. Earlier, some of them had been holding up a finger on each hand which I presumed meant it was 1–1 at West Ham. But by now, I thought United must be ahead.

What I didn't know was that United had laid siege to the West Ham goal for most of the second half and that Andy Cole had missed a hatful of chances. Even now, it makes me nervous thinking about it. I watched a replay of the two games and thought that Cole was going to put one of them away and that I wasn't going to be able to go up and collect my medal. They had the Premiership trophy ready for us at Anfield but I thought in those moments after Jamie scored that they would have to drive it over to Manchester, ready for United to parade it around when they got back from London.

After Jamie's goal, we all just tried to compose ourselves. I looked over at the bench. I was looking for help but I got nothing from them. They were as devastated as me. They felt it was inevitable that United would score, too. In that moment, I really thought it was all over. I felt devastated. If we had blown it that day, we would all have been scarred by it for the rest of our careers. We would have been labelled bottlers for the rest of our playing days. It would have been something that would have hung over us.

Then as we walked back towards the centre circle for the kick off, time seemed to drag into slow motion. We were trying to get back to our positions and motivate each other. We were encouraging each other without really believing that we could force our way back into it. We were attacking The Kop end and the goal seemed to be moving further and further away by the second. But as we got up to the halfway line, the Blackburn fans over in the corner behind us started going ballistic. The final whistle had gone at Upton Park. United had only got a point.

I didn't believe it at first. There have been so many instances of added heartbreak being caused that way. One season, when Manchester City were fighting to avoid relegation, their manager Alan Ball told his players to play for a point because he believed from the crowd that that was all they needed. So City were taking the ball into the corner and wasting valuable time when the reality was that they needed a win. So I looked at the bench again because I trusted Kenny.

I saw him there. I saw everything about him quicken. There was a commotion on the bench. I lost sight of him for a second. Then I saw him clapping a policeman on the back. Then I saw Tony Gale, one of our substitutes, leaping in the air. I saw Kenny being congratulated by Ronnie Moran, Liverpool's faithful old servant who had been captain in the early days of Bill Shankly. I saw Kenny and Ray hugging each other. God, that was a beautiful sight. I tried to stay calm but it was hard. We all started giving each other high fives. The ref was trying to get play started again but Alan just told him to blow the whistle and a few seconds later he did. And that was it: we were champions. We had won the title. It was ours.

We had gone through such extremes of emotion in such a short space of time that even to this day I find it hard to come to terms with the fact that we actually won the Premiership. I had resigned myself to the fact that we had lost it. There were scenes of madness back in the dressing room, people spraying champagne, players coming in in their boots and falling over on the wet floor. Alan started to fizz up some champagne and his old mate Neil Ruddock shoved him into the dressing room because he didn't want to get sprayed and Alan fell over. Then we went back out onto the pitch for the presentation. A lot of the Liverpool fans had stayed behind for it. I'll never forget that. They seemed to feel that we deserved recognition; and, of course, they were happy for Kenny. They were brilliant.

That evening, we had a celebration party in Preston. It's funny, really. Preston's hardly the most glamorous venue for the celebrations of the Premiership champions but I noticed that when Chelsea sealed their first title under Jose Mourinho in 2004/05 with an away win at Bolton Wanderers, they stayed that night at a hotel in ... Preston. Their reason for being there was that they were staying in the north for a Champions League semi-final against Liverpool a couple of days later. We went there out of choice.

It was an odd kind of night. We'd been to the restaurant a few times before. A lot of the waiters and waitresses were part-time musicians so as soon as they had stopped serving the food, they morphed into their alter egos. They'd appear in different clothes, singing stuff from the Blues Brothers, Gladys Knight and the Pips, and other Motown classics. Everyone else was there with their wives and girlfriends but I was there by myself so it was all a bit strange for me. We had a great night but after that kind of achievement, any celebration is going to be an anti-climax. After a marathon league season, a celebration in one night at a restaurant is never going to do it justice.

That was it, however. That night in Preston was pretty much the end of the good times at Blackburn Rovers. Everything we had worked so hard for was frittered away in double-quick time. History has tended to judge our title victory that year as a blip, a title that was bought and paid for by Jack Walker. Blackburn's triumph now is treated as the great anomaly in Premiership history but I resent the idea that we bullied our way to the title financially.

As I have said, money isn't everything anyway. You need to buy the right players and you need to have the right team spirit. If the players don't have the hunger as well as the ability, a team would never win anything. Jose Mourinho created that desire at Chelsea and Kenny instilled it in us at Blackburn. Of course we had players who cost a lot of money. But Blackburn also made signings that were very shrewd. That's why you can't bracket us with the new Chelsea. The new Chelsea don't go in for bargains. They can afford to pay £24 million for Shaun Wright-Phillips and stick him on the bench. John Terry is the only player in that squad that has not cost a king's ransom. Their spending power is on a different level to what Blackburn had. Jack Walker was a rich man but he wasn't Roman Abramovich rich.

Our winning the Premiership would be the equivalent now of Wigan Athletic winning the competition. It was the last chance for a club to break the monopoly of the big teams. We sneaked in under the radar and by the time Manchester United, Newcastle, Leeds and Arsenal realized what was going on, it was too late. We did it and then circumstances broke the team up. Kenny went 'upstairs' to be director of football; Ray became manager; and everything fell apart. We were only at the summit for the flicker of an eye but what we did with Blackburn Rovers will never be done again.

FIVE

Going Batty and Turning Sour

In the summer of 1995, a few weeks after Blackburn had clinched the title, I played for England in the Umbro Cup against Brazil at Wembley. I scored with a volley from 25 yards, a screamer that dipped over the arching dive of the goalkeeper who could only push it into the roof of the net. It was the only goal I ever scored for England. I wheeled away to celebrate and the first person to dash over to give me a hug was my Blackburn team-mate, David Batty. We were all smiles and jubilation. The camaraderie between us didn't last.

Everything seemed possible at that moment. I had just started seeing Mariana and she had come to watch me play for the first time. I thought Blackburn were going to be challenging for the title for the foreseeable future and at the end of the 1995/96 season, there was the tantalising prospect of the 1996 European Championships, which were being held in England. The excitement about that was beginning to build fast and the way things were going for me with

England, I felt like I could play an important part in the tournament. I thought I could help England win it.

If I thought that goal against Brazil might be a prelude to another great season for me, I was wrong. I got the first hint that I was about to be thrust into a long nightmare when my friend's car was stolen while I was on holiday in the south of France later that summer. He had left it outside a restaurant when other diners suddenly started yelling that someone had leapt into it and was trying to drive it away.

By the time I got outside, it was being reversed up the street. I sprinted after it and when I got alongside, I tried to wrestle the passenger door open. Luckily, it was locked. Luckily, because as I kept trying to force my way into the car, I peered inside and saw the driver reach into the inside pocket of his jacket and pull out a gun. At that point, I stopped running very quickly and just let go of the handle. Fifty metres further on, another car was blocking the road so the driver of our car could make a clean getaway. They were well organized, I'll give them that.

When I got back to Blackburn, there were more nasty surprises. We were told that Kenny Dalglish had taken a position as director of football and that Ray Harford was now the boss. I liked Ray a lot but I just thought it was such a shame that the changes had been made. It seemed bizarre. Why change a winning formula? One of the things that made it terribly ironic was that one of Ray's favourite sayings was 'If it ain't broke, don't fix it'. All that happened was that they changed it and then they broke it.

It was so short-sighted of everyone. Why oh why did they do that? Kenny moving upstairs changed the whole dynamic of the set up. The chairman, Robert Coar, said a few things that upset everyone, too. In particular, he said we'd won the league a year too early. We all felt that that showed a lack of ambition and a lack of gratitude. In essence it was an admission that they hadn't prepared right for the defence of the title. They didn't know how to deal with the success we had achieved – they hadn't done their homework and they hadn't signed anyone. As the season approached, we didn't see Kenny at all. Before, he had been involved every day; now, he was the man who wasn't there.

Kenny's position as director of football caused a huge distraction. Even though it's a common feature in continental football, it was pretty much the first time that experiment had been tried out in the English game and everyone developed a morbid fascination with how long it would take for it to fail. The media became obsessed with the issue. *The Sun* followed him round for a week, trying to find out what Kenny actually did. They found out he spent four out of his five days on the golf course. They had a lot of fun with that.

Kenny had decided he didn't want the pressure of it. He probably thought he had a difficult act to follow after winning the Premiership. Perhaps he realized that the club had reached the limit of its ambition and that the hunger to compete with Alex Ferguson and Manchester United year after year just wasn't there. If that was his thinking, he was right – because the club didn't bring in new players; they didn't strengthen. They made the mistake of being too loyal to the players who had won them the league. We needed fresh blood. The club lost its ambition and because of that some of the players lost their ambition. It became a less hard-working, less driven kind of place. We had lost our leadership. Even the players felt we couldn't sustain the success we had achieved and some were having their heads turned by offers from clubs that suddenly seemed to have more potential.

Everyone was very familiar with Ray and so he couldn't be a Kenny-type figure. Ray was the classic example of the man who was a brilliant number two but who was just too nice to be the boss. He was an extremely able coach and a great football man but he didn't have Kenny's ruthlessness. He couldn't be the person you need at a club who commands a kind of fear. Everyone respected him but he had always been like a father to us – that was why he was such a great assistant. As soon as Kenny went, there was no one there who could really control the players. That was quickly reflected in the way we trained and played and in our results. Ray didn't socialize with the players but it didn't change the fact there was no emotional distance.

It was amazing how quickly it all began to unravel. Just a couple of months after the high of winning the league, it was as if the glue that had kept us all together had begun to dissolve. It all got a bit niggly between the players and groups started to form. The players who pushed the boundaries a little bit started to get away with more. Tim Sherwood, Batts, Chris Sutton and Mike Newell, the stronger characters, got away with things that wouldn't have happened under Kenny.

That started to break the unity of the team. I could feel the atmosphere changing. It was all breaking down and as it broke down we began to turn on each other. Suddenly, we were desperately vulnerable. We were in the midst of raging against the loss of our dominance when we travelled to Moscow that winter to play Spartak in our doomed Champions League campaign and where the fight between me and David Batty came to symbolize Blackburn's fall from grace.

Things had gone badly right from the start that season. We lost the Charity Shield to an average Everton side and after we had won our first league game of the season, we lost four of our next five. By mid-September, we were one place above the relegation zone and it was already apparent that we were not even going to be contenders in the Premiership.

The Champions League, about which there had been so much excitement, turned into a disaster. We didn't know anything about the teams we were playing against. We finished bottom of our qualifying group, below Spartak Moscow, Legia Warsaw and Rosenborg. I had had three incredible years at Blackburn and now in the fourth year, it had all changed. We were being subjected to a lot of criticism in the media, much of it based on the pleasure of seeing the so-called rich boys falling on hard times. Things deteriorated very quickly.

It was against this backdrop that David Batty and I fell out so spectacularly in Moscow. People started looking after themselves rather than playing for the team and there were a couple of games where David and I had had a bit of a go at each other on the pitch. David was one of those players who would always come really short to get the ball and some-times he would be almost on top of you so you had to give him a five-yard pass. Occasionally, I'd tell him he didn't need to come so close. If I didn't pass to him and ended up losing the ball with a different pass, he'd have a go at me. Gradually, that started to get worse. Two weeks before the incident in Moscow, something happened in training. We'd had a five-a-side and I'd nutmegged him and he got the hump about it. So he came after me in training and I got a bit prickly about that. There was just an edge developing.

The following game, he said something to me during the first half about being selfish and I came in at half-time and had it out with him in front of everyone. I told him to say what he'd said to me again and he wouldn't. He sort of backed off. I thought that was it. I was frustrated at the way things were going and I knew he was, too, but after that I thought it was over and that we'd got rid of the problem. And then we travelled to Russia.

It was a horrible atmosphere in Moscow. It was bitterly cold and the pitch was frozen. The dressing rooms at the Spartak Moscow stadium were cold and miserable. It was a really grim place. I felt weighed down by a general air of anxiety even before the game started. They scored early on and things felt like they were unravelling. Everything just felt like it was going from bad to worse. It felt fraught.

It was still the first half when I set off after a loose ball. I was running up the touchline and the ball was in front of me and I was going to intercept it. David was coming across the pitch to try and get the ball as well and a couple of their players were in the vicinity. So we were all battling for this ball that was in no man's land. David and I both got there at the same time and we ran into each other. I hit the deck and then as I got up, he came at me very aggressively.

I'm looking a bit grumpy with all that gear on...

...but it wasn't long before I was breaking into a smile.

My older sister Jeanette being protective of her newly-born brother. She's still like that now.

Life's a beach. Early sun-drenched days in Jersey with Mum, Dad and Jeanette.

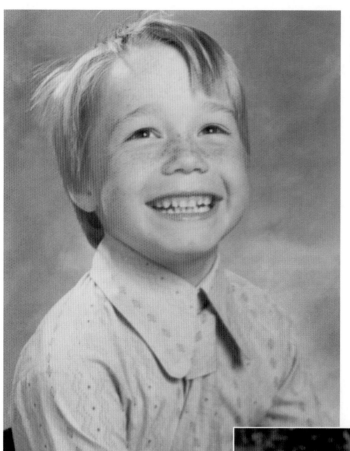

We all have a picture like this somewhere!

Shirt tucked in like a model professional. Aged five, in my first football kit, outside the family home in Jersey.

Me at thirteen, with my youngest sister Alison who now lives in Canada.

Early Chelsea club photo, 1998/99. The kit design is almost as bad as the hair.

In full flight for Chelsea against Southampton. Fifteen years later, I would be playing alongside Jason Dodd when Gordon Strachan signed me for the Saints.

My lowest point during my first spell at Chelsea. I think the faces in the crowd say it all.

My finest goal – and my only international goal. This volley from 25 yards out couldn't prevent Brazil winning 3–1 at Wembley in 1995.

Post-match with Terry Venables. Even after defeat, Terry still found time to share his thoughts on the game.

On the ladder to success with Matt Le Tissier. We were both Channel Islanders, born within days of each other, and debuting for England in the same match.

What a great way to finish the season. Losing to Liverpool but winning the 1994/95 league championship with Blackburn.

Alan Shearer and I demonstrate the team spirit that made Blackburn such a force. This was my goal in our 7–1 annihilation of Nottingham Forest in November 1995.

The bust-up with David Batty during the Champions League game against Spartak Moscow. A terrible moment that we all had to deal with.

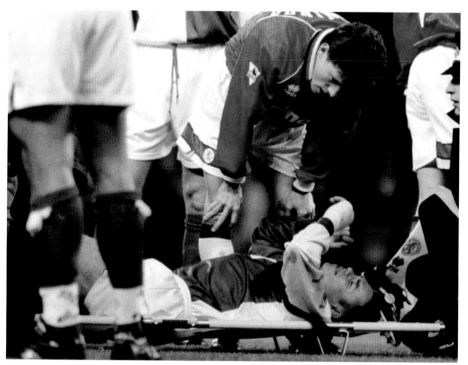

Every player's greatest fear. Juninho shows sympathy after I broke my ankle in December 1995. It was serious enough to cost me my England place for Euro 96.

Reunited with my Chelsea shirt in August 1997.

He was being threatening. He was screaming things at me as well. But in a way, what he was saying was irrelevant. It was just that he was right in my face and I felt I had to protect myself. I just swung at him. I connected and I knew immediately I'd broken my left hand. I'm not a fighter. I hadn't closed my fist properly. Tim Sherwood ran over to intervene and I thought he was going to hit me. But he just pulled us apart. He was embarrassed. So was I. I was in a lot of pain from my hand which just made me feel even more ridiculous. I knew I couldn't come off.

Mainly, I was in shock at what had happened. We came off at half-time and Ray had a go at us. He said he was ashamed. He said he hadn't been able to believe what he was seeing and that no manager had ever been asked to deal with that kind of situation before. I was getting my hand strapped up. David didn't really say anything. He seemed okay. I suppose he might have had a sore cheek. The whole scene was very weird.

Chris Sutton started having a go at the way we were playing so Derek Fazakerley had a go at Chris. Chris said: 'What do you know, Faz, you're just a budgerigar.' I don't know why he said that. It makes me smile now, that Monty Python moment, but I don't think anyone laughed at the time because it wasn't that kind of situation. It was a terrible situation. It was all a bit surreal. I was in bits because of the state of my hand and the realization of what I'd been involved in.

Both at the time and in the years that have passed since that incident, there has always been fierce speculation about what David said to me. Most people have assumed that it was a homophobic taunt that made me snap. But I never thought of it as being similar to what Robbie Fowler did to me. It wasn't in the same league. What David said was between me and him and if anything it was my reaction that increased the likelihood that it would become public.

I'm not condoning what he said, obviously, and I'm not condoning what I did either. In the heat of the moment, it angered me. The incident was a product of deep frustration. People had started to lose respect for each other within the situation that had developed at Blackburn. Europe was the most embarrassing part of that campaign and I don't think it was a coincidence that that was where it all flared up. We were just two men who were deeply pissed off at what was going on at our football club and who felt powerless to stop the slide. We were in an inhospitable environment, getting beaten, heading for more misery, more criticism, more under-achievement, and when we ran into each other, we just lost it.

It was just that the whole thing had been getting worse and worse and that was the moment when it all exploded. His face was so contorted with anger and he was so venomous and aggressive, it was like he was going to rip my head off. Hitting him was more of a pre-emptive strike than anything. If I hadn't hit him, I felt he was going to hit me.

I was upset about what he said and that he was accusing me of being selfish; I was also upset that we weren't doing well as a team and I reacted because of the way he came at me. It was a combination of four or five things. It wasn't just him saying something. It is one of the great urban myths that he was hurling a stream of homophobic abuse at me. He wasn't. But after that, his respect for me changed quite dramatically. Our relationship had been deteriorating rapidly but the moment that happened, it became more balanced again. Maybe it was one of those things that had to happen. I just wish it hadn't happened in a Champions League game.

God, the aftermath was awful. We were miles away from home in Russia, we'd been beaten 3–0, I had a broken hand and I had just hit my own team-mate. When we were on the coach heading back to Moscow airport, I sat by myself. The atmosphere was terrible. We were a long way from home and we had got battered – and we had imploded in the public gaze. It was a great day for the media: they were rubbing their hands in glee.

When we landed back in England at Blackpool, a couple of the press lads actually got on the bus to try to talk to me. I was sitting there alone waiting for the other guys to come out. I knew it must be a bloody big story if they were getting on the bus, which is always out of bounds for the press boys. But Matt Dickinson and Martin Samuel approached me anyway. I was cowering at the back. I didn't really know what to say to them but I gave them a couple of lines.

For me, there is nothing but regret for what happened. There was no justification for it. I apologized to David after the game in the dressing room in front of everyone. I sat down with him in the airport lounge and we talked about it. To be fair to him, he was absolutely fine about it. He was calm. He told me not to worry, which was never going to be an option. But still, it was nice of him to say it.

I talked to Mariana on the phone and I told her I felt like I wanted to die. I went back to my house in Waddington and I was so anxious about what the repercussions were going to be that I couldn't get to sleep. It was awful. I didn't leave the house the next day. I didn't get any newspapers but I know they were bad. People called to tell me. I really battened down the hatches. I had a sense of impending doom.

I turned all the phones off because they were going ballistic. The club was calling me because anyone and everyone was calling them to try and get a quote from me. I just tried to contain it. I made a public apology. Ray Harford was distraught: he felt it was a poor reflection on him and his management; he felt it showed he must be doing something badly wrong. Poor Ray – he didn't deserve that. When managers are under pressure, they take all the cares of the world on their shoulders; it must be a horribly lonely job. More than anything else, it is the one thing I wish I could erase from my career – including my injury.

The fight between David and me pretty much finished our season off. We ended up bottom of our Champions League group. Our style of play wasn't really conducive to European football. We were a very young side in terms of experience and we didn't adapt. Again, much of the blame for that lies with the club for not drafting in international-class players who had performed at the highest level of European competition before.

Soon, the finger-pointing started. Colin Hendry and Kevin Gallacher had quite a rough time with the other lads. They got the mickey taken out of them. Colin was Mr Blackburn. He was quite an easy target and the lads used to tell stories about him all the time. There was one doing the rounds about how he put up a sign outside his house saying 'No FA Cup tickets left' because he was so sick of being asked if he had any spares. During that season, Colin was getting a house built and he was forever bringing balls and shirts in to get them signed for his builders. So the lads used to say they felt as if they were paying for the bloody house with their autographs and that sort of thing. It was just that Colin was a generous guy. But every time they signed a ball, they'd say something like, 'This is for the conservatory'. He had a tartan made, a Hendry tartan, and that caused a lot of hilarity, too. It soon got out of hand. Newelly and Colin had a ruck in training. It had turned into an appalling year. For me, it was about to get much, much worse.

It was December and we were playing Middlesbrough at Ewood Park. It was a fairly uneventful game and midway through the second half, I was running back in the direction of my own goal with the ball, trying to shepherd it away from Juninho. He was shadowing me on my left, the goal side, and I tried to get away from him by doing a Cruyff turn, flicking the ball behind my standing leg, sending me quickly the other way. As I started to turn, Juninho brushed me with his shoulder and even though it was only a slight contact, it knocked me off balance and I started to twist. I was wearing adidas boots that had blades, not studs, on their base and as I twisted, my heel got stuck in the turf. My body went forward and around and my ankle just stayed where it was. I heard a crunching and a cracking. Everything was breaking – I could hear it and I could feel it. I didn't know it as I hit the ground but I had fractured and dislocated my right ankle, fractured my fibula and torn ligaments in my foot. Generally, it was a bit of a mess.

It wasn't pretty. It's hard to describe the pain – I had been hurt before but this was on a completely different level. I called out to the referee to help me. I looked down and saw my leg as he was running past. I screamed out to him. 'For God's sake, help me,' I yelled. He stopped the game immediately. Blackburn were wearing white socks with a blue band with the word 'Asics' written on it. When I looked, the band had gone totally distorted: 'Asics' was nowhere near where it should have been.

I thought I had broken my leg higher up. A couple of guys grabbed my hand. I was yelling like an animal. The more I yelled, the more I was hoping the pain would go. The Blackburn physio, a guy called Steve Foster, came on and realized he couldn't deal with it. He panicked. The Middlesbrough physio, Bob Ward, used to be my physio at Chelsea. He came on as well and took over completely. They didn't give me any gas and air or injections on the pitch, but the pain got a bit better. I think the body just shuts down and goes into shock. I was on the pitch for about ten minutes before they took me away on the stretcher.

On the way off the pitch, I nearly fell off the stretcher because they hadn't strapped me in. Within ten minutes of getting the injury, I began to panic that my career was over. Once the pain is under control, your mind starts racing. I was wondering if I might be permanently disabled, too. I got into the tunnel and Alan Smith, the England physio, and a surgeon called John Hodgkinson were both at the game. Thank God they were there. Mr Hodgkinson ended up operating on me later that night. I was rushed into the treatment room where they took off my boot and moved my ankle back around because they were worried about the blood vessels being twisted and me losing my foot.

They had to pick my foot up and try and move it back round while I held onto someone's hand and did the equivalent of biting a piece of leather. The first time I had any pain relief was when the ambulance came and they gave me gas and air. I was in tears and I could see by Alan's expression that he was shocked. The first thing I said to him was 'Will I be all right for the summer'. He told me not to worry about the summer.

I kept pressing him. I kept asking him if I was ever going to play again. It wasn't fair of me to put him in that position but Euro 96 had become my dream and now I was sensing that it had been ripped away from me. I only realized how much it meant to me once it began to sink in that I wasn't going to be playing in it. Alan couldn't look at me. Once I got back into the treatment room, I knew it was serious: I could see everyone in there was worried, everyone was a bit flustered. Alan came with me in the ambulance to Blackburn Royal Infirmary. They gave me some medication and some pethidine and I had some x-rays. Once I had the pethidine, I was fine. Actually, I was ready to go out and hit the town. I hadn't had any food or anything so I was stoned – it knocked me for six.

Once they realized how bad the injury was, arrangements were made for me to be taken by ambulance to a private hospital in Rochdale. I got scared then. I was operated on that night. Mr Hodgkinson was out for dinner with his wife but he had to skip dessert. He operated on me for a couple of hours and then I was wheeled away into my room. It was the week before Christmas.

I'd been intending to drive down to Suffolk after the game because Mariana and her family were staying at Center Parcs near Lowestoft. I was going to go down and have an early Christmas with them. I even had Christmas presents in the back of my car for Mariana and her family. Now, all I could think about was letting them and my dad know that I was okay – well, okay in a manner of speaking. Someone got through to my dad but I couldn't make contact with Mariana because there was no mobile phone reception where she was. She found out when a picture of me flashed up on the television news that night. They had the sound turned down so she thought I must have scored a goal. She turned the volume up and realized what had happened.

I woke up the morning after the operation and didn't know where I was. I was wheeled to the x-ray room and then wheeled back. I threw up. My ankle was in plaster but it was so sensitive and painful that I couldn't even rest a bedsheet on my foot. When I got back to the room, the ankle was aching and burning. I turned on the television and the first thing that came on was the draw for Euro 96. I burst into tears. I saw England's name up there with Holland, Scotland and Switzerland and I was just crying my eyes out.

Blackburn didn't do a lot to alleviate my distress. I know people have got used to footballers whingeing and complaining at every turn but even now I feel that the club's attitude towards me beggared belief. The Blackburn physio, in particular, played a real blinder. I know he had to stay and watch the game but as soon as it finished he should have been in his car on his way down to see me. Football club physios are usually dedicated people who treat the players like a doctor treats a valued patient – but this guy. made no effort to contact me. I was incensed by the fact that he had no compassion and didn't seem to care.

I never heard from the club, either. Most of the players came to see me but there was no word from the chairman or any of the officials. The day after the operation, I received a massive basket of fruit from the Middlesbrough manager, Bryan Robson, and all the Middlesbrough staff wishing me a speedy recovery. That made Blackburn's lack of action all the more hurtful, particularly as it was a close-knit club. Kenny and Ray phoned me but that was it. No official from the club came to see me.

The club didn't even make any effort to find out how I was getting home. I couldn't walk – I was on crutches. I was so angry and upset that I asked my agent if anyone had ever handed in a transfer request while they were in hospital. Sadly, it all seemed to sum up the way the club was going. That was the end for me and Blackburn. After that experience, emotionally, I was finished with them.

I spent a week in hospital. Mariana's brother-in-law, Andrew, drove her up to Rochdale and she stayed on a camp bed in my room. I went home for a day and then I had to go back into hospital because I started getting pains in my shoulder. They were worried I had a blood clot but it must just have been the way I fell when I was injured or the way I was using my crutches because the tests didn't show anything up. I had to inject myself in the stomach with some blood-thinning agents. It wasn't easy.

I got a lot of support from friends but I got one particularly nasty surprise from Manchester United fans. One of the United fanzines ran a cut-out advert on one of their pages with a message. The message was: 'Dear Graeme, we are just writing regarding your horrific injury. Just to let you know, it's the best Christmas present we could ever have. Don't get well soon.' They suggested the readers cut it out and send it to me – and about thirty of them did. The girls who opened the mail at Blackburn wouldn't give them to me. I walked in one day and they were a bit coy. I could tell they were hiding something. In the end, they showed one to me. Very pleasant. Every time I played at Old Trafford after that, I always remembered the note. Every game I played against United was for the guys who sent that message to me. I used it as my motivation. I thought of what they had written and I knew they were hard core fans who would be at the game and that would be my response to them.

I spent Christmas in London with Mariana. I was in plaster up to my knee for two months and in the New Year, I went back up to Blackburn and started exercising. I refused to work with the Blackburn physio. I did two or three days work in London each week and then went up to Blackburn but I'd drive to Sheffield to do rehab with Alan Smith. Blackburn knew exactly what they had done and were shamefaced about the way they had abandoned me. I just told them how I was managing my rehab. I did all my fitness programmes under the supervision of Alan Smith. Even if I'd wanted to stay in Blackburn all week, there was no way I could be by myself up at my cottage because there was no one to look after me and I couldn't get around the place on one leg. It was all stairs and nooks and crannies.

I started my rehab doing a Cindy Crawford fitness video – as it was the only thing I could find in Mariana's flat. Robbie Fowler would have loved it if he could have seen me doing that. But I was desperately motivated to get fit right from the start. I was passionate about football so I was equally passionate about getting fit. I got a lot of help and support, too. When England met up, for instance, I met up with them as well. Terry Venables was brilliant like that – he made me feel I was still part of the group.

When the plaster was taken off after eight weeks, my leg looked like the leg of an elderly person: wrinkly and skinny. It was strange walking on it again but it is amazing how quickly you get your confidence. I started with two crutches so that they took most of the weight and I rolled my foot through the motions. Then I was down to one crutch and eventually none. It was very stiff all the time. I did a lot of swimming and walking in water and I made a lot of day trips to Sheffield.

In the spring, Mariana and I went to the Maldives for a couple of weeks for our first holiday together. From a romantic point of view, it felt like a honeymoon. From a football point of view, I made a massive leap forward in my confidence about the injury. I was walking in the sand, I had the sun on my back, good weather and good food. We snorkelled for three hours a day, and with flippers on it was the perfect exercise for me. I started to jog for the first time on the sand out there and I felt like I had won a gold medal.

I always felt really positive about coming back. I never thought that I wouldn't play again. It wasn't an option. There was one time when I was really scared – when I was about a third of the way through my rehab. I had picked up the intensity a bit and had done a bit of jogging on the treadmill and for a brief period I experienced a sharp pain in the back of my ankle every time I put my heel down. It felt as if something was digging into my ankle – then it disappeared as quickly as it had arrived.

The rehab was monotonous and draining, but it was very methodical and I could see the progress I was making. It went through jogging, running, kicking the ball, putting all my weight on the foot and tackling. I was anxious about anything that got close to recreating the action of the foot when I did the injury. I did some set up block tackles. When I went back to the club, I could sense in training sessions that my team-mates were being very cautious around me.

Euro 96 was very hard for me. I didn't get close to regaining my fitness in time. It was never going to happen. Nevertheless, I went to all the games and did a bit of promotional work with Microsoft. Terry invited me to the squad's headquarters at Burnham Beeches during the tournament and I did a few training sessions on the lawn in front of the hotel. Now and then a few of the lads came to see how I was getting on: there was probably an element of 'There but for the grace of God go I'.

The first proper tackle I did when I got back to Blackburn for pre-season was on Jason Wilcox and for a few seconds I was waiting to make sure there was no reaction. I played in a reserve game at Ewood Park and a really good crowd turned out. That was a great moment for me but inside I still knew I didn't want to be at the club. I started playing again for Blackburn in October. We had had a terrible start, losing five of our first six games – in fact we were relegation material. Things had gone from bad to worse after the disappointment of the season before when we had eventually rallied to finish seventh. Alan Shearer had left for Newcastle by this time and David Batty had gone, too. We picked up a couple of points in October but we didn't win a Premiership match until November and Ray was sacked. All the warning signs had been there that the spirit was falling apart but nobody had done anything about it.

Tony Parkes, football's favourite caretaker boss, stepped in again for a while. I had a problem with him. He was on a power trip and he didn't like the way I had behaved in the aftermath of my injury: he thought I was being disloyal to the club because I had made it known I wasn't happy. The lads used to call him BBC. It stood for Balls, Bibs and Cones because that's all he used to do. When Kenny and Ray were there, he was okay. He was quite feisty, a good little footballer, good fun and a good organizer. He always had an edge to him and when he took over as manager, he got a bit carried away. I told him I didn't want to be at the club. He told me that if he was the full-time manager, he'd let me rot in the reserves. I said to him: 'Well, you're not manager, you'll be doing balls, bibs and cones again soon, so don't worry yourself about that'.

There was one occasion when we were coming off the training pitches and Tony kicked a ball over towards the car park. It came right towards me so I headed it. He laughed. 'There's a first time for everything, son' he said. I was already wound up about everything so I just flipped my lid. I ran at him and he turned on his heels and started heading off towards the pitches. I confronted him and the rest of the players grabbed hold of me, keeping me from getting to him.

It all started to get a bit nasty. I had a couple of meetings with Jack Walker who flew over from Jersey to try and get me to stay. We had a few chats at a hotel called Northcote Manor, near the training ground. I had put in a transfer request by then. Jack was really upset with me because he regarded me as one of his boys. He took it personally. He offered me a lot more money but I told him it wasn't about the money. I told Jack I'd be a worse person if I signed for more money because my heart still wouldn't be in it. I wanted my career to be successful. Jack took it quite hard.

Things had changed so quickly for the worse. Once you lose people's goodwill, it's all over. It became quite a difficult time towards the end of that season. The supporters knew I was unhappy but I never said why. I always tried to keep that to myself. The club tried to stop me from going but that was just counterproductive. It wasn't as if I had some massive deal sorted out with another club and I was trying to stir it in order to get away. I just didn't want to be at Blackburn any more and the club wouldn't accept it. In an impasse like that, you end up fighting the world: you become negative and disruptive and that's not my nature. I trained okay, but I joined the crew of moaners. The relationship with Blackburn was over.

I played for the rest of the 1996/97 season. I even had a meeting with the new manager, Roy Hodgson, before he took over. I liked him. 'Good luck to you,' I said, 'but I won't be here.' He asked what I meant and I explained the whole thing to him. I said it was nothing to do with him. I told him that the way my attitude towards the club was, he wasn't going to want me around. He was an experienced guy and I think he probably told the board to get what they could for me and let me go.

So they came to me and said they would let me go for £7.5 million – which was, in effect, the same as saying they weren't going to let me go. I had some really good clubs after me. Arsenal were interested in me: I had spoken to Arsene Wenger and Pat Rice and I could tell they were on the verge of big things. Then Chelsea came in. Ruud Gullit was in charge and the sexy football thing was all the rage. I thought that would be a chance for me to make amends for the first time around at Stamford Bridge but I was scared as well because I thought it might be difficult going back to a place where I had such a lot of history – and not all of it good.

Juventus, Atletico Madrid and Inter Milan all expressed an interest, too, but when Blackburn put the price tag on my head, they all faded away. It got to another transfer deadline day and this was when I was at my most disruptive. We had a team photo at Ewood Park and I told them there was no point me being in it. The chairman said I had to be in it. I said I'd go on the end so that they could crop me out once I'd moved.

We finished the photo and I got back to my car where I discovered that I had twenty missed calls. Things were starting to happen. I phoned Jon Holmes and Struan Marshall at SFX, my agents at the time, and they said Blackburn had accepted an offer from Chelsea and that we could talk to them. 'Anyone else,' I said. 'What about Arsenal?' They told me Blackburn hadn't given us permission to speak to Arsenal.

When Chelsea sold me in the first place, they had a sell-on clause whereby they would get 10 per cent of any future sale. The price Blackburn were asking was £5.5 million but they were going to get their 10 per cent back so it brought it down to £5 million. Arsenal had offered £5 million as well but they were told the price was £5.5 million. There was a £500,000 discrepancy and Arsenal didn't know why. They thought Blackburn were trying to fleece them. Arsenal had a board meeting to discuss it but it was inconclusive, and time was running out.

So that evening, Mariana and I drove down to London and stopped at a service station on the M1 to meet with Struan and go through the contract details. How very football – contract details at Watford Gap. When we got to London, we met the Chelsea chief executive, Colin Hutchinson, and went to Charing Cross Hospital for the medical. After that, we travelled west to a hotel at Heathrow where I signed the contract. It was past midnight.

I didn't feel any regrets about leaving Blackburn then. I'd fallen out of love with the club. I thought that they valued me but the way I was treated in the aftermath of my injury disillusioned me. Maybe I was naive about that. Roy Keane said something in his last couple of years at Manchester United about how football clubs treat their players like pieces of meat. But what happened at Blackburn still came as a shock. Up to that point, I'd had the happiest years of my career at Ewood Park but even if it meant taking a risk by going back to the place where I had been so unsettled before I moved north, I knew I needed to get away.

SIX

International

It surprised me when Terry Venables became part of the England hierarchy in the wake of Sven-Goran Eriksson's failed campaign at the 2006 World Cup. In fact, it astonished me – not because I doubted Terry's ability but because I knew just how able he was. I played under him all too briefly when I was at Blackburn and he was England manager in the build-up to Euro 96. I knew just how good he was, I knew how much the players would respect him and respond to him and I knew that he would probably overshadow the manager, Steve McClaren. I didn't think it was a partnership that would work.

It wasn't because I thought Terry would be Machiavellian – that he would scheme and plot to bring Steve down and get the job for himself. That's not what he's like. Terry doesn't need to be tricky to succeed. It's just that he has this great football knowledge, a fascinating tactical brain and a charisma that marks him out as the main man wherever he goes. What I'm saying is that he's the least likely number two I've ever had the pleasure to work with.

What struck me immediately about the McClaren–Venables partnership that the FA sanctioned after the miserable end of the Eriksson era was that it was an inversion of the natural order. McClaren enjoyed his best times as Sir Alex Ferguson's assistant straddling the turn of the century. He was a brilliant number two. In his first season at Old Trafford, he helped to inspire Manchester United to the Treble. The United players thought he was an innovative coach who made training interesting, challenging and fun.

However, when he was his own boss, McClaren didn't make quite the same impact. His record as manager of Middlesbrough was patchy. He got the England job on the back of a dramatic run in the UEFA Cup twinned with progress to the semi-finals of the FA Cup. He seems like a decent bloke and a fairly astute man but you've got to be something special to be in the same league as Venables. Venables won La Liga with Barcelona and took them to the European Cup Final. He guided England to the semi-finals of Euro 96, beating Holland 4–1 on the way. So when the FA formed the partnership, instead of McClaren–Venables, it should have been Venables–McClaren, although that was never a realistic possibility.

I suppose I would say that. Terry was the best coach I ever worked with. On top of that, he gave me my England debut so I'm bound to be biased. When he got the job after Graham Taylor had fallen short in his efforts to get England to the 1994 World Cup, Terry called me up for his very first squad, a friendly against Denmark at Wembley in March 1994. A year earlier, David Webb had bombed me out of Chelsea and told me he didn't think we'd ever hear of

Graeme Le Saux again and now I was in with a real chance of winning my first England cap. I've got plenty of reasons to be grateful to Terry Venables.

There was no fanfare about that March call-up. I found out by fax. The FA sent it through to Ewood Park and one of the secretaries at Blackburn Rovers told me about it when I popped in that day to get my mail. There was my name on a list of names. There was my name with green marker pen stroked through it. I never thought I would be included in Terry's first squad so I was pleasantly surprised rather than swept off my feet. In fact, Kenny Dalglish, a proud Scotsman, helped to ensure my feet were firmly on the ground. As I was leaving the Blackburn changing room that day, he poked his head out of the shower and said: 'Rag, well done on the England call-up ... I hope you get fucking stuffed.' As I left, I could hear him chuckling.

Graham Taylor had called me up a few times. I was in the squad for a game against Russia but I didn't get on. I played in a couple of B-internationals, too: one was against Switzerland at Walsall under Lawrie McMenemy. On the occasions I did get called up to the full squad under Taylor, I felt totally marginalized. There were giants in that squad, men like Gary Lineker, who I regarded as being from another world. And then there were people like Paul Stewart, who was definitely from this world. He was an average player who came across as so arrogant, blanking new boys like me and making me feel the size of an ant. I felt out of place and unwelcome in that squad.

I'd never come close to getting on the pitch under Taylor. I couldn't really blame him. Stuart Pearce was the dominant

England left-back at the time and Tony Dorigo was his understudy so I never got much of a look-in. I had been in and out of the side at Chelsea anyway, busy chucking my shirt at Ian Porterfield and raging against the iniquity of what was happening to me at Stamford Bridge, so I had hardly been pushing my claims at international level and I certainly didn't feel then that I was at the same standard as Pearce. That changed with the move to Blackburn and our push higher and higher up the Premiership table.

Even though I was doing well at Blackburn, I didn't think I'd be called up. From outcast at Chelsea to the England squad is a pretty steep curve – it's a lot to get your head round. I was pleased and excited but there was apprehension as well. I knew I was going to be stepping out of my comfort zone. I thought 'This is serious'. I knew how much pressure an England international gets put under: all the main press boys would be there, I thought, and if it went wrong we were all right in the firing line.

I was also affected by the memory of how brutally the press had treated Graham Taylor. *The Sun* had mocked up a picture of him as a turnip after England lost to Sweden in a World Cup qualifying game – it was the kind of humiliation that made you wince. It's become commonplace now to lampoon the England manager to that degree but back then it was still shocking in its severity. I knew that at that level, the press didn't hold back and that was one of the reasons why the England call-up was intimidating as well as exciting. I felt the same mixture of joy and trepidation that I think a lot of players feel when they are asked to step up. That's why sometimes a player will be included in an England squad and then his career will fall away. It's as if he doesn't want to push himself any more, as if he doesn't want to take the risk. You are quite happy where you are. Do you really want to expose yourself to a new test? Do you want to run the risk that you, a top player in league football, will be found out at the highest level? Wouldn't you rather remain the big fish in the small pond?

I did my best to quell those thoughts. As soon as we started training that week at Bisham Abbey, I tried to work out where I fitted into the manager's plans. The fact that this might be my ticket to Euro 96 never entered my head – it was too far away, too distant a prospect. A large part of me thought this call-up would probably be a one-off. Stuart Pearce was there as well, of course, and at first I assumed he would start and if I was lucky I would be on the bench. I thought I was along for the ride but I still felt involved from the second I arrived. I was very excited and very nervous but I did at least have the comfort of knowing Alan Shearer and a couple of the other Blackburn lads there.

By the day before the game, though, it began to look more likely that Terry would play me. When he announced the team at Bisham that Tuesday, we were all standing in a circle. After Terry said 'Le Saux', I didn't hear any of the other names. He could have said Mickey Mouse was playing centre-forward and I wouldn't have laughed. The shutters came down. I was in. If you had asked me afterwards who else was playing, I wouldn't have had a clue.

Stuart Pearce was very magnanimous and very gracious. I was in awe of him a little bit but he was lovely to me. He was extremely professional and very generous. It was almost as if he was handing the shirt over to me, and I don't mean in a pompous way. He just told me I had earned it and I could tell that he really wanted me to do well. I respected him for that – I still respect him for it. The way he reacted really helped me: it took a little bit of pressure off. If he had tried to intimidate me, I would have had that in my mind but he was very supportive and I took that as a tremendous honour.

Venables taught me an awful lot very quickly. I was fertile ground for a coach like him because I still had so much to learn and I was eager to listen. I was new to international football and from the moment I met up with that England squad for the Denmark game, I felt my development begin to quicken. For those few days, I was playing with the best players in the country every day and I felt so sharp it was amazing.

I liked the way Terry communicated with players. He made everyone feel at home and very comfortable. He was very bubbly and he had that gift of being able to relate to everyone, however different the various characters were within the squad. The best coaches make you feel you want to do it for them. You almost develop a father-son relationship with them. Paul Gascoigne definitely had that with Venables but then I think part of Terry's gift was that he made plenty of the players feel that way.

All of us wanted to please him because he was very much a players' manager. He gave you a bit of responsibility. He allowed you to have a bit of fun, play a bit of golf, go out for a drink if the time was right. He was good at that incentive-based way of dealing with players. I thought of his man-management techniques when I heard McClaren had allowed the England players to have mini-bars in their rooms again when he took over. That sounds like a small thing but it means a lot to the players: it shows a player respect but asks that the respect be reciprocated on the pitch and off.

Terry often worked on specific things in training. The most useful piece of information he ever gave me – and it was like a penny dropping when he told me – was about how to defend against a fast winger. He said that if you are marking your winger and the opposition has the ball and your winger makes a run down the line, don't run alongside him when you are anticipating the pass because the ball can get played inside you and then you are out of the game. Instead, he said, run towards your near post and then you have got a chance of intercepting the ball and you are also closing down the angle for the passer. If he does pass it to the winger, he has to pass it outside you and that means that you are still not beaten. It was like a revelation to me, like having the answer to a question passed to you on a piece of paper.

The next few times in training, I had to override my natural tendency to sprint along with my winger and make a conscious effort to run towards the near post. It was so simple but no one had ever told me before, and it made a radical difference to my game. Apparently, Venables imparted the same information to Gary Neville soon after that and he was similarly impressed. If there is one coaching tip I will always remember, it's that one – it was invaluable. It also came in one of the first coaching sessions I ever had with him – I hadn't even played a game under him and already he was having a radical effect on my football.

Terry was very good at empathizing with every player in the squad – I never felt that he had favourites or that he neglected people. Part of his talent was being incredibly inclusive. When training had finished and we were walking back to the coach, he would always be with someone. He would be with one player with his arm round him or walking along talking. Often, he'd keep Gazza back and have a chat with him, aware that he needed constant reassurance and encouragement. Terry planted little seeds of interest and stimulation in your mind all the time. That was just him as a person: he was a bright man, with a mind that never rested.

If you look at what Terry has done in his life, you have to be impressed: he was a top player; he invented a board game; he ran a nightclub; he wrote the screenplay for a television series; he had a song in the pop charts; he was a manager and a chairman. He's an entrepreneur. He's not been frightened to try anything and his own mind is constantly churning with new ideas. When he was a player, he rebelled against the accepted norms of behaviour. He was never as much of an outsider as me but he didn't want to spend large swathes of his life in pool halls and smoky bars. He wanted to challenge himself with other things and I think that's brilliant. I respect that. Terry made training and playing with England a real pleasure.

When I broke my ankle and it quickly became obvious I was going to miss Euro 96, I needed Terry more than ever, and he didn't let me down. He phoned me up after it happened and I could hear in his voice that he was genuinely devastated for me. Alan Smith, the England physio, kept in touch with him about me and Terry invited me to every England squad after I suffered the injury. There was no question of him banishing me or freezing me out, no suggestion that he might not want me around in case it unsettled the other players. He was confident enough not to worry about things like that.

So during Euro 96, I was up at England's base at Burnham Beeches in Berkshire most days. I was running well by then and I trained with Alan on the lawn in front of the hotel. Terry had a suite at the top of the hotel and one day I saw him looking down at me through the curtains. It made me think about what might have been if the injury had never happened. I would love to have known what was going on in his mind at that moment but it made me work harder knowing that someone like that was backing me.

I hadn't even been thinking about Euro 96 when Terry included me in the starting line-up for the Denmark game. I was wholly preoccupied with the magnitude of the prospect of playing for my country. The coach journey from Burnham Beeches to Wembley that evening seemed awfully long. The occasion was made even more daunting for me by the fact that it would be the first time I had ever played at Wembley. It was a mythical place for me, a kind of dream stadium, somewhere that represented an aspiration as much as a stadium. I also knew it was the first England game under a new manager and a massive opportunity. It didn't get any bigger than this for me.

I sat next to Matt Le Tissier on the coach and we reminisced about all our good times playing against each other for Jersey and Guernsey. It was funny how our careers and our lives seemed to follow such a similar pattern: born within a few days of each other and now about to make our

England debuts within sixty-six minutes of each other – I started the game and he came on midway through the second half. Matt had always been the golden boy of Channel Islands football, the scorer of spectacular goals and the guy who got the big contract with Southampton. He never quite fulfilled his potential with England – and there were those who thought he missed out on the big time by not moving to a bigger club. His performances and status at Southampton were remarkable. Perhaps being in that comfort zone meant he feared he might not be able to recreate his commanding performances at an elite club. But that was the way he was. There was never any real rivalry between us beyond a kind of unspoken competitiveness but there was great pride for both of us in making our debuts together that day.

When the coach got close to the ground and began to crawl down Wembley Way, I began to feel overwhelmed by what was happening. The coach drove right up to the ground and began to turn into the area behind the Wembley tunnel to park. There was a great throng of people blocking its way – it was absolutely heaving and the whole process seemed to take an age. With every minute I was getting more and more nervous. I started thinking 'Do I really want to play?' There were a couple of telegrams waiting for me in the dressing room and I got even more tense.

I played on the left side of a four man defence with David Seaman in goal. Paul Parker was the right-back and Gary Pallister and Tony Adams were the centre-halves. Gazza and Incey were in the heart of midfield, Shearer and Peter Beardsley up front. It was a useful side, good enough to have qualified for the World Cup, I thought. But, sod's law, I got Brian Laudrup to mark and he was a wonderful player.

So I had a headache for the entire Denmark game, literally and metaphorically. Partly, it was because I was stressed. My dad and Alice had come over for the game. In fact, half of Jersey seemed to have made the journey. I had loads of friends there and I felt the pressure of that. I felt I was representing two countries in one game and I was desperate not to let anyone down.

The other part of the headache was Laudrup, the younger brother of Michael, who was also in the Denmark side that night. I was marking him and when I look back on my England career, I still regard him as one of my toughest opponents because of that match. He played for Chelsea later but never settled and even though he was having a tough time on loan at AC Milan when we played Denmark, he was at his peak. He was a superb wide player with great vision and silky skills. He was tremendously cultured, too, a player it was impossible not to admire.

Laudrup was deceptively quick. He had a long body and short legs but he could shift. There were a couple of really scary moments where he got past me and I had to recover. But I was like glue – I stuck to him. I just about managed to nullify him but it was exhausting mentally and physically. A couple of times, I felt like I couldn't breathe. Wembley felt massive and the combination of the size of the pitch, the heavy ground and the great atmosphere left me totally drained.

I was delighted I managed to prevent Laudrup doing any real damage and I also had a hand in England's goal in a 1–0 victory. I played a long ball down the channel for Shearer to chase and we won a throw. I took the throw and a couple of touches later David Platt had put the ball past Peter Schmeichel and in the back of the net. Okay, I know that my part in it sounds a bit tenuous now but at the time I felt incredibly proud of my contribution.

I must have taken about twenty match-programmes home with me that night. I also took the socks home and my slip, my shirt and my shorts – in fact I took everything I could lay my hands on because I really thought it might have been my last game. That wasn't because I thought I'd played badly but because I still couldn't quite believe it was all happening. Ray Stubbs asked me in a post-match interview what I was going to do with my shirt and I told him I was going to sleep in it. When I see that interview now, there's a real innocence about me. I saw my dad and Alice an hour or so after the game had finished and I wondered what was going on inside his mind. What would it have been like if my mum had been there? How proud would she have been? You feel the loss more keenly than ever on nights like that.

Anyway, I did play for England again. Two months later, I was in the side that stuffed Greece 5–0 at Wembley. Then it was a draw with Norway, a win over the USA and so on. It became almost routine. All the games were friendlies because as hosts of Euro 96, we qualified for the finals automatically, but they were the kind of friendlies everyone wanted to win because there was so much at stake. Indeed, they didn't feel like friendlies. They felt like qualification through a process of maintaining form and building a momentum. We all felt we had a genuine chance of winning the first tournament on home soil for thirty years and no one wanted to miss out on a chance of being in the starting line-up.

The matches came thick and fast. By the summer of 2005, I'd won ten England caps. I had become a regular and I began to get more used to the rituals of England weeks. I never lost the excitement of pulling on an England shirt but after a week staying in a hotel with a group of people I did not really know, I felt at times more like a prisoner than a privileged guest. There's a lot of food and, at first, you really look forward to meal times (apparently prisoners have the same attitude). Then after a while you realize that even the most skilful cooks can only do a limited amount with chicken and pasta and I am afraid that I rather began to dread dinner.

There was the option of having a massage and it was one that most players, to pass the time, would take up at least once a day. By the end of the week, the most exhausted members of the party would be the overworked team masseurs. There would also be the occasional card school in the bar and at the 1998 World Cup we had race nights and golf days. There were team meetings and videos to watch as part of our preparations but there was still a lot of time to kill.

When I broke into the squad, my Blackburn team-mates Shearer, David Batty and Tim Flowers were also being called up. I knew some of the other lads because I'd played against them but it did help if you were surrounded by players from your own club, and when it came to the one with more representatives in the England team than any other, Manchester United won easily. By the late 1990s, David

Beckham, Gary and Phil Neville, Nicky Butt and Paul Scholes were all in the squad. They spent their time together, especially meals. If you got down late to lunch and the only remaining seat was on the 'United table' it was always a bit awkward. They, as any club players do, had their own jokes, their own discussions about their club and, although they were never unfriendly, it was a not an easy world for an outsider to walk into.

The best thing about the England camps was the training. I always felt that I came back from international duty a better, sharper player. For a start, the sessions were intensely competitive because, unlike a club side working day-to-day, there were often a couple of places up for grabs and, if you were playing well, you could leapfrog one of the more established players. That brought something extra to training. There was a greater level of quality because in those days you were probably playing with better players than those at your club side – although for some of those in the England team now, that may no longer be the case. The ball seemed to be passed around faster, moves did not break down as quickly and it would build my performance up to a peak over the course of the week. It was such a clear indicator of how much playing with good players improved an individual.

Terry Venables made a smart move in recruiting Don Howe. Don had coached briefly at Chelsea under Ian Porterfield until a heart attack had forced him out of the game. He was a great man to work with, especially for a defender. He had a favourite video which he would have made us watch all day if he could. It was footage from his perfect game, AC Milan's 4–0 victory over Barcelona in the

1994 European Cup Final. Milan destroyed Barcelona that night but Don loved the game for the way it illustrated Milan's mastery of pressing and defending. It showed how all these superstars worked together as a team. He would freeze the frame and show that whenever Barcelona had the ball, there were always three Milan players in the picture. Don had great principles and was very much the old school, enjoying telling stories. He was the perfect counterfoil to Terry who was more of a players' manager.

Terry only lost two games throughout the two years he was in charge of England. One was the defeat on penalties to Germany in the semi-finals of Euro 96, the other was a match against Brazil in a mini-tournament called the Umbro Cup that we played in June 1995. That game isn't etched in my memory because we lost, though – I remember it best because I scored my only goal for England that day and it was a stonker.

I was incredibly excited to be playing against Brazil anyway. Even as an international player, it was still a treat to play against the world champions, still a great challenge to match yourself against players like Ronaldo and Dunga. It was also the first game that my new girlfriend, Mariana, came to watch. She got a rather exaggerated idea of my goalscoring potential because of that game. Blackburn v. Middlesbrough at Ewood Park on a wet Wednesday night never quite compared to Brazil at Wembley.

Before the match, Terry told me that when we had a corner, he didn't want me to stay on the halfway line, which was my normal position, but to move to the edge of the box. 'If the ball comes out to you, just smash it in the goal,' he said. Seven minutes before half-time, we got a free-kick that might as well have been a corner so I moved up to the edge of the box as instructed. Stuart Pearce was playing in that game as part of a three-man back line and he took the kick which was headed out to me.

I backed off a little bit to let it bounce and took it on my chest. It sat up nicely and I let it drop and then I volleyed it. I hit across it and it looped and bent towards the goal. Their goalkeeper, Zetti, got a hand to it but he only managed to push it up into the roof of the net which made it look even more spectacular. England fans voted it the eighteenth best England goal ever in a poll a couple of years ago. I was submerged by Batty and the rest of my team-mates congratulating me and then I ran towards the bench to let Terry know I had remembered what he'd said to me. We went in at half-time 1–0 up and I thought we might win it. I was dreaming about being the hero.

It didn't happen. Brazil were too good for us. They had a young Ronaldo up front. He was playing for PSV then but he was exceptional. Juninho equalized nine minutes after half-time, Ronaldo got the second and Edmundo grabbed the third. And that was it. I made one hard challenge on Dunga that earned me a nasty stare. The next time I saw him was for the build-up to the Soccer Aid benefit game eleven years later. I was talking to Angus Deayton and I said I hoped Dunga didn't remember me. Angus gave me the perfect put-down. 'I think there's probably a bit of water passed under the bridge for him since then,' he said.

So we lost 3–1 to the world champions and moved on towards Euro 96. We drew with Colombia in September and then again with Portugal on 12 December. Four days later, I played for Blackburn against Middlesbrough, broke my ankle and that was the end of my dream of playing in Euro 96. I never played for Terry Venables again, which is a lasting regret.

I spent the tournament in a kind of shadow land, training at Burnham Beeches, hanging round the lads a bit and working for Microsoft doing webchats. I went to all the games as a spectator so I saw Stuart Pearce gain his personal redemption when he scored in the penalty shoot-out against Spain. I was so pleased for him. He had come straight back into the side when I was injured and that was a reward for his drive and strength of character.

Sometimes, a thought nags at me, though. I would love to know if I could have made a difference in Euro 96. I'd love to know if I could have helped us get further than we did. I think of what might have been. I imagine myself playing against Germany in that semi-final and wondering how I would have tackled it. I wonder how I would have performed on a stage like that when I was at my peak with Blackburn. I would have been flying in that tournament but it wasn't to be. By the time I was fit again, Terry had gone. Glenn Hoddle was now in charge.

SEVEN

England under Hoddle

I quite liked Eileen Drewery. I never asked her for a short, back and sides like Ray Parlour did – I never felt the need to mock her. I had a laugh about her with some of the other lads when the prominence that Glenn Hoddle accorded her within the squad began to grow to bizarre proportions. I didn't buy into everything she said but nor did I feel unreservedly cynical about her. I understood the scepticism some of the other lads expressed about her and ultimately her presence became a divisive and damaging diversion. But anyway, I enjoyed talking to her.

Eileen had her own room at the England team hotel at Burnham Beeches. She put a simple dining chair in the middle of the room and sat you down in it. The first time I went to see her, she explained a little bit about what she did and how she worked. It was straightforward enough. She didn't make any extravagant claims about supernatural powers or anything like that and I just regarded her as someone to talk to. Some of the other lads felt embarrassed in there but I didn't find it awkward at all. Glenn asked us to be open-minded about her and I was.

I never became a disciple of Eileen's – not remotely. I didn't think she could help me with my injuries in the way that someone like Darren Anderton appeared to do. But I had lost my mum and I had never had any help getting over that and Eileen was the sort of person you could talk to about it. Her whole approach was to try to get you to share your worries or concerns, not just about football but about life in general, so I talked to her more about my mum than anything else and, in a strange kind of way, I found it comforting.

I wouldn't say she counselled me but she lent an ear. I didn't think of her as a mystic and I don't believe she had any special powers. I did feel a warmth coming off her hands when she put them above my head but I think if I put my hands above someone's head, they could probably feel a warmth coming off them, too, if they concentrated hard enough. I didn't really think there was anything unusual about that.

Eileen didn't try and pretend that she'd spoken to my mum and tell me that she was doing fine up there. She didn't say she'd been in touch but it was just good to share my thoughts about mum with someone else. I'd kept it inside for so long and guarded it so carefully from everyone else that it was quite a relief to chat about it – it felt like shedding a burden. I came out of there and I felt I had got something off my chest. I certainly never felt that I could have gone in there and openly made fun of her as some of the other guys did. Nor did I set any store by her like Darren did. Darren had

had a lot of problems with injuries and he felt that she was able to aid the healing process. Whether her methods just acted as a placebo or not, I don't know, but if someone derives a benefit from it, then who cares.

The thing was, quite a lot of people did seem to care. The press became obsessed with Eileen Drewery, and Glenn's devotion to her became the issue that dominated his time as England manager. It distorted his time in charge – it warped everything. It overshadowed what he was trying to do on the football pitch and swamped discussion about his tactics and his ability as a coach. His dependence on Eileen came to define him and allowed his critics to write him off as a nutty quack. I didn't have a problem with her but I could see very clearly, very soon, that her presence had become an issue. It created a difficult atmosphere within the squad. Most footballers are conservative by nature and deeply suspicious of something alternative like that. Spiritualism's a niche thing and yet suddenly it was being forced on a group of footballers, some of whom felt hostile towards it and threatened by it.

Things like that work okay when they are under the radar, when they are low-key. But Eileen wasn't low-key – she was high profile. It wasn't long before she was doing interviews about how she'd thrown up a force field around the Italy goal during England's goalless draw in Rome in October 1997 that sealed our qualification for the 1998 World Cup. The rationale, she said, was that if England had scored, there would have been a riot and people would have got hurt. That was all very Uri Geller. It began to feel as if she was using the England team as a publicity vehicle and a lot of the players became more and more uneasy about her.

Quite a few of the guys felt they had been placed under unfair pressure to go and see her even though they didn't want to. Hoddle never told us directly that we had to go. He never ordered us but we were invited to pay her a visit and the inference in the invitation was clear. He believed in her totally and so if you didn't go and see her, you felt as if you were questioning the manager and that he knew you were questioning him. Suddenly, all the media wanted to talk about was whether you'd been to see Eileen. It was all very cloak and dagger, like a murder mystery.

When we got back from a session with Eileen, Glenn never really asked how it went but there was a general worry that she reported her conversations with the players back to him. In my case, I wondered if she told him about my mum. I began to worry that maybe she thought I was emotionally fragile and not ready to play. He had such faith in her powers of analysis that you felt he might be guided by her opinions. Then, when she started appearing in the newspapers, the lads started worrying that she was going to divulge the details of what they had told her.

The boys who laughed at her felt they were being discriminated against. Steve McManaman and Robbie Fowler went in to see her and asked her if she could tell them who was going to win tomorrow's 3.15 at Wincanton so they could go and stick a bet on. They and other Eileen-sceptics ended up being marginalized by Hoddle. Maybe they would have been marginalized anyway but Eileen's presence gave them a reason to believe they were being victimized and that was not good for morale within the squad.

For a long time, I found it difficult to be critical of Hoddle and his methods. I still do. I can't see him for who he is and what he is because I can only see him as someone I idolized when he was a player. I have still got a tremendous amount of admiration for him and then I tended to look at him through rose-tinted spectacles. Even though he was not nearly as good a communicator as Terry Venables, he was very astute tactically and I always thought of it as an honour to be playing for him.

Even I could see, though, that the closer we got to the 1998 World Cup, the more intense Glenn became. It wasn't just his devotion to Eileen but also his man-management and his obsession with an alternative medical regime. The players felt their bodies were being flooded with all manner of strange substances. We had no idea what we were taking and it seemed very alien but we never had any suspicion that it was anything illegal or unnatural. Combined with the presence of Eileen, the insistence on vials of liquids and intravenous drips began to give the England squad the feel of a rather eccentric health farm.

In the run-up to France 98, Glenn became obsessed with our physical preparations and got really carried away with an extensive programme of vitamins and anti-oxidants. He had been influenced by Arsene Wenger, who had managed him when he played at Monaco and whom he regarded as his footballing mentor. At Arsenal, Wenger had got all the players on a supplement called creatine that helped explosive muscle reaction and it had obviously worked for them: in 1997/98, they won the Double. So when we met up with England at the end of that season, we were deluged. The

Arsenal players in the squad were comfortable with this, but the rest of us were not. I recall Tony Adams having to reassure players about everything. I didn't take creatine because I had tried it at Blackburn and it didn't agree with me. It used to make me very heavy-legged and give me cramp in my calves. But I couldn't escape the rest of what Glenn had planned. He had brought this guy with him to France called Philippe Boixel, an osteopath, physio and nutritionist who had worked with Wenger, and suddenly we all began to find that we were caught up in a very intense regime.

At Burnham Beeches and, later, at our team hotel in La Baule near Nantes, there was a big box full of glass vials of liquid in every player's room. There were detailed instructions about what you had to take and when you had to take it. You had to snap the top of the vial off, hold it above a glass, and then snap the bottom off so that you created a flow. We all had to drink a couple of these vials half an hour before breakfast and the first morning we were given them, five or six players came down to the breakfast room with tissue wrapped round their forefinger and thumb because they'd cut themselves trying to snap the bloody vials apart. There was a lot of hilarity about that but it was quite a rigmarole. We were told it was all herbal and we had to take it but there was an awful lot of trust involved. We didn't know what we were taking but according to the law of strict liability we were the ones who were responsible for what was in our system. We should have been told more.

That wasn't the end of it, either. A couple of hours before each World Cup game, we were offered to be hooked up to an intravenous drip. You'd be sitting there in your hotel room a couple of hours before one of the biggest matches of your life with a tube in your arm. It was surreal and it was also counterproductive because somehow it made me feel reliant on something I had never felt reliant upon before. It undermined me because it took away my personal responsibility – it was a crutch I didn't need.

I hadn't been well before the World Cup, picking up a bad throat infection at the end of the Premiership season, and so Boixel put me on a special regime to clear it up. It worked brilliantly – it was fantastic. I felt trapped then because I felt like I needed whatever he was giving me to keep me healthy and to aid my performance. The first game against Tunisia, I had this intravenous drip in my arm before the match and I felt great. I had a really good game and I connected the two things in my mind and so I took it for the next game.

I was drug-tested after our second-round defeat to Argentina and I was fine. If it had gone wrong, I was the one who would have been banned, of course. Under the laws of strict liability, every athlete is responsible for what is in his own body. But we take stuff like that because we're told it's harmless and because we're told it will make us recover faster and give us more stamina. All my footballing life I took vitamin supplements. Well, what are you going to do? Everyone else is taking it. You are looking for a way of finding an extra yard and for better recovery and it is up to the individual or his coach to decide what lengths you are prepared to go to in order to get it.

There are people in football now who are looking at how they can bend the rules and push things to the limits of legality. There were times during the 1998 World Cup when I thought 'I hope all this is above board'. I know, too, that some clubs weren't happy about what their players were taking but there wasn't a lot they could do. There was, once again, no suggestion whatsoever that any of it was illegal. I wasn't totally sure about it but if I had felt a really serious doubt, I would have insisted that I didn't take it. Of course, it would have been hard because it would have been construed as wilful disobedience of the coach and that's what I imagine makes it easy for some athletes to get pushed into taking stuff they don't really want to take. If eight out of ten people are taking it, how are the other two going to feel if they refuse?

I know the Manchester United players felt very suspicious about creatine. They didn't want to take it. They were sceptical about it because they had heard how much store the Arsenal players set by it and the two clubs were bitter rivals. The whole nutritional regime was alien to most of us and that created a problem. If things are done differently to the way they are conducted at your club, there is an inner conflict. That implies that your club is doing something wrong and if you believe in your club, as the United lads did, that constitutes a conflict.

Ultimately, the obsession with vitamins and vials and antioxidants was futile. It was introduced too late. If you are going to be doing something like that, you have got to do it for a year – you can't introduce it two or three weeks before a tournament. So everything was essentially experimental. In the end, I took one supplement too many and it disabled me when I could least afford it, on the biggest possible stage.

Before the World Cup epic against Argentina, I took a caffeine tablet. It went back to the idea that I thought I would be at a disadvantage if I didn't take one. All this stuff was on offer and I started thinking 'Oh, actually, I do feel a little bit tired'. I persuaded myself I felt a bit lethargic and I thought it would make me sharper. So the medical guys gave me the tablet. It was a bloody big thing, like a horse pill. It made my whole mouth dry out. The thing was, I was wired for that game anyway. I couldn't have been any more hyped up for it. But you always have a bit of down-time before the game before the adrenalin kicks in and that's when I took the tablet. So by the time kick-off came around, my mouth was absolutely parched and I felt like I couldn't produce any saliva. As the game went on, I began to feel more and more uncomfortable. I had to come off a few minutes before the end of normal time which was very unusual for me but my calves were cramping badly and I'd become a liability – I could hardly move. Why was that? Was it because I was more tense than usual or was it because I had taken a tablet I wasn't used to and it had taken water away from my muscles? The fact was, by the time of the Argentina game, I had an imbalance of vitamins in my body which gave me cramp. I didn't have cramp because I wasn't fit enough – I had cramp because I was overloaded.

I felt I had let everybody down by coming off. For me, it was the ultimate indictment of the nutrition regime we were encouraged to adhere to under Hoddle. Because elements of it were random and unfamiliar, it ended up hobbling me rather than imbuing me with new levels of stamina and energy. I do believe in a modern approach to nutrition but over a sustained period of time. It was such a shame that it ended up like that under Glenn, such a shame that there was so much paranoia around – about the vials, the tablets, the drips, about Eileen. It sapped some of the energy out of a squad that was capable of winning that 1998 World Cup. It became a distraction when we didn't need a distraction.

We should have been going into that World Cup on a high after we qualified automatically from a difficult group. I made my England comeback, after a broken ankle, in the home tie against Italy at Wembley. We lost that to a lovely goal from Gianfranco Zola and I felt guilty because I couldn't help feeling pleased with myself at the end of the game. I was so happy that I came through it and played well that it blotted out some of the disappointment of the defeat.

We recovered well from that. We won an important game away to Poland in Katowice. Not a welcoming venue, Katowice – also known as the Hell Hole of Silesia, apparently, and I can understand why. I remember it mainly for the moments before the game. We were lining up in a metal tunnel underneath the main stand when the Poland players filed out of their dressing room. It would be fair to say they were pumped up for the game. Suddenly, I heard this shouting and then a metallic clanging. I looked round and their centre-half, a huge skinhead bloke, was leaping up and down and headbutting the tunnel roof. Okay, I admit it, a bit of a shiver went through me at that moment. When the game began, we turned the tables on them, though. Alan Shearer scored after six minutes and David Batty cut their midfield playmaker in half with a scything tackle and he had to go off. That seemed to take away some of their spirit. We won 2–0 with a late goal from Teddy Sheringham wrapping it up.

In the end, it came down to the last game of the group, the return tie with Italy in the Stadio Olimpico in Rome. We needed a draw and we got it with Paul Gascoigne playing an incredibly disciplined game in the centre of midfield. We nearly scored near the end when Ian Wright hit the post but Italy broke incredibly quickly and I knew there was a danger that we were going to be exposed. I hurtled back into defence but when they crossed from their left towards Christian Vieri at the back post, I thought we were finished. I jumped with him and did everything I could to put him off but I knew he was a lot taller than me and one of the best headers of the ball in the world so I feared the worst. Thankfully, he headed wide and we were through. Maybe Eileen had put a force field round our goal, too.

Everything appeared to be going so well. With our results and performances, I was feeling positive and was looking forward to the team being successful under Glenn.

The Italy game was Gazza's last appearance for England in a competitive match. As the World Cup approached, his mental and physical condition began to deteriorate. He played a part in the warm-up games against Morocco and Belgium in the King Hassan II Cup in Casablanca at the end of May but when we got back to our base at La Manga in southern Spain, he began to crack. I value him tremendously as a friend and it was sad to watch as his lifestyle began to catch up with him. That last season before the World Cup, he really went downhill. He was losing his pace, his sharpness and his fitness and he was losing them fast.

The whole La Manga experience was horrible even for those of us who were reasonably confident we were going to make the squad. We knew that at the end of our few days there, Hoddle was going to axe five players from the squad and send them home. And with Glenn, even if you thought you were in, you could never quite be sure. Irrespective of whether you thought you would get in or not, there was a voice in your ear saying you might be in trouble. John Gorman, Hoddle's deputy, was a lovely bloke but he just went round telling everybody what they wanted to hear. I think he told every member of the squad that they were in at one time or another which made the disappointment all the more severe when they were bombed out. Every time some-body praised Phil Neville or Andy Hinchcliffe at La Manga, my ears pricked up because they were my rivals for what I assumed would be the two left-back spots.

The effect was to create a terrible, almost unbearable tension and rumours began to circulate that Gazza's place might be in jeopardy. Gazza sensed it, too, and he began to implode. We had quite a few evenings in the Piano Bar in our hotel in La Manga and Gazza was often to be found at the piano singing. He'd get the pianist to play 'New York, New York' or 'My Way' and rearrange the lyrics so it would be 'We'll win the World Cup at a doddle, come on, please, take me Hoddle'. There was a lot of laughter, but it was uneasy laughter.

On the day when we were each due to hear our fate, Gazza went out on the golf course in the morning and started drinking early. I didn't see it happen but some of the lads said that when he got back, they'd thrown him in the swimming pool to sober him up. We had each been given a time for an individual meeting with Glenn in his room that afternoon and as it was a sunny day, most of us went to sit out by the pool while we waited for our slot to come around. There must have been a better way of doing it than that, surely. Hoddle turned it into Judgement Day. It was unnecessarily cruel, even though I'm sure it was unintentional.

When a player's slot time came around, John Gorman would come down and tell him it was time to go. The player would get up from the pool and head for the hotel. It felt like waving somebody off as they go to face a firing squad. We could see the window of Hoddle's room from the pool. Some of the lads came back down. Some of them didn't. Gazza didn't. He went berserk when Hoddle told him he wasn't going and smashed parts of the room up. He chucked a lamp and booted a table so hard that he gashed his shin. Some of the lads who were close to him like Dave Seaman and Paul Ince went up to calm him down and take him back to his room.

I felt desperately sorry for Gazza. He had been such a great player and he loved football so much. He had a complicated personal life and a tortured personality beneath all the joking and the bluster. The football field was the only place he felt he could escape his problems and now that route had been taken away from him, too. He had become a superstar at the World Cup in Italy eight years earlier and he had set his heart on playing in it again. Being left out was a crushing blow for him but in a way I respected Hoddle for doing it. It was a hard decision. You could even say it was a ruthless decision – but it was the right decision. At that stage, there wasn't any evidence that Gazza would be at his best for that tournament or anything close to it.

I was next in after Gazza. I knocked on the door and walked in. It was a big suite. The mirror was still a bit lopsided, a couple of pictures weren't straight either and the table Gazza had kicked had been removed. I looked for blood on the floor but I couldn't see any. I sat down opposite Glenn. He seemed a little bit flustered. I'm certain that he wasn't enjoying it. He must have known there was a possibility it would turn into a melodrama. Anyway, he told me I was in and that he was expecting a lot of me in France. I found out quite how much when I realized he hadn't included another left-back in the squad: Phil Neville and Hinchcliffe were both on the plane home with Gazza.

The fun and games still weren't over, though. When we got back from La Manga, we were given a couple of days off. Teddy Sheringham went to Portugal for a short break and some pictures of him appeared, smoking a cigarette and having a drink. Hoddle was furious. He made him apologize in public which Teddy did through gritted teeth. Then, on the way to La Baule, we stopped off in Caen and played a game that was supposed to be 'behind closed doors'. The security was ridiculous: there were police everywhere and there even were snipers on the rooftops. No journalists were allowed in – Hoddle was adamant about that – but there were a group of locally invited VIPs in some of the executive boxes. So the English journalists just stopped them on their way out and asked what the team had been. It was all very silly. Teddy, by the way, was left out as a punishment.

After the smoke had cleared and the frenzy about Gazza's exclusion had subsided a little, it was clear that we were still left with a very good squad. Despite the sense of siege that was settling over us because of Hoddle's paranoia, despite the worries over the pills that we were popping and the mysterious liquids we were drinking, there was a lot of optimism about our chances in France. We had a lot of very good experienced players and a kid like Michael Owen who was threatening to turn into a phenomenon. We played a 3–5–2 system, which was a bold move from the manager, but we all knew our jobs within it and we were comfortable with our responsibilities and confident in each other.

Player by player, we were as good as anyone. David Seaman was at his peak as a goalkeeper. I always felt that he was in control which is what you need from your keeper when you are a defender. Gary Neville, mainly, was on the right side of the back three. He didn't do much wrong then and he doesn't do much wrong now. He's still terribly underrated as a player. I looked at him when he broke into the England side and I knew he was going to be playing for England for a long time. He is quick enough and his intelligence and his positional sense give him an extra edge.

There was a great mental strength about Gary, too. It was obvious that he was the leader of the Manchester United set that was at the core of that World Cup squad. The United boys were never really part of the gang and even though that didn't bother me in the slightest, it created some resentment amongst some of the other lads. The United boys were very serious. They had their own table at meal times and even

161

that became an issue. The Liverpool players got a bit chippy about it. Hoddle went through a period when he tried to ban them from sitting together, which seemed bizarre. I didn't understand why them sitting at their own table was supposed to be a threat. If that was what they were comfortable with, that was fine.

There were other groups, too. Players like Paul Ince and Robbie Fowler, and to a lesser extent Steve McManaman, were the guys – The Lads. They were the ones who liked having a laugh at the expense of others, a set of practical jokers. Then there was the group who always sat at the front of the bus playing cards when we were on the road: this comprised Shearer, Batty, Tim Flowers and Gareth Southgate. I wasn't a card player, which was another one of my great social failings. I just never got that integration thing cracked. I should have done my research about how to behave around footballers. If I could have played cards or golf or done impressions, I might have been a lot more popular.

Then there was Tony Adams. He didn't play cards, of course. He was going through the process of confronting all his problems and he was puritanical about not drinking or gambling. He had to be, I suppose, and I respected him for that. Still, it was fascinating the way he changed overnight. The old Tony wasn't really interested in me but the new Tony was reading books on philosophy and thinking deeply about everything and, for some reason, he identified me as a kindred spirit. He must have thought 'Who can I share all this with?' and arrived at me because there was this perception that I was some sort of bookworm, some sort of

Guardian-reading intellect. So he would suddenly come up to me an hour before training when you were strapping your ankles in the physio's room before getting on the bus and would start talking to me about Jean-Paul Sartre and I'd be nodding my head and thinking 'I haven't got a clue what you're talking about, Tony, but I'm sure it's really good'.

The transformation in Tony was astonishing really. He had gone from one extreme to the other: from a kind of out-of-control lager lout to an aesthete, from the soul of the party to someone who was reflective and considerate. I was equally as confused by the new Tony as I had been by the old one. He was trying to change everything and he became this new person and maybe he thought I could relate to that – but I couldn't. I like reading but I don't know the classics. The fact that I was regarded within football as some sort of Oxford don said more about football than it did about me. Just because I read *The Guardian*, liked a different kind of music and went to the cinema and the theatre now and again didn't make me a leading academic. It was just that most footballers seemed to think it did.

Everybody respected Tony for the changes he was making. Within the England squad, he was still granted the same status. No one took the piss out of him because he was very serious about it. Paul Merson was a bit more light-hearted about the problems he was facing. A couple of years earlier, I'd been with him, Tim Sherwood and Tim Flowers at the bar in the Wembley Banqueting Halls after an England game. They were all intending to go on to the Atlantic Bar in Soho for a drink but it was before Merse had gone public about his addictions and he said he had to go back to his local pub somewhere in north London to get some 'gear'. 'Don't worry about it, mate,' Tim Flowers said. 'They'll let you in dressed like that.' Merse didn't mean that kind of gear.

On one England away trip, Merse came and sat with me and Gareth Southgate and he talked about all his issues quite happily. He was talking about all the people he hung out with and how much time he had on his hands and the disposable income he didn't know what to do with and the type of pub his local was. We asked him how he'd got caught up in the spiral he was in. He said one thing led to another. 'Put it another way,' he said, 'if you go to a hairdresser's seven days a week, eventually you are going to get a haircut.'

But if there were players in that squad intent on putting personal problems behind them, the most troubled individual on the eve of the tournament was David Beckham. David always wore his heart on his sleeve so you could tell when he was upset about something – and he was definitely upset going into the 1998 World Cup. His relationship with Victoria was gathering momentum and Hoddle claimed that David was not properly focused on his football. There was a lot of tension between them and everything burst out into the open when Hoddle left him out of the side for the opening game against Tunisia, which we won comfortably 2–0, and picked Darren Anderton on the right side of midfield instead.

David made his disappointment about being left out very obvious and the problem got worse and worse. Hoddle forced him to do a press conference which incurred Alex Ferguson's wrath at Old Trafford. Ferguson was appalled at the way David was being treated, which probably made

David feel empowered. Managers always say they are looking for a reaction from someone when they drop them. Well,
Glenn got a reaction but it might not have been the one he
had anticipated – certainly not the one he was hoping for.

David trained hard and worked hard but he rebelled a bit
and that went against him. He was surly about it. Hoddle
went with Anderton but the general feeling in the squad was
that David deserved to be in the team as well – his training
and his performances demanded that. But Glenn had made
his decision and wasn't going to change it. He thought he
had put David in his place. That works with some people
but David is a deceptively stubborn and bloody-minded guy.
It didn't work with him.

Sometimes, Glenn's manner in training was all about
showing you how it should be done. He was still bloody
good technically even though his playing career had been
over for a few years. The things he did in training, his touch
with both feet, his passing, were all fantastic. You talk about
players impressing you when you first come across them in
the context of England training but when Glenn joined in, he
was unbelievable: his balance, his poise, everything. His ability was spellbinding.

It occurred to me now and again that he may still have
harboured frustrations about his own playing career. The
England team should have been built around him when he
was at his peak – but it wasn't. Sometimes, it seemed he was
frustrated by members of our England team who were
praised to the skies by the critics but who he may have felt
did not possess his talent. There was a time before the game
against Argentina, for instance, when he criticized Beckham

and Paul Scholes because they couldn't master a free-kick they were trying. That upset David and Paul. In fact, it upset the whole of the United contingent. It isn't hard to make a connection between Glenn's treatment of David and David's sending-off against the Argentines.

Glenn got very impatient with players' technical deficiencies. I don't know if it was an innocent thing stemming from the fact that he believed that if he could do it, current players should be able to do it, too. Glenn was a tactless man in some ways. He probably just didn't realize that he was offending the sensitivities of people as much as he was. Whatever his motives, he rubbed David up the wrong way. It got personal between them and David started to mope around. It was just a matter of time until he blew.

David got back into the side after we lost to Romania in our second game. Judging by some of the stick I got afterwards, perhaps he should have thanked me for that 2–1 defeat in Toulouse. What happened against Romania was a hell of a jolt for me because I was made the scapegoat for a loss that no one was really expecting. Hoddle made it plain that he felt I was at fault for Romania's late winner by my Chelsea team-mate Dan Petrescu, and some of the other England boys gave me the cold shoulder, too.

I'd done well against Dan for most of the game. He was on their right, I was on our left, so we were matched against each other and we knew each other's games well. I caused him quite a few problems but we didn't play well as a team, especially in midfield, and then Paul Ince came off, claiming injury. Romania were a good side as well. We'd played against them at Wembley a few years before and there was one spell where they kept the ball for about ten minutes. Gheorghe Hagi was a veteran by then but he was still a world-class playmaker who was incredibly difficult to pick up and they were also solid at the back.

Romania took the lead in Toulouse and they deserved it but it was a bad goal to give away. They had a throw-in on my side of the pitch, level with the edge of the area, and we failed to defend it. I couldn't quite get to the throw and it dropped to Hagi. He lobbed it over Tony Adams into the path of Viorel Moldovan and he volleyed it past David Seaman. It stayed that way until close to the end when Hoddle brought on the wonderboy, Michael Owen, and Michael grabbed an equalizer in the seventy-ninth minute.

Then Dan scored the goal that put me in the stocks. I was playing as a left wing-back and I saw Dan start to make this speculative run from our side of the pitch across towards the centre. I watched him for about ten yards and thought he would get picked up by someone else and that I should keep my position, but no one picked him up so I started to follow him. Then I hesitated because if I went with him and someone made a break down my flank, I would have been stranded and the team would have been exposed.

But still no one picked him up. So I tracked him and as I did that, he suddenly darted right towards the goal. I was playing catch up then and the ball was played through and our defence opened up. I was trying to catch up with him and I was running alongside him playing like a right-back. I was thinking that he was right footed so he would probably try and turn inside back onto his right foot, particularly as the angle was so tight for a left foot shot. Because of that, I didn't try and get in front of him but stayed along-side him.

As we were running, his arm caught me in the face and knocked me back. In fact it caught me in the teeth and jolted me back so that I almost stopped for a step. Then I carried on. Perhaps I should have gone down holding my face but I kept going. He had his forearm across my neck, too, so at the vital moment when the bouncing ball was dropping, my head was forced upwards and I wasn't looking at the ball. Some might say he shielded it well, others that he fouled me. Anyway, when it dropped, he sidefooted it past Seaman. He shot with his left foot and it went in at the near post. I couldn't fathom that. Dave was standing there and I was surprised he had been beaten at his near post. I just bent down and held my head because I'd got a whack in the face from Dan.

A couple of minutes later, the final whistle went. We'd lost. Suddenly, we were in danger of not qualifying for the second round. I was in shock. I felt terrible. In the dressing room afterwards, everyone's chins were on the floor and when Glenn came in there was suddenly this sense that it was all my fault. Tony Adams just said 'What happened there?' and Seaman seemed bemused about it and wanted to know how it could have happened. Then Glenn came in and started quizzing me, too. He said I hadn't defended properly, that I hadn't been strong, that I should have shrugged off that elbow in the face and not let it rock me back. They made me the chosen victim and I got slaughtered. I didn't read anything in the newspapers but a lot of people phoned and said I had been roasted.

The next few days were horrible: I felt it was going to be all down to me if we were knocked out. There was no one else to replace me at left wing-back even if Hoddle had wanted to replace me but I still felt alone. I felt nervous in training. I lost my confidence overnight. Hoddle didn't do anything to reassure me because he wasn't that type. I tried to keep my head down but the backlash was quite severe. I had been a consistent player for England and I had never been made to feel directly responsible for the team conceding a goal before. Now, none of that counted for anything. It was whack, have that.

I thought the criticism was excessive and I thought the reaction from Hoddle was unnecessary. The blame culture kicked in. I know that as part of a team, it's up to each individual not to make a mistake but sometimes you are going to make a mistake and you hope that when you do, the reaction is relative to the action. If Dan had scored because I'd been loitering out on the left wing picking my nose and couldn't be bothered to track him then fine, I would have deserved everything I got. But I tried to do the right thing, made a poor decision and got punished for it.

If I had stayed on the left where I was originally, I wouldn't have got blamed. But because I was an honest player, I tried to do what was best for the team and to deal with that situation. I could have said Dan Petrescu wasn't my man once he moved across. Still, I do blame myself. When I got smacked in the face, I should have carried on. I shouldn't have let that knock me out of my stride. I should have anticipated him hitting it with his left foot. The decisions I made proved to be the wrong decisions. It was a tight angle and I thought the only way he was going to score was if he had cut back. I thought that was the danger because Dave had the near post covered. My job was to stop him checking back. I admit all that but I still think it was counterproductive for me to be turned into a scapegoat.

Football is like that, I suppose – success is frighteningly transitory. I'd swung in the free-kick from which Alan Shearer opened the scoring in the game against Tunisia and everyone was raving about the quality of the delivery. Now, the venom directed at me was unbelievable. The result was that I went into the final group game against Colombia in Lens absolutely petrified. I played on my nerves; I played with fear. I was nervous that if I made another mistake I would be crucified. I had a couple of chances to score but I was so tense, I didn't connect. I felt I was under severe pressure.

I just about got out of there alive. David Beckham came back into the team and started alongside Darren Anderton and they scored our two goals. I was mainly concerned with not doing anything wrong and trying to keep the Colombia talisman, Carlos Valderrama, out of the game. It was an experience playing against him. Everyone knew Valderrama because of his clever skills and his big hair but I hadn't realized that he was festooned with necklaces and bracelets. He had so many he rattled and clanged. Whenever I had the ball, I knew if he was trying to chase me down because it was like Santa's sleigh bells coming up behind you: there was no chance of him sneaking up on you. As it turned out, he didn't have that much influence on the game and when Beckham scored with a terrific free-kick to put us 2–0 up, we were through.

By now, the hotel in La Baule was starting to grate on everyone, too. It was outside the town and we weren't even allowed to go to the shops unless we were accompanied by security guards and had Glenn's express permission. There weren't really many social areas at the hotel, either. It wasn't easy for us to mix. There was a central pool and a small restaurant but Glenn always sacrificed comfort for isolation. He had a thing about us being accessible to anyone – he couldn't stand that.

The rooms in La Baule were arranged in a kind of horse-shoe shape around the pool. They were like little apartments There was a kitchenette and then you went upstairs to your bedroom and there was a sliding door that went out to the terrace that looked over a golf course. It sounds nice but there was nothing there at all. One of the first things I did was get one of the security guys to take me into town so I could buy a stereo for the room. I had done a couple of inter-views with Steve Lamacq, the Radio 1 presenter who did *The Evening Session*, so I asked him if he could get someone to tape me the shows and send them out to me every week. I used to save these up and play them when things got particu-larly dull and I felt particularly desperate. As for the TV, it wasn't a lot of use as there were no English television chan-nels. To be fair to the FA, they had converted this kind of garage area into a youth club. There were pinball machines and racing car games and a pool table but it all felt a bit juve-nile. Rio Ferdinand was really young then and he and a couple of the other lads seemed to be in there all the time.

So we all just fell into a strange routine. It was like being a prisoner smack bang in the middle of the world's greatest sporting event. When it is that monotonous, it's a real shame. I know you're there to play football but when you're at a World Cup, you've got to try and make sure your players enjoy the atmosphere and have fun: that's how you're going to make the most of it. Be focused, of course; be as focused as you are when you are playing for your club. I didn't give any more for England than I did for my club so why should the preparations be so radically different? How was England going to get more out of me than that?

When we got knocked out and I actually got to see Mariana and the family, I would be lying if I said there wasn't an element of relief. I know that's a horrible thing to say but that was what the whole set-up made it feel like. I was 95 per cent disappointed and gutted but there was that element of a weight being lifted off my shoulders because psychologically we had been on a treadmill. That says everything and that can't be good. If you have got some friends who have come to see you play, why can't you spend the evening with them afterwards? After all, you're not going to go to sleep after the game, that's for sure – too much adrenalin flowing. So it's either go back to the games room and play some mind-numbing arcade game for four hours or meet up with some people if you are in the right location and wind down.

That's what you would do normally. At Chelsea, we would go to a restaurant in Knightsbridge called San Lorenzo and have some pasta and a glass of wine and unwind that way. That was great. Inevitably, you'd end up talking about the game so you had a debrief anyway. As for keeping us separated from our wives and families for so long, that was just counterproductive. The whole 'Wags' issue was presented as a reason why we played so badly in Germany in 2006 but I don't see how that could be. You're telling me that players can't focus because their wives are spending money? That's ridiculous. It didn't create a great impression and it shouldn't have been allowed to turn into the circus it did but there was nothing that abnormal about it. The Wags had been shunted up the news agenda because of the celebrity culture we live in, and because thankfully hooliganism wasn't such a big issue for the news reporters any more. That was the reason for their prominence – that and the fact that England performed badly. The wives and girlfriends of Australian cricketers accompany them on tour and nobody ever mentions it – because they're winning all the time.

The way Hoddle handled that aspect of the tournament was bizarre. What are the benefits of keeping players isolated when you compare them with the negatives, such as boredom? You can't focus on football all day every day. You need to let your mind switch off a bit and when you are isolated like that, you can't. You have got nothing else to think about or talk about. You are creating a situation where players miss things more and they want to rebel against it. That never actually happened but it became more and more stressful for everyone as the tournament went on because you had no normality. For me to spend a day with Mariana down at the beach or shopping four or five days before a game would hardly have done any harm. I would do that before a Champions League game; I would do it before a title-deciding match for Blackburn. So what's the difference?

The goldfish bowl effect was about to increase now we were through to the second round. Because we hadn't won the group, we were playing Argentina for a place in the quarter-finals. They were one of the tournament favourites but I knew that the build-up to the game was going to open up a can of worms for me. My wife, Mariana, had been born and brought up in Argentina. Her maiden name was Crawley and her family moved to England when she was four because of the political situation over there. Her father Eduardo had been the editor of a newspaper in Patagonia called *Sur Argentino*. It wasn't a campaigning paper but it was a turbulent time in the early Seventies when the Peronistas were in charge and Peron's widow, Isabelita, had succeeded her late husband and was running things. Before that, her father had been at a paper called *La Opinion*, which was the most prestigious daily in Argentina and where ten journalists out of a staff of just over one hundred had been killed or had joined the ranks of the 'disappeared'. Statistics at the time said there were two and a half political killings a day. *Sur Argentino* had protected fugitives now and again and it got to the point where Eduardo began to feel that he might be in danger if he stayed in the country. So in 1974, he took his family to England.

When the Falklands War broke out, Mariana's father was often on British television as a commentator and analyst. Mrs Thatcher objected to him because she felt that Argentines should not be portrayed as intelligent, reasonable men like Eduardo, even though he had fled the country before General Galtieri even took power. Thatcher was particularly incensed by an interview Eduardo gave to the BBC's Michael Cockerell in which he borrowed all the 'principles' Thatcher kept quoting, said he fully agreed with them and then went on to say that those were the very principles the Argentines were upholding. It was difficult for Mariana when the war broke out. She was only twelve, she had dual nationality and sometimes she was made to feel a little uneasy by an occasional stray comment.

So England v. Argentina in the knock-out phase of the World Cup was pretty special in our family. I wouldn't say it was a touchy subject really because even though they loved their country, Mariana's family weren't really football fans. I got Mariana's father, her brother and brother-in-law tickets for the game in St Etienne but they were coming to support me and be part of the atmosphere, not to shout for the opposition. But if the subject wasn't loaded for us, it was for the English media. They had a field day with it.

I was doing some articles for *The Sun* during that World Cup but that didn't stop them doorstepping Mariana's parents at their home in Hertfordshire to try and get a scoop about how the wife of an England player was going to be supporting Argentina. They didn't find her parents as they weren't in. So they ended up harrassing her eighty-year-old grandmother. Her gran didn't speak much English and got thoroughly confused about what these people were doing jabbering away at her about me. She was bewildered by it all and Mariana and her family were very upset.

When I found out about it, I was furious. I phoned Steve Howard, the journalist who was doing the columns with me, and told him I wouldn't be doing any more. He said it was nothing to do with the sports section and that the features department had sent these journalists round to hassle Mariana's gran. Reporters always say that. They always say it was another part of the paper but when it happens to you, it's difficult to distinguish between different departments and editorial policies. All you know is, it's causing you a problem.

I was a long way away and I felt helpless. It was a tense build-up anyway and that kind of upset was the last thing I needed. I was very much on my guard after that. There were a lot of questions about my family and I could tell a lot of the journalists were fishing for a headline. Everything was getting very jingoistic and quite unpleasant. English newspapers love nothing better than matches against the 'Krauts' and the 'Argies' – great footballing nations but countries we've fought wars against. People resort to the lowest common denominator. It's sad.

Apart from that nonsense, I felt we were well prepared for the Argentina game. There was still tension in the camp over the monastic life we were expected to lead. Nonetheless we were still optimistic. We were very pumped up for the game and tactically we all knew what we were doing and what to expect. We knew we were playing one of the favourites but we didn't doubt our ability. I felt totally confident that we'd win. There was a feeling we had an exciting match-winner in Michael Owen. That made everyone feel good because he was so fresh and so fearless and he had the pace and unpredictability that scares even the best defenders rigid. Michael's emergence added to the feeling that the team was evolving during the tournament in the way that many of the best sides do.

Domestic glory, collective celebration. Chelsea 2 Middlesbrough 0, League Cup Final 1998. My second spell at Stamford Bridge was a much happier time for me.

Enjoying European success with the 1998 Cup-Winners' Cup, alongside my captain and good friend, Dennis Wise.

Brian Laudrup was one of my toughest international opponents, especially on my first call-up for England.

Receiving instructions from Glenn Hoddle, a manager for whom I had a lot of respect.

After the 1998 World Cup, I'm trying to make a lasting impression on Her Majesty The Queen.

The England XI line-up against Columbia, 1998 World Cup. Apart from the left wing-back, what a team.

The defining image of our World Cup campaign. The tide turned against us from the moment David Beckham received his marching orders against Argentina.

Dan Petrescu's winner for Romania means World Cup heartache once again. My wrong decision proved costly. I took some heat after that goal.

Deep in discussion with a footballing hero from my childhood, Kevin Keegan.

I have to take evasive action as Paul Ince dives in.

A robust challenge and a frustrating match at Wembley in 1999. Little did I realise it would be my final England game.

I can't hide my disbelief. Urging the linesman to intervene after Robbie Fowler's 'gesture' at Stamford Bridge in February 1999.

An all-time great. Gianfranco Zola was magnificent to watch. And he likes my jokes.

Man of the match for our final-day win over Liverpool in May 2003 that got us into the Champions League.

I'll always be grateful to John Hollins for giving me my first real opportunity as a professional footballer. The gamble paid off, I think.

Tough times at Southampton. Identical expressions on the faces of Jim Smith, Harry Redknapp, Matt Oakley and Jamie Redknapp. I've got the same feeling of hopelessness.

A sad farewell to St Mary's and a great set of fans as Southampton are relegated in May 2005.

For ITV's *Extinct*, I travelled to Rwanda in November 2006 and was welcomed into a new family. Here I'm surrounded by 28 mountain gorillas – an emotionally overwhelming experience.

Pitchside at Old Trafford for the BBC alongside the legendary John Motson. Having grown up listening to his commentary, it was an honour to finally work with him.

Wedding bells. Tying the knot with Mariana in June 1997 was the most special day of my life.

Mariana and I at the Cumberland Hotel in early summer 2007.

Family holidays are a lot more enjoyable now that I'm no longer playing. With our two children Georgina and Lucas.

My mouth was really parched when we started because of my horse pill caffeine tablet but it felt like we'd just kicked off in the World Cup Final. To beat Argentina would have sent out a powerful message to the remaining teams. I was up against Javier Zanetti, the Inter Milan player, who was strong, quick and had good endurance. I had my work cut out with him. He was a very clever player, one of the best I have ever played against. We had a real sparring contest. He was hard to get past because he read the game well and he made me think about my game. At that level, you have to solve the problems your opposite number gives you on the pitch.

Argentina went ahead with an early penalty from Gabriel Batistuta but we equalized soon after with a penalty from Shearer. Then Michael scored that goal and I watched wide-eyed with 40,000 other spectators. When he picked up the ball near the halfway line, I thought I'd sprint to try and support him to give him an option. I'd gone a few yards when I realized there was no way I was going to get anywhere near him. I was just willing him to keep going. He suddenly took off and it was all instinctive. He became isolated, there was no one else around him except Scholes, and when he knocked the ball to the right and went past Roberto Ayala, I didn't think he had a good angle to shoot across the goalkeeper. I thought Michael would aim low to the keeper's near post but he went high to the keeper's far post. The ball bulged the net. It was incredible. Now we had all the momentum. Half-time was getting close. I thought we were going to be difficult to beat.

Then, on the stroke of half-time, they got a free-kick on the edge of our box. I had peeled away from the wall to the left, just a few yards, so I could mark Ariel Ortega who was out wide. I was trying not to go too wide but I was also aware of not being too narrow. If I gave Ortega too much space, I'd leave the team vulnerable to the possibility that he could receive the ball and cross it behind our defence into the box and then you're dead. If anyone touches it, it goes in. I knew something was afoot because there was a lot of consultation going on between the players standing over the ball. Zanetti wandered behind our wall – whoever was marking him just let him go. Juan Sebastian Veron ran up as if he was going to shoot and then passed to Zanetti who had darted out from behind the wall. If Scholes had stuck his left foot out, he would have intercepted it – it was that close to him – but he was bracing himself for a shot and he was part of the wall so it wasn't his fault. Zanetti got it, took one touch, swivelled, shot and scored.

When we went in at half-time, I got roasted by Hoddle for not picking Zanetti up. I told him Zanetti wasn't my man. I felt I had to defend myself. If I had left the man out wide, they would probably have scored, too. The management's criticism wasn't particularly constructive at that point but everyone was frustrated because we had conceded an equalizer so close to the interval. If we had come in 2–1 up, that would have given them plenty to think about. How would they have coped with the chasing Michael Owen was giving them? How would they have coped with the way we were playing?

Our frustration was compounded by the fact that they had scored from a set-piece and we didn't know about it. Had they done it before in the tournament? Had they done it in preparation for the tournament? If they had, we weren't told about it and that suggests a gap in the preparation of the coaching staff. If it was the first time they had ever done it, it was a stroke of genius and it cost us more than a goal. It cost us the psychological advantage of the high of Michael's goal. We still felt we were winning on points but that was about to change.

Ten minutes after half-time, Beckham was sent off. He was fouled by Diego Simeone, Argentina's midfield enforcer, just inside the England half. Simeone pretended to help him up but pinched his skin as he did it. It's an old trick and Beckham bit. He flicked his leg out and caught Simeone behind the knee. He went down as if he had been shot, Batistuta came running over waving an imaginary card and the referee, Kim Milton Nielsen, did the rest.

I thought it was a yellow card offence. I was incensed at the behaviour of their players and the way they influenced the referee. There is a clear parallel with what Cristiano Ronaldo did to help get Wayne Rooney sent off in the 2006 World Cup. David shouldn't have reacted the way he did, obviously but I've done some things on the pitch that I wish I had had time to think about first. It wasn't a rational thing to do. It was stupid but sometimes you just react. It was such a nothing offence, such a harmless thing to do really. It was such a cheap way to get sent off.

I didn't blame David but it did illustrate what Hoddle's problem with him was at the time. It also reflected the way David had been behaving during the early stages of the tournament. He had been surly and down and his reaction to things that had happened had given Glenn the excuse not to play him. As a player, you have to put your anger and your disappointment to one side, fight and show the manager you can be trusted. It must have been difficult for David psychologically. I know that. Part of you thinks you should have been in the team all along and by trying harder you are almost giving the manager justification for his actions. At the same time, you don't want to give him that satisfaction. David showed all his emotion and his resentment in that one moment when he kicked out at Simeone. In that moment, I'm sure Glenn cursed the fact that he had given him a chance but then if he had handled him properly, if he had judged his character more accurately, he would have chosen his words towards David much more carefully. Hoddle had created this seething resentment in him and laid the foundations for him to react the way he did to Simeone. As I said, it was only a matter of time until Beckham blew in that tournament.

When David got home, the reaction from the press was absolutely appalling. A lot of people wrote about ten brave men and one silly boy. His actions singled him out, and when that happens you know you are going to get criticised but the level it got to and the hatred expressed was unbelievable. The whole situation got out of hand. I'd had a taste of being the scapegoat after the Romania game but what he went through was many, many times worse.

When you lose a player in a match, it is soul-destroying for a few minutes. You wonder how you will be able to adapt. Then your mentality changes. There is a much greater element of caution but there is also a spirit of defiance that kicks in like adrenalin. I was wing-back but I adjusted my position and became much narrower. I was so focused on what I was doing, the game became a blur. I thought that to have a chance of winning, we had to score in the ninety minutes. It had been a hard game even with eleven men and I thought if it went to extra-time, they would wear us down.

We defended stoically. We dug in. It was backs to the wall. There is something quite enjoyable about that – in the way that it galvanizes the team. We were all shouting and yelling, encouraging each other. We were determined not to concede a goal. Then, with about fifteen minutes of normal time remaining, I started getting absolutely horrendous cramps in my calves. There was one point where Zanetti ran past me and if he had got the ball, he would have been away and free and I would have been utterly helpless with him in on goal. I just couldn't run. Thankfully, the man in possession didn't see his run and we got away with it, but I knew I had to come off.

Immediately, I felt I had let everyone down. We had all fought so hard together and there I was calling over to say I couldn't carry on. Nonetheless, I had become a liability and there was no point pretending just to try to keep up appearances – but it hurt to admit that my game was over. I watched from the bench while the team performed more heroics in extra-time. At one point, we thought Sol Campbell had scored but it was disallowed and before we realized it, Argentina had taken the free-kick and were breaking away. I felt like running onto the pitch and tackling someone because we were so outnumbered. It was an incredible panic. We were so angry because we couldn't work out why the free-kick was given against him. It was a perfectly good goal. It's destiny, I suppose.

I was very nervous when it went to penalties. It was just horrible. I didn't want to be there but I was. It was completely out of my hands. I didn't feel we were overly prepared – we hadn't practised, not really. We had done the odd shoot-out in training. but it was all very light-hearted. It's hard to re-create the pressure you're under when it happens for real. I was a fantastic penalty taker in training – all footballers are – but I never took one for real in my whole career. I would have taken one – I was confident enough in my own ability to do that – but I wasn't on the pitch.

The people who took them that night have my eternal admiration. Whether someone scores or not, at least they have had the balls to stand up and take one. You can't blame people for not taking them but you have got to be true to yourself as well. If you are a senior player, you have to accept responsibility. Players don't judge other players on penalty misses – apart from Peter Crouch when he chipped one over the bar in an England World Cup warm-up game. That was just showing off. Zinedine Zidane pulled it off in the World Cup Final but then he's Zidane.

When Carlos Roa saved David Batty's decisive spot-kick, it just felt terribly, terribly cruel. I can still see David giving that little skip of despair in the instant he sees the goalkeeper parry it. I was shattered. We had all invested so much, not just in that game but in buying into Hoddle's whole philosophy and making the choices and the sacrifices to try to be the best. I bought into the whole Hoddle regime on the basis that it had to work but it wasn't always the easiest regime to adhere to. It would have been worth it if we had won the World Cup. Now, it felt pointless.

As soon as we came off the pitch, I was marched off for a drugs test. I didn't speak to anyone for an hour. I didn't get to talk to the lads in the changing room. You want to be with your team-mates at moments like that almost as much as when you have won. Ortega was the Argentine who was taking the test with me. I spoke to him a little bit in Spanish and congratulated him. He looked elated in the way some-one does when they know they have just got off the hook.

When I got back into the dressing room, it was like arriving late for a funeral. I don't know if Hoddle had debriefed the players but a lot of them had already gone. I felt as if I had missed out on a ritual. I felt I hadn't been given the chance to discuss everything that had happened. David Beckham was still sitting in there with his head down. Tony Adams had spoken to him. I thought about trying to comfort him but it would have been overkill – best to leave him alone I thought, not that there was much I could have said. Anyway, on the surface he seemed very composed about the whole thing. He wasn't distraught. People don't realize that beneath that gentle voice and the showbiz reputation, there's a very hard competitor.

When I got outside to the area where the team coach was, the Argentina players were already on their bus which was parked right next door to ours. They were really rocking. They were waving out of the windows, screaming their delight. They were just a few feet away from the glaring faces of some of our players, separated by a bit of glass. They weren't blatantly mocking us but they were celebrating like crazy – just like we would have been. Some of the England players reacted quite aggressively to that – Incey and the like, the usual suspects. There was a lot of gesturing and name-calling going on.

I was more concerned with seeing Mariana and my family. I got half an hour with my wife, who was quite heavily pregnant with our first child. It was the first time I'd seen her throughout the whole tournament which was part of the crazy monastic lifestyle Hoddle had imposed on us. He'd set aside one night for everyone after the Colombia game but I just thought that was degrading. People were having dinner and basically shoving food down their throats so they could get upstairs. It was like watching a dog grab a leg. Outside that stadium in St Etienne, I felt like saying to the rest of the lads 'You go on, I'm going to stay here with my wife'.

But I left with the squad and we got on our plane back to La Baule. We sat up all night with a few beers and talked it all through. We chatted away and played pool, packed our bags and got on Concorde. As I said, part of me felt relieved that I was coming home, that all the restrictions the regime had imposed on us had finally been lifted and that normality was about to flood back in. It hadn't been as enjoyable as it should have been. In parts it had been a bit of an ordeal.

We came back heroes – out in the second round and we were heroes. Despite our failure, everybody said we had done ourselves proud. There were a lot of people to meet us at Heathrow, fans as well as television cameras and news reporters. Everyone was talking about the 'if onlys' and Beckham's sending-off. He fled to America with his girlfriend to try to escape the hounds of hell. I never expected that tumultuous reception for the rest of us. Then, before you know it, everyone has melted away. Everyone has gone and the World Cup moves on without you.

All that remained for Hoddle was a sad epilogue. He published a World Cup diary that autumn, ghost-written by the FA's communications director, David Davies, which the players felt broke the unwritten code of silence within the dressing room. Perhaps it was just that he got in first because plenty of people did World Cup books but it seemed wrong that the manager should be doing one when he was in a position of responsibility and the players trusted him. People were particularly upset that he went through all the details of Gazza's breakdown so soon after the event.

We lost a European Championship qualifying game to Sweden in Stockholm that September and then in February Hoddle gave an interview to Matt Dickinson, a journalist from *The Times*, which made its front page. Among other things, he said he believed disabled people were being punished for the sins of a former life which was very offensive to a lot of people. Glenn said he had been misquoted. Others pointed out that he had made similar comments in a radio interview not long before. When Tony Blair expressed his doubts about whether Hoddle should be allowed to remain England manager, the FA lost their nerve and sacked him.

The truth is that I think it was over for Glenn before he even gave that interview. His authority had been fatally undermined by his diary. When you think of the suffocating control he subjected us to throughout the tournament and the peculiar emphasis he placed on secrecy, it seemed deeply hypocritical for him to do something like that. When we got back together for the Sweden game, everyone was talking about it, everyone was whispering about the betrayal. No one confronted him about it but suddenly everyone was starting to see a negative side to him.

Hoddle had lost the dressing room by the time he gave the interview to Matt Dickinson. Managers can't please you all the time and the book was a catalyst for the things the players didn't like about his style of management to come to the surface and create one big problem. That is when the balance of power is lost by a manager. It's not that you go out thinking you don't want to play for him but you have to buy into your manager's philosophy and if you don't, then it's the beginning of the end. If you start to disagree with a manager, if you feel he has betrayed a confidence within the dressing room by writing certain things about players, people start to withdraw. I didn't quite believe in him any more.

I didn't doubt he was trying to do the best he could. But the dynamic of the team changed and that was reflected in our results. The interview in *The Times* also proved that his mind was on other issues a lot of the time – all the stuff with Eileen and his spiritual views took up a lot of his thinking. If we had been charging along playing fantastic football, would the FA have helped him through that? I think they would. But by that stage, there was a media campaign against him and he had lost the support of the players. He was a football manager, not a student of the scriptures. He completely overlooked the people he was going to offend – which was everyone. I expect that if he had his time again, Glenn would have done things differently in the buid up to, and Finals, of the

World Cup. I believe that managers should be judged on football issues but it had become more complicated than that. The timing was very convenient for the FA. They gave Howard Wilkinson the reins for a game. Then they switched from a false prophet to a messiah. After Hoddle, they went for Kevin Keegan.

EIGHT

Ruud, Luca, and Sexy Football

I rejoined Chelsea in the summer of 1997. Some things had changed. Some hadn't. The biggest difference for me was this: for the first time in my career, I discovered I had become one of the lads. I was popular. I could be myself. Gianfranco Zola laughed at my jokes. In fact, when I speak to him now, the first thing he says to me is 'Please tell me one of your jokes, I love your jokes'. I think he may be being sarcastic but I don't care. I got on brilliantly with Franco and with the rest of the new wave of players who had arrived at Chelsea in the period since I had left, four years earlier. Never call me a Euro-sceptic. I loved the band of foreign stars and the new atmosphere they had brought to my old club. I loved everything about Ruud Gullit's sexy football. I look back on my second spell at Chelsea and I think 'How lucky was I'.

There was nobody like John McNaught there any more; no one like Graham Roberts throwing his weight around; no one like Peter Nicholas with his biting comments and his sharp tongue; nobody arriving at training half-pissed. All the venom had gone. There was a positive spirit about the place now. There was a sense that everyone was pulling together, it was much more inclusive. There was still a lot of joking and leg-pulling but I was part of it now rather than the target of it. It was a gentler place than it had been. I felt for the first time as though football was beginning to move towards me. Suddenly, now that the culture of the game was changing and becoming more cosmopolitan, I fitted in.

Sometimes, it seemed almost unbelievable to me that Chelsea were at the forefront of the change. When I was there in the late Eighties, they were the last club I would have imagined leading English football into a new era. Glenn Hoddle had started the revolution before he left to become England manager and Gullit had continued it. So I wasn't rubbing shoulders with players like McNaught, Roberts and Nicholas any more. I was playing alongside exotic superstars like Zola, Gianluca Vialli, Frank Lebouef, Gus Poyet and Roberto di Matteo.

People often talked in disparaging terms about 'Chelsea's foreign legion' in those days and there is still fierce debate now about the damage the influx of players from abroad has done versus the benefits they have brought. But at Chelsea, we managed to bring young players through as well. The outstanding example is John Terry. But I know that playing with someone like Marcel Desailly helped JT develop into the player who has risen to be England captain. I know that playing with people like Franco inspired me. Even now, look at the huge strides that Frank Lampard has taken over the years he has been at Chelsea and ask yourself if he would have taken those strides without a group of foreign superstars around him. We had a good base of British players at the club, like Dennis Wise, Kevin Hitchcock and Mark Hughes, and some young English talent as well.

Even given the sweeping changes in personnel, there were still plenty of happy idiosyncracies about the place. Even during my second spell at Chelsea, the training ground was still frequented by all manner of strange characters who devoted their lives to watching our sessions. There was a lady called Felicity, who would bake every player a cake for his birthday – we were never quite sure if they were safe to eat but she took great pride in her gifts and her face was a picture of horror when JT accidentally dropped his. Vialli gave her one of his manager's coats when he was in charge and, from then on, she never took it off, even though it was far too big for her.

Then there was Alan, a retired British Airways worker, who would appear on his bike every day and collect any of the balls that found their way into the bushes behind the goals. He just turned up out of the blue once and, this being Chelsea, before long I would bump into him in the tunnel at Stamford Bridge. Later the players found out that he had been put in charge of picking up the UEFA delegates from Heathrow and bringing them to Champions League matches. I have no idea if he was paid for this service.

One official who is still held in the greatest affection by the players, and continues to serve under Jose Mourinho, is Gary Staker. You will see him at Stamford Bridge around the tunnel, a cheery bloke who started off as a match steward but, because he had Italian parents, ended up as the official translator for the Italian players and, eventually, Ranieri. Now he takes care of all the details around the club's travel and helps out with players' individual needs. Of course, all these people had to be approved by the chairman, Ken Bates, and at Chelsea in those days you never knew who would become a club official.

I bet no one works for free at Chelsea now, and I wonder whether Felicity still makes the journey down to Cobham to the new training ground where the long drive is protected by security guards and the perfectly prepared pitches are hidden by trees. I would imagine that Mourinho has never called her over on a Monday, as his predecessors once did, to plant a kiss on the cheek of the weekend's goalscorer. It was a guaranteed way of embarrassing even the most experienced professional footballer.

But in many ways, the club was thinking big at the time I rejoined. It was paying big transfer fees for good players and putting them on considerable salaries. Di Matteo had cost £4.9 million from Lazio; I cost £5.5 million; Gullit, Zola and Vialli were all earning massive wages, and plenty more were to come. Zola, in particular, was a delight, on and off the pitch. If there was one person you would want as a role model for a young player, it would be Franco. He had all the qualities of the ultimate professional but with the humility and the humour and self-deprecation.

Franco was a family guy but he was also at the core of the team spirit we built at the club. He was a very affectionate person and that affection was reciprocated. I think every football fan in the country respected him. His balance, his speed, his goalscoring – they were all top class. He worked hard, too, and clearly loved his football. Everything in his life was positive. He was an easy target because he was little and he looked a bit like the Fonz but he dealt with it easily enough. 'I might look like a horse,' he said, 'but I have a beautiful wife.'

One of the things that made me laugh most about Franco was that he drove a huge Range Rover into training every day. If you pulled up next to him in the car park, he'd wave at you but when he jumped out of the car, he would disappear completely from sight on the other side of it. He was a bad, bad driver, too. He came into training one day and I started telling this story about how his wife had called him up when he was driving home from training down the M4.

'Be careful, Franco, darling,' she said, 'there's a lunatic driving the wrong way down the carriageway.'

'I know, I know,' Franco said, 'there's hundreds of them.'

It wasn't true but it got a laugh. Everyone knew he wasn't the best behind the wheel.

We had sublime players like Franco but, still, it was typical of Chelsea and Bates that they didn't follow their policy of signing gifted and high-profile individuals through to its logical conclusion. They shelled out all the money for these superstars with their magnificent skills and then made them train at the same old dilapidated training ground at Harlington, with its London University groundsman and its temperamental showers. Because it wasn't private land, anyone could wander in – and they often did. One day, because the security was what you might call 'relaxed', someone waltzed into the changing rooms and nicked £25,000 in cash and watches. The changing rooms had astroturf on the floor now but apart from that there was no difference from when I had been there before. The pipes didn't have enough pressure in them to water the pitches properly. When you went into the dingy old changing rooms at Stamford Bridge, you felt like there should be a surgical hand-scrub offered on the way out. The club couldn't see beyond that first layer of lavishing money on players and a high-profile manager. The rest was left to take care of itself.

We didn't have the facilities the Chelsea players have now and we never had a tried and tested great manager either. I admired Ruud and Luca massively as players and as people but they were both new to management. They were novices who were being thrown in at the deep end against wily old veterans like Alex Ferguson and Arsene Wenger. Neither Ruud nor Luca had particularly well-developed man-management skills and neither lasted the course so we were never given the consistent direction we needed. In a way, we almost over-achieved, given the foundations that we had and the lack of facilities. The spirit and quality of the players took us a long way.

Later, when Claudio Ranieri had taken over and we were on the team coach on a long journey back from Old Trafford, we had all got so disillusioned with the state of the training ground that we got to talking about what we could do to try to improve things. It had got to the point at Harlington where you had to turn the bath taps on just to lower the temperature below scalding in the showers. In the winter, it often went to the other extreme and the hot water ran out altogether. The pitches were rutted and hard and it took five or six of us to lug the huge iron-framed goal posts out onto the pitch in the morning. So we started making suggestions.

Franco had already bought a defensive wall out of his own pocket so he could practise his free-kicks day after day at the end of training. He was saying now that he also wanted to buy some lightweight aluminium goals so that we didn't have to go through the daily weightlifting ritual. I said that squad members should chip in £100 each because it wasn't fair that Franco footed the whole bill and then people started weighing in with other proposals. Jimmy Floyd Hasselbaink, who'd just joined the club, suggested we should pay a groundsman's salary for a year so that we had our own guy to look after our training pitches. He said if we all put in £1,000, it should cover it. Someone else said that if we put another £500 each in the pot, we could get the showers retiled because people had started to cut their feet on the jagged edges. Marcel Desailly said that if we put in another few hundred quid we could get a jacuzzi. Then Eidur Gudjohnsen piped up. 'Fuck it,' he said, 'why don't we put in £100,000 each and buy Ronaldo.'

Snapshots like that were what the early years of my return to Chelsea were all about. I loved the diversity of the place and the feeling of it being a melting pot. I loved the humour and the fact that when we had to stop talking at training when Concorde was taking off, Marcel would suddenly stand to attention and start singing the Marseillaise. 'Look at that,' he would say as the plane rose above the tree line, 'French industry and British engineering. What the fuck have the Italians ever done for this world?'

I enjoyed the comical situations the cosmopolitanism threw up. I liked seeing Franco wandering around the training ground with his massive Anglo-Italian dictionary quizzing me or Dennis Wise on the finer points of the English language – and Wisey doing his best to teach him. I liked misunderstandings like the one when I heard Di Matteo and Franco whispering 'Le Saux, Le Saux' to each other in the dressing room. 'What are you saying about me,' I asked them and they looked at me as if I was mad. 'Come on,' I said, 'I heard you saying my name.' They still looked blank. Then the realisation hit them. 'We weren't talking about you, Graeme,' Franco said. 'We were saying 'no lo so, no lo so'. It's just "I don't know" in Italian.'

During my second-time round at Chelsea, I got to know Dennis Wise a lot better. He was one of the most important figures at the club, a great survivor, and I found him to be a close ally. We were completely different in character and our take on life, yet we felt comfortable in each other's company. I think Wisey was quite amused by some of the things I said, stuff that he wouldn't necessarily relate to but found entertaining nonetheless. I'm pleased he went on to have some managerial success at Millwall – getting them to a Cup final – then at Swindon and Leeds. He's shown himself to be a lot shrewder than many people give him credit for.

I felt relaxed at last – I felt I was among friends. Partly, it was because I'd changed, I know – I was less up tight. I had won a league title and I wasn't trying to prove anything any more. That was why my time at Blackburn was invaluable. It gave me the credibility that I had struggled to find at Chelsea on the first time round. Acceptance within the sport is important. If you are not perceived as 'one of us', the only way you are going to achieve acceptance is by rising to such a level on the pitch that it's impossible for people not to respect you.

Chelsea paid £5.5 million for me and even though that was a burden in some ways, I also saw it as a vote of confidence. It meant they felt I was a major player, not someone they were going to mess around. I wasn't seen as a bit-part player, someone who was on the margins. I was central to their vision of success. By then, I was much more secure in terms of who I was and what I was capable of. That cuts through a lot of crap. So I had definitely changed. I wasn't fighting the system or fighting for where I wanted to get to. I had got there; I had become consistent.

A lot of the things that had upset me when I was a developing player wouldn't have upset me the second time around if they had happened again. I had a certain amount of security because I had achieved. I had won a league championship. I had the medal and the memories and the inviolable confidence that brings. I played as hard as I always did but I didn't have to fight the system any more. The atmosphere at the club was the happiest one I've ever been involved in. And I felt popular. At Blackburn, I got on well with the players but I never felt popular. I felt I could be who I really was at Chelsea the second time, that I could say what I wanted. If I made a joke, people knew where I was coming from. I felt appreciated more than I had been before. I felt part of everything and that I was an important component of the dressing room. For much of my second spell at Stamford Bridge, I was club captain, with Dennis Wise as team captain, and we dealt with a lot of the big issues that came up. I enjoyed the responsibility and because there were a lot of foreign players, they appreciated my input. It wasn't that they looked up to me but they did value my advice.

I was very anxious about how I would be received by the Chelsea fans when I ran out in the team's colours again. I felt the shadow of the incident when I hurled my shirt at Ian Porterfield was still hanging over me. I knew that some people had interpreted that as me being disrespectful to the club even though I'd made it clear I'd never intended that. Anyway, I didn't sleep at all the night before my first game back for the club, in August 1997 against Coventry City. I was excited but nervous when I ran out at Highfield Road. The adrenalin was pumping and I sprinted straight over to where the Chelsea fans were. They gave me a great reception and I was so elated. I felt as if I had scored a goal. God, I miss that feeling.

We lost the game 3–2 but my first season back with Chelsea was one of great excitement, intrigue and general melodrama. There was a feeling we were on the up. We were the glamour boys of the league, the team that appeared to be rising fast. Gullit had taken the club to its first major trophy for twenty-six years the previous spring when Chelsea beat Middlesbrough 2–0 in the FA Cup Final. And despite losing at Coventry, we picked up where my predecessors had left off. By February 1998, we were in the semi-finals of the League Cup and the Cup Winners' Cup and were second in the league. Then, without any warning, Ruud was sacked and replaced immediately by Luca. It was blamed on a row over money – Chelsea Chief Executive Colin Hutchinson famously said Ruud had asked for a manager's salary of £2 million 'netto' – but it was about much more than that.

Ruud had tremendous charisma. He could walk into a room and command it: you would stop chatting and look at him if he walked in. He had that kind of presence.

But he could be aloof, too, and despite the tremendous atmosphere among the players, a schism had developed between Ruud and Luca. Luca had signed from Juventus in 1996 after he'd led them to victory in the European Cup and when Ruud decided that Luca wasn't his first-choice striker all the time, Vialli took that very badly. Things got nasty. Ruud left him out of the starting line-up for the FA Cup Final in 1997 and only brought him on in the last minute. I wasn't part of Chelsea then. In fact, I was on my stag weekend in Paris but I watched it in a bar and even I winced when that happened. It seemed to be an obvious show of power from Ruud.

By the time I got there, their relationship had deteriorated further. Luca still played and he still scored but he was often left out of the big games. He scored four against Barnsley in a 6–0 win at Oakwell. He scored another hat-trick against Tromso in the Cup Winners' Cup and then was dropped for the next three games. It was a battle of wills as much as anything. The boys gave Luca a lot of stick one week when the *Match of the Day* cameras caught him making a face at Ruud behind his back when he was sitting on the bench and Ruud was up on his feet gesticulating to the players.

There were three or four players who had problems with Ruud's management style and the way he behaved but equally, there were plenty who acted as if they were his disciples. Wisey had an affectionate relationship with him, and Frank Leboeuf was his big mate. Our form, however, was uneven and around the turn of the year, stories started appearing about crisis meetings among the players, which weren't true. We had a couple of meetings, but it was the management who suggested them. When news of Ruud's sacking was announced, the vast majority of us were in total shock. Luca might have known that Ruud was going to get the bullet – in fact there were rumours that Luca had met Brian Laudrup a couple of days earlier to discuss his impending move from Rangers – but nobody else did.

The day before the news broke, Ruud wanted us to do some running in training. Wisey asked him if we could postpone it for a day because we were all knackered. We'd played a lot of matches and Ruud saw the sense of what Dennis was saying and relented. The next day, he got the sack so we never got to do our running and Wisey felt awful. He was worried that Ruud would have thought he knew what was going on. His sacking happened so suddenly that we didn't even get a chance to say goodbye. I know that happens in other walks of life, too – people told to clear their desks and marched out of the building – but it seems particularly brutal when you can't even thank someone who has had a big impact on your life.

Like everyone else, I was shocked about Ruud's departure. I was disappointed, too, and unsettled. It was Ruud who had signed me and I had only played for him for six months. Now someone else was taking over. I didn't have any particular worries about my job security because I got on well with Luca, who was installed almost at once, but that doesn't necessarily mean your place is going to be safe. Furthermore, as soon as Luca changed from a player to a manager, he shut himself off: he made a lot of enemies very quickly.

At first, revenge must have tasted sweet for Luca. This man who had marginalized him and belittled him, who had cast doubt on Luca's talent just as he must have been beginning to feel insecure about his age, had been ruthlessly deposed and Luca made the beneficiary. Even though it was masterminded by Ken Bates, it felt like a particularly Italian kind of coup: a bit of Caesar, a bit of Machiavelli and a bit of the Borgias mixed in there. However, like a lot of revengers, Luca quickly became tortured by the act of retribution to the point where it poisoned his whole attitude while he was in charge. Luca was the man who had complained most about Ruud but unwittingly he began to take on the traits he had disliked in Ruud. From the minute he took over, he was suspicious. He saw plots everywhere. It was inevitable, I suppose. He took over in a behind-your-back way and so he took over knowing that the same was probably going to happen to him. He became afraid. He had been part of a plot and he knew that if they could do it to his predecessor, they could certainly do it to him: not really the ideal circumstances in which to take your first job as manager. He never got beyond that really – never got beyond the fear that his demise was only around the corner.

The atmosphere also changed when Luca took over. It wasn't quite so carefree any more, not quite as much fun. Luca had enjoyed his greatest success with Juventus in the mid-1990s when the emphasis had been on physical fitness and endurance. Some of the methods were discredited later amid rumours about the physios and medics running the club like a pharmacy. Luca didn't do that but he did take things to extremes. His regime was physical beyond belief. We were doing things I didn't agree with such as jumping with weights on our backs – with my suspect ankle, that was the worst thing I could have done.

Luca brought in a Juve fitness coach called Antonio Pintus, who was a lovely man but sometimes he seemed more like a medieval torture expert than a fitness trainer. Things started to get bizarre. There was one session we did regularly in the gym where we had to put pads on our legs with electric leads in them: when you were ready to lift some weights, an electric shock was sent through the pads and that fired your muscle so that you could lift weights far heavier than you would normally be able to. The machines were forcing your muscles to contract. It was horrible.

There were a lot of rumours about the methods Juventus used during the time Luca was there as a player. It was interesting that many of the Juve players played at their peak at Juve and then fell away pretty quickly – Luca himself was an example of that. Juve got their pound of flesh out of their players. It was a full-on regime and you didn't have a lot left at the end of it, but what he didn't take into account when he took over at Chelsea was that the match scenario in England was more demanding than in Serie A. The intensity of the Premiership game was higher – there were no lulls like in Italy – so the players found it hard to think that this was the right way to go.

Most of us felt things were going too far. I have always believed that the crux of training is making a connection between it and playing competitively. Under Luca, I couldn't make that connection at all. Mourinho is good at that. Fitness is all football-related. You don't go running on sand dunes because you don't play football on sand dunes. Under Ruud, everything had been football-related and training with Graham Rix had been challenging and interesting. Rixy was still there but now the training had lost some of its focus.

Luca was a perfectionist, too. Nothing wrong with that, really, but his perfectionism manifested itself as a kind of eccentricity. The lads who had roomed with him said that his travel bag was always full of clothes that were meticulously folded. There was a touch of Obsessive Compulsive Disorder in there, I think, and it manifested itself in training, too. The cones that we dribbled in and out of had to be in a perfect straight line. If they were a couple of centimetres out, he would get someone to move them back into position before the drill could start. Some of the lads used to nudge them on the way past just to wind him up.

Just as Ruud's relationship with Luca had broken down, so Luca's relationship with former friends like Robbie Di Matteo and Franco deteriorated, too. I had been good friends with Luca when he was a player as well but now he made a conscious effort not to be mates with me. He went from a gregarious, urbane, sociable guy to a cold and austere man. I think that was a sign of insecurity. Just because I might have gone out for a drink with him wouldn't have meant I expected to be picked for the side. He should have realized that this applied to all of us. His way of dealing with any problem was just to train us harder and harder. It got to the point where, towards the end of games, we were beginning to tire dramatically because we were so knackered from training, but if we told Luca that, his reaction was that we weren't fit enough.

To begin with, things went astonishingly well under Luca. In his first game in charge, we beat Arsenal 3–1 in the second leg of the Coca-Cola Cup semi-final, a result which put us through to the final. His first game at the helm and already we were in a final. We won it, too. We beat Middlesbrough at Wembley and Luca had himself a trophy just forty-five days after taking over. Then, as now, it's not the most glamorous trophy of them all but it was my first domestic cup final so it meant a huge amount to me. It was an inspiring game for me to play in.

Our form held up in the league, too, and we finished fourth. But it was the Cup Winners' Cup that was our greatest triumph that season. I played in every game on the way to the final, including a dramatic semi-final against Vicenza where we overturned a first-leg deficit in the return at Stamford Bridge. We even conceded an away goal at home before winning 3–1, which meant 3–2 on aggregate. We were due to play VfB Stuttgart in the final and then, a fortnight before the game, I got a small tear in my calf.

I still thought I'd be okay. It would have been one of the biggest club games of my career and I was desperate to play. I dragged myself back almost to full fitness and it looked like I'd be on the flight to Stockholm where the final was going to be played. I was stepping things up nicely at Harlington, doing sprints with Dennis Wise, who was also recovering from injury, when I broke down a few days before the game. I'd finished a sprint and was jogging before the next one when I felt my calf go again. Wisey looked back at me and thought I was joking but I wasn't. He was upset for me. He kept going on about how much they needed me. I felt I'd let the team down as well as myself but I just muttered something about how the important thing was that he made it through to the game. Funny how you try to disguise your disappointment even at moments when you feel everything is falling apart.

I travelled to Sweden with the squad but there was no chance of me playing. A young lad called Danny Granville played instead of me – and got a massive move to Leeds off the back of it. It was a tight, tense game in the Rasunda Stadium but when Luca brought Franco off the bench after seventy minutes, he won the game for us. He had only been on the pitch for seventeen seconds when he raced onto a through ball from Wisey and smashed a half-volley past their keeper that was still rising when it hit the back of the net. Dan Petrescu was sent off six minutes from the end but we hung on. The celebrations were great. I was fit enough to take part in them. In my suit, I ran up and down the pitch with the rest of the lads and flung myself on the turf in front of our fans time and time again. Occasionally people mention to me now how upset I must have been not to have won the Cup Winners' Cup, but I did win it. I played in every game up to the final. I would love to have played in Stockholm but I played my part in that victory, nonetheless.

The next season belonged to Manchester United but it nearly belonged to us as well. We lost to Coventry on the opening day (again), after Darren Huckerby gave Marcel Desailly a fearful introduction to the Premiership, but we didn't lose another match until the last day of January and we were top of the table at Christmas. Then when things tightened up in the run-in, so did we. We lost at home to West Ham and then drew with Middlesbrough, Leicester and Sheffield Wednesday, one after the other. United and Arsenal edged away from us right at the end but we still finished only four points behind the champions, in third place. We lost just three league games all season. We lost in the semis of the Cup Winners' Cup to Real Mallorca and the quarters of the domestic cup competitions but for the first time in our history, we'd qualified for the Champions League.

Take out a couple of those draws with teams we should have beaten and we would have been champions and United wouldn't have had their treble. That's how close we were – that's how good we were. I feel now that when people look back on that Chelsea side, they bracket us with a team like Tommy Docherty's Manchester United in the 1970s, a great cup side but lacking the character and the determination to produce the consistency to win the league. I understand that comparison but it's not quite fair. We were a better team than that: the fact that we got so close to winning the Premiership that season proves it. But we had a couple of players who were on the downslope of their careers, and when it came to the crunch we were not quite good enough to climb above Arsenal and United.

I don't think we ever quite saw the best of Desailly, for example. The game had taken its toll on him before he got to Chelsea. He put in a few phenomenal performances and there were glimpses of the great, great player he had once been but he had had a long career up to that point already, he had climbed a lot of peaks. He didn't let anyone down but he made more mistakes than in the past. The game had caught up with him a bit but he had incredible will and he was an unbelievable athlete. He was a fantastic character, too. He was very softly spoken and laid back and calm about everything and on the bad days at Harlington, in the depths of winter, he used to do his best to lift the spirits. On really cold days, he had so much stuff on you could only just see his eyes. 'Lads,' he used to say, 'in an hour, we'll be sitting in our cars with a cigar.'

Frank Leboeuf had his detractors, too. He was a nice guy and a great player but the more success came his way, the more self-interested he became. Playing in the winning team in the 1998 World Cup had a big effect on him in that respect. It got to the stage where if someone was disrespectful to him during a Premiership match, he would turn around and stare at them. 'Don't you know that I won the World Cup,' he'd say. There were plenty of opponents who pointed out in forthright terms that he was only in the side in the final because Laurent Blanc was suspended.

I think that Frank came to be regarded by some of our opponents as our Achilles heel. We were always seen as a side that didn't quite fancy it on the less glamorous, more physical type of occasion. When Frank got hurt, he would overreact and in central defence, that's perceived as a sign of weakness. But he was a fine player on the ball, and he read the game so well. His passing was something else. He would hit a ball with the top of his foot and strike across it so it would have a bit of fade on it. He produced so many defence-splitting passes. He was a pleasure to play with if you were playing in midfield. If you were in space, he would see you. With other players, you'd have to jump up and down and set fireworks off just to get them to notice you but not with him.

That 1998/99 season was the best it got for me at Chelsea in terms of results. I loved my football through all that second spell at Stamford Bridge and I got a lot of satisfaction from playing with Celestine Babayaro on the left side. Every game I played with Baba, I told him I was going to work as hard as I could for him but that I expected him to do the same for me. A trust developed between us. He knew that if he went past me on the overlap, the chances were I was going to give him the ball. It used to kill me as a full-back if I over-lapped a midfielder and made a sixty-yard run and they didn't give it at least once out of three times. Baba and I had an understanding that it was a dual effort. I said to him that whatever happened we were not going to concede a goal from our side of the pitch.

It started with me at left-back and him at left midfield and then we switched later on. I loved playing midfield. I played with much more freedom. Your responsibility as a defender is to defend. You have to be safe. Everything is about not getting carried away. Everything is restricted. You have more responsibility to your role. There is a greater pressure of the consequences of failure on you. When I was in midfield, I felt like more of a free spirit. I knew I had defensive responsibili-ties but I felt much more creative and positive when I had the ball. I always felt happier on the pitch in midfield – you could try things. I wish I'd played there more.

I missed a large part of the following season because I had two more operations on my ankle. I squeezed in thirteen minutes of the 5–0 thrashing of United at Stamford Bridge on 3 October which had a lot of people tipping us as hot favourites for the title. We were irresistible that day although we were helped by the fact that Wisey managed to goad Nicky Butt into getting himself sent off midway through the second half. However, we couldn't maintain that kind of form and gradually we fell away. We lost to our rivals at the top but we also lost to Watford, Derby, Sunderland and Sheffield Wednesday.

I managed some of the early stages of the Champions League at the start of the season, too, and those games were fantastic experiences. I came on against AC Milan in the goalless draw at Stamford Bridge and played against Galatasaray in Istanbul at the Ali Sami Yen. What a stadium that was. There were 15,000 people inside it but it felt like 150,000 with the amount of noise they generated and the fervour that contorted their features. That game against Galatasaray probably sent more adrenalin coursing through me than any other in my career. I was scared before the start and sometimes as a footballer, it helps to be scared.

I loved Istanbul. We stayed at a hotel called the Ciragan Palace, right on the Bosphorus. At night, you looked out of your window and you could see the dark shapes of ships gliding silently along the great waterway that separates Europe and Asia. It's a spectacular place and the people are fantastic, passionate individuals. When we landed, there was a greeting party waiting for us: all these supporters standing next to the team bus, staring you right in the eyes and drawing their hands slowly across their throats. It amused me, really. I always took it for part of a melodramatic act. I still think it was, although obviously the tragic fate that befell two Leeds United fans when their team played against Galatasaray in Istanbul in April 2000 put those gestures in an altogether more sinister light.

When we got on the bus to go to the stadium, no one wanted a window seat. Even going to the game, the atmosphere was really intense. We had fans in cars chasing after us. It was like Turkey's version of *The Italian Job*. As we got nearer the stadium, things started getting thrown and one of the windows came in. It was like a war zone. I got that flight or fight adrenalin rush, fear versus professionalism. I felt someone could get hurt when the game started because I had never experienced that kind of intimidation before. The stadium seemed to be a mass of flairs and fire. The whole place felt as if it was on the verge of anarchy.

Plenty of English teams had had problems there before. Eric Cantona had been coshed by a policeman when United played at the Ali Sami Yen in 1993 and Bryan Robson was attacked in the tunnel that night, too. When you came out of the changing rooms, you had to walk up some stairs to the pitch. As I looked up the stairs, I saw these riot police with their riot shields fashioned into a kind of roof. I could hear missiles pinging onto these shields – coins and bits of stones. Then suddenly we were out on the pitch. It was a capacity crowd for the warm-up and they seemed very highly motivated to say the least.

Although it was hostile and incredibly intimidating, it wasn't as if these people were drunk. They were just incredibly passionate. The match started and because I was intimidated and a bit fearful, when I ran, it felt as if my legs weren't mine. I had so much energy. It was as if my body was telling me I ought to be running away from this situation. But none of us ran away. In fact, this group of players – who were later to come in for so much criticism because six of us refused to travel to Israel for a UEFA Cup game in the wake of 9/11 – produced one of the best performances they'd ever seen in the Ali Sami Yen.

Galatasaray were a good side, packed with class players: Hakan Sukur, Gica Popescu, Hagi, Arif, Tugay and Emre. They even had a guy called Capone, which seemed just about right given the lawless feel of the place. After a nervy start, Tore Andre Flo scored half an hour into the match and then we took them to pieces. We beat them 5–0 and at the end, we were applauded off the pitch and it was the Galatasaray players who were stoned – quite a turn around.

Soon after that, my injuries intervened. I missed out on the quarter-final with Barcelona when we beat them 3–1 in the first leg at Stamford Bridge and came within seven minutes of going through in the return at the Nou Camp. But they got a late goal to go 3–1 up on the night and then eased away from us in extra-time to win 5–1 and 6–4 on aggregate. Because we'd been inconsistent again in the league, all we had left in the end was the FA Cup Final against Middlesbrough, the last one at the old Wembley. I still wasn't fit so I organized the players' pool, which was a bloody thankless task, and did a few articles in the papers.

One of those articles cost me my friendship with my old Blackburn team-mate Chris Sutton. Luca had signed Chris from Blackburn for a club record £10 million at the start of the season but he insisted on playing him on his own up front when it was obvious Chris was at his most effective with a strike partner. He was a tremendous finisher and a great link man but he wasn't built to play on his own and he struggled dreadfully. He had a couple of clear chances in the opening game of the season against Sunderland and missed both of them badly. From then on, he was low on confidence and a target for the press.

It was as if Luca expected him to be able to do all the things that Franco could do but Chris wasn't in Franco's league technically. He was a very clever player and a very bright bloke but he needed someone with him in attack. It didn't help that he moved to London and enjoyed London to the full. There were some of our young lads coming through making the mistakes young English footballers make and Chris got caught up in that a bit. It turned out to be a really bad move for him, even though he did add a different kind of wit to the dressing room.

You had to make allowances for his humour because it was so caustic. If there's something obvious about someone that might make them uncomfortable – a wart, a birthmark, a nervous tick – you and I would go out of our way not to mention it, but Chris was the opposite. He used to pick on our goalkeeper, Ed de Goey, who it would be fair to say was not blessed with great looks. Chris, inevitably, picked up on this early even though Ed was quite sensitive about it. On one occasion we were in the treatment room before training and Chris and Ed started having a bit of banter – which was always dangerous with Chris because he just turned up the heat.

'You're not the best looking guy are you Ed,' Chris said.

Ed rose to it. 'You're not exactly handsome yourself,' he said.

'Actually,' Chris said, 'are you sure you weren't born in Chernobyl?'

Ed went ballistic and jumped on him and started playfully whacking him on the head. He let go in the end and then Chris started apologising, gradually edging towards the door. 'Look,' he said, 'I'm out of order with that. But if you weren't born in Chernobyl, was it somewhere nearby?' Chris shot out of the door at that point and soon Ed was chasing him round the training pitches.

But Chris could be sensitive, too, and I blew it with him and his wife, Sam, in the run-up to the Cup Final. I did a player-by-player run-down of our team in *The Sun* that was published on the day of the game. It was all supposed to be jokey and light-hearted. I didn't think carefully enough about it, really, or imagine the consequences and because I was such a big fan of Chris, I also had a sense that he was going to have a big influence on the match. In the end, he didn't even make the bench.

Anyway, in the piece in *The Sun*, I made a reference to the fact that we were going to be dressed in Armani suits. I said that Chris might be a good-looking bloke but he wasn't the best dresser and that even if you put him in an Armani suit, he'd still look like a tramp. I thought it was a harmless joke, a throw-away comment, but *The Sun* did this huge caricature of Chris dressed as a tramp and made it the main feature of the whole page. Chris's wife went nuts. She phoned me up and accused me of betraying him. He was low anyway, she said, and now I had kicked him while he was down. I tried to apologize but she wouldn't accept it. Chris seemed okay but there was a distance between us after that.

We beat Aston Villa in the final and we beat United to win the Charity Shield the following August. That made Luca the most successful manager in Chelsea's history but it wasn't enough to save him. We had only finished fifth in the league in 1999/2000 and even though Bates allowed Luca to spend £26 million in the summer on players like Hasselbaink and Gudjohnsen, he sacked him after five games of the new season. The fears that had been festering inside Luca since he stepped into Ruud's dead man's shoes had come to pass.

Luca's departure was in many ways typical of Chelsea at that time. It didn't take a lot before a manager was deemed a failure. It was the demise I had predicted in my own head when he took over. He was increasingly insecure and he lost control of where we were going. A few players harboured ill feeling towards him and so when things got a little difficult or there was a fundamental difference of opinion over something like the amount of physical work he was making us do, there was no goodwill for him to fall back on.

Players didn't necessarily go against the manager – it was more a case that they were not 100 per cent behind him. It wasn't so much that Luca lost the dressing room as that he suffered an erosion of support. It was a strong dressing room then. Gus Poyet, in particular, was quite vocal and very passionate about the team and the game, and there were a few who were good mates with Luca and then fell out with him when he took over. Robbie di Matteo and Franco both felt that way – they both lost respect for him quite quickly. Luca ended up doing to Franco what Gullit had done to Luca.

Because Franco had been party to Luca moaning about Ruud – 'How can he do this?', 'What is he trying to do to me?', all that kind of stuff – Luca probably started wondering who Franco was talking to about him. It was like a circle of paranoia, it complicated things and it all added up. At one stage, we went to him and said the lads were getting tired in the last twenty minutes of games and we were feeling like we ran out of steam because of the intensity of the training regime. Instead of Luca backing off, he decided we weren't fit enough.

Because it was his first job, Luca was very dependent on Rixy tactically, but Rixy had his own problems. In March 1999, he was sentenced to twelve months in prison for having underage sex with a fifteen-year-old girl. He got out six months later and Chelsea took him back but he was a troubled man and a registered sex offender and when Luca left, he left, too. Rixy has been wandering around the margins of football since then like a lost soul.

All in all, it felt as if there was an inevitability about Luca getting the sack. It was still a shock to us all when it actually happened and I wanted to contact him to reassure him that no one had known what was going on. He thought one of the players had knifed him in the back, which, once again, came back to the way he had witnessed what had happened to Gullit. He imagined all sorts of machinations going on behind the scenes. He came out with some mysterious quote about not being able to trust 'the quiet man'. We were moving from Julius Caesar to Agatha Christie now.

I felt a bit guilty even though I'd had nothing to do with it. I think it was just that Bates and Colin Hutchinson were ruthless men and they sensed the club had entered a period of drift. They had spent so much money they couldn't afford drift. So even though Luca lost only one of the first five games of that season, the fact that he won only one damned him. I played in his last two games, the 2–2 draw with Arsenal and the goalless draw with Newcastle at St James' Park. Then he was gone. They got him in the end, just like they got Gullit, just like Luca always knew they would.

NINE

Chelsea and Ranieri

We finished sixth at the end of Claudio Ranieri's first eight months in charge, one place behind Ipswich Town. Ranieri had taken over on 18 September 2000, a few days after Luca's sacking, and I was starting to get used to the bizarre selection habits of the Tinkerman. I didn't like them but I was getting used to them. In the close season, he bought Frank Lampard from West Ham for £11 million. 'How much,' we all spluttered. It seemed like an awful lot – just shows you what we knew. Off the pitch, rumours were starting to proliferate about the club being in dire financial trouble. Dennis Wise, who had been the heartbeat of the club for a decade, was sold; so was the ever popular Gus Poyet. At home, Mariana was heavily pregnant with our second child. I went into the 2001/02 season feeling as though a great upheaval was coming.

11 September 2001
Commercial airliners hijacked by terrorists took to the
skies above America and slam into the twin towers of the
World Trade Centre in New York and the Pentagon in
Washington. Flight 93 plunges into a field in
Pennsylvania. Chelsea's UEFA Cup first-round first-leg
home game against Levski Sofia, scheduled for 13
September, is postponed and rearranged for 20
September.

12 September 2001
Claudio Ranieri gives Chelsea players the day off on
compassionate grounds. A few go home to their families
and watch the world changing. A few others go on a
bender. It takes them to the Airport Bowl near Heathrow
where they launch themselves head first down the lanes,
playing human tenpin. They're wasted. They lurch on to
the Posthouse Hotel and lark around in the bar. They
don't verbally insult American tourists but the News of
the World finds out about their behaviour and Chelsea
throw them to the wolves.

23 September 2001
Ranieri brings me on for the last twelve minutes of a
frantic game against Middlesbrough at Stamford Bridge –
Tinkerman at it again. We're winning 2–1. The surface is
slick with rain and I haven't got time to adjust to it. In
the last minute, the ball skids up off the turf and hits me
on the arm – Rob Styles gives a penalty. The only one I've
conceded in my career so far. Alen Boksic equalizes.

Chelsea and Ranieri

27 September 2001
Chelsea beat Levski Sofia 2–0 in Bulgaria in the second
leg of the UEFA Cup tie. We win 5–0 on aggregate.

28 September 2001
Osama Bin Laden is being blamed for 9/11. Bin Laden
says the world should blame Israel. The foreign office
tells Britons not to travel to Israel. The draw for the
second round of the UEFA Cup is made. We get Hapoel
Tel Aviv. The first leg is away in Israel on 18 October.
Unh-oh. All hell breaks loose.

29 September 2001
My son, Lucas, is born.

I was club captain by then. When it became clear we had to
fulfil our fixture against Hapoel, I made up my mind I didn't
want to go. It sounds stark when you say it like that and I
was accused of being a coward, as were the other five players
who didn't want to go. I felt dreadful about it. I felt I was
letting my team-mates down. Of course I did. But if I'd gone,
I would have been letting down my wife and family. I knew
which was more important.

Two of my best friends, Greg and Lisa, lived a couple of
blocks away from the Twin Towers in Battery Park. Their
daughter went to a nursery in the World Trade Center
complex. They lived through the hell of the attacks. They
were not killed but Mariana and I didn't know that for three
days – it took us that long to contact them. They were
desperate to get out of New York. Like everyone else there,

they were traumatized by what had happened. They came to live with us in Amersham and the two wives, both expecting babies imminently, felt the horror of what had happened with the special keenness of people who are about to bring new life into the world.

Everyone was still in a state of suppressed panic and deep uncertainty. Israel had an international game against Poland and were ordered to play it in Cyprus, but we were still told we had to play in Tel Aviv. I told Colin Hutchinson, the Chelsea chief executive, that the lads were very anxious about going to Israel and that he should do everything he could to make sure we could play the game somewhere else. It shouldn't have been that big a deal but the club didn't really take it seriously. They didn't stick up for us with UEFA. They seemed to think it would be character-building to play a game of football in an area of such great volatility. Our chairman, Ken Bates, revelled in that kind of perversity.

As the game got nearer, it started to get really difficult. No one wanted to go although some felt more strongly than others. We all talked after training every day and everyone was worried about it. We played a league game at Stamford Bridge and suddenly Ronnie Rosenthal, the ex-Liverpool forward and Israeli international, was brought into the dressing room and started talking about how nice Israel was and about the beaches and the promenade at Tel Aviv. It was as if he was working for the Israeli Tourist Board. The lads were all looking at each other in bemusement – it was quite funny really. The club had got him in to tell us Israel was very different to how we might be imagining it. The idea they wanted to get across was that it was a bit like going to

Ireland during the Troubles. Just because there was a heightened sense of tension in the Middle East, it didn't necessarily mean you were going to be putting yourself in the way of danger. This, however, felt very different. We were a Western team and we were sponsored by Emirates, an Arab airline. An Arab airline emblazoned on your shirt in Israel a month after 9/11 – don't tell me that wasn't a recipe for trouble. Even the club acknowledged that point: when they travelled to Israel, they played the match against Hapoel without the 'Fly Emirates' logo on the shirts.

As the game got closer, unbeknownst to me, Mariana phoned the Foreign Office. She was very worried about my trip. Lucas was a few days old. She also found out about another close friend of ours who worked for Lehmann Brothers, whose offices near the World Trade Center had been damaged, and who had told him they didn't want him flying anywhere for a couple more weeks and that he had to stay grounded. Elsewhere the Ryder Cup was cancelled. The American team didn't want to leave home. Nobody really wanted to leave home. The world suddenly felt very dangerous. The Middle East now felt even more dangerous. The Foreign Office told Mariana they advised against travel to Israel.

So I started to agonize about it – really agonize. I felt I had a responsibility to my family more than to anyone else. Eventually, the club said they recognized this was a special circumstance and that each player should have a free choice about whether they travelled to Israel or not. It was up to us. It wouldn't be held against us if we didn't go but whatever happened, a Chelsea team of some sort would fulfil that fixture because UEFA had ordered that the club should travel. Colin Hutchinson's argument was that if we had pulled out then, not only would it have resulted in a ban but it would also have sent the wrong message to European football. He said that if we had refused to go to Israel then some clubs may in the future refuse to go to places like Russia or Turkey. It could have marked the beginning of the fragmentation of football in Europe.

The worst thing about the affair was that we were publicly split. Most of the players didn't want to go – it was just a question of levels of reluctance. The newspapers loved it because they knew we were divided. My belief was that if there was one person who didn't feel comfortable going, then no one should have gone. Otherwise, those who don't want to go get isolated and the unity of the team is disrupted. Some people, however, are just pleased to see a club divided. It got to the point after the home win against Leicester on 13 October that we stayed in the dressing room after everyone else had left so we could have a vote on it.

The deal was that if you didn't want to go, you had to put your hand up. Of course, no one wanted to be the first to put his hand up: it was embarrassing, it was mortifying. It got to the point where we had to say, 'Put your hand up on the count of three'. No one wanted to sell out. Those of us who didn't want to go all felt we were letting the other lads down. Eventually, it became clear in the dressing room that there were six of us who wouldn't make the journey: me, Marcel Desailly, Emmanuel Petit, Eidur Gudjohnsen, William Gallas and Albert Ferrer. We all felt strongly that we had a responsibility to our families.

I made it clear that I wouldn't hold it against the ones who went on the trip as long as they didn't hold my decision against me. Then we sat in the dressing room and had a bit of a clear-the-air chat about it. Five of the six of us had either just had kids or had wives that were heavily pregnant. Marcel was the only one that tended to hum and ha a bit and eventually ended up having a problem with his tooth or something, which was a bit of a cop-out. It would have been more honest if he had come out and said he just didn't want to go but in those circumstances he could be forgiven for working on his alibi.

The day the team flew out, I felt terrible. I felt I was really letting everyone down. The chairman was on the phone to me telling me to make sure I went or I might end up regretting it. Thanks for that, Ken – so much for the free choice. He said he was going with his partner, Susannah, and he would be at the front of the plane. I wished him good luck and I meant it. I thought it was madness to go. While the team was in the air, Israel's Tourism Minister, Rechavam Ze'evy, was assassinated with two shots to the head outside his room at the Jersulaem Hyatt Hotel. The atmosphere everywhere in the country was incredibly tense. Thankfully, nothing happened to the team. There were no threats. There were no incidents. But in the four days that I would have been away, how nervous would Mariana have been? She was vulnerable anyway, having just had a baby. I found it hard to forgive myself for not going but I would have found it harder still to live with myself if I had gone.

I felt terribly guilty about it for a long time. Sometimes, I still feel guilty about it now – but I would have felt worse if I had gone because I would have been letting down my own family. Does that make me a coward, a yellow-belly? I was called both of those things but I think it was braver to make the decision I made than to go just because I might be worried about what the press and the public thought. If I had really felt worried about the consequences, I would probably have gone. There was nothing pre-meditated about it. I wasn't bothered about how I was going to be perceived.

So I didn't go to Tel Aviv, and the lads were beaten. They played terribly but you would expect that. Mario Melchiot was sent off early in the second half and we conceded two goals in the last five minutes. We lost 2–0. The six of us who didn't go were blamed for it. It just made me feel worse about the whole thing but when the lads came back, they were true to their word: they didn't hold it against those of us who hadn't gone and we set about rebuilding our team spirit and our unity as fast as we could.

That process began the next Sunday at Leeds. We played that game like furious men, determined to show we were not divided. As you can imagine, I felt especially pumped up. Coward, turncoat, yellow-belly – I thought 'I'll show them'. I went for everything – including Danny Mills. We went for a 50–50 ball in the first half. He went over the top of the ball but I saw him coming and went over the top of him. He had my stud marks all the way from his knee to his thigh. I wasn't proud of that but the challenge was part release of tension after the Tel Aviv affair and part self-preservation. Leeds' manager, David O'Leary, was so disgusted with my tackle and the fact that the referee, Paul Durkin, only gave me a yellow card and didn't send me off that he got sent off instead. I knew instantly I deserved a red card for it. I've no idea why I escaped: after all, the evidence was there in the bright red gashes on Mills' leg.

I wasn't thinking 'I didn't go to Israel so I'm going to kick you' but under the surface I was unbelievably tense when we walked out for that match and I knew we had an awful lot to prove. We had been publicly hammered before that game – everyone was ridiculing us. We spoke about it before the Leeds match and we were so fired up. We were not renowned for standing up for ourselves as a team. Sometimes we got bullied but that day we didn't. That day, we stood up and fought back together. We drew 0–0 at Elland Road but it felt like a victory to me.

I played in the second leg of the Hapoel game at Stamford Bridge. Bates had shown his sensitive side in the build-up by cracking a joke about the Hapoel ticket manager ringing up and asking if he could have a discount for a block booking. Ha, ha, ha. I thought helping Chelsea overturn the two-goal deficit that night would cleanse me of my guilt and allow everybody to forget about the first leg more quickly. I felt as if we had to win and that if we won, everything would be all right. But we couldn't do it. We actually fell a goal behind before Franco equalized and even though we subjected them to constant pressure, we couldn't force another. Now the recriminations redoubled.

Bates branded me the ringleader and our relationship, which had always been very cordial up to that point, was never the same again. He clearly felt let down and I was upset that he had criticized me in public. I felt it was a very personal thing for him to do and had expected better of him, particularly given the relationship we had had. He called me in and we had a chat about it. For once, he backed down. He wrote an apology in his programme notes and we tried to get over it. Instead, things quickly got worse.

As well as being club captain, I was the Professional Footballers' Association representative at Chelsea. At that time, it didn't entail much apart from administrative duties: I handed out forms for the Player of the Year vote; I was a point of contact for players if they wanted to do a course of some sort; I handled the players' pool when we got to the Cup Final – it was that kind of stuff. I supported the work the PFA did and felt that the Premiership players had a responsibility to those in the lower leagues. That's why I sometimes looked at the PFA's in-house magazine, *Players Club*, and found it distasteful that it was packed with advice on the best yacht to buy and the best Miami condo to invest in. Sometimes, it felt as if the union focused a lot more on the high-profile players than the ones at the bottom of the ladder.

Nonetheless I was happy in my administrative role: I had no ambitions as an agitator or a campaigner. Then suddenly, that autumn, an almighty row flared up between the PFA and the Premier League over the PFA's share of revenue from the new television deal and I found myself being branded a militant. But I'm not a militant and I objected to being labelled as one. When the PFA's chief executive, Gordon Taylor, started talking about strike action from the players, I had deep misgivings about it. Gordon was demanding £27 million a year from the Premier League, the Football League and the FA as the union's portion of the three-year deal, which was worth more than £2 billion. Richard Scudamore, the Premier League chief executive, wanted to pay £16 million a year.

The media said the players were being greedy but they chose to ignore the fact that this fight wasn't being conducted for the millionaires of the Premiership. It was being fought on behalf of lower league players who often needed help retraining when their short careers finished and on behalf of those whose careers were cut short by injury. It was to finance insurance and education and all the other good services that the PFA provides. However, I quickly realized that it was going to be a very hard sell when the public was seeing pictures every day of Premiership players driving into training grounds in Ferraris and Aston Martins.

I supported the PFA in areas of its work but when Gordon started talking about a strike, it made me uneasy. It was particularly difficult for me because Bates was one of Gordon's most vociferous critics. He said the Premier League chairmen were sick of being 'ridiculed, insulted and slagged off' by Gordon. He said Gordon just made baseless allegations. Bates was up for an all-out fight with the PFA and I started getting nervous.

Gordon sent a strike ballot round to the clubs and I distributed them dutifully among my team-mates at Chelsea. The result was that 99 per cent of PFA members backed the call for a strike. It so happened that the testing ground for the strike, the first match to be affected, would be Chelsea's league game against Manchester United, due to be shown live on Sky on 1 December. We were going to be the guinea pigs. Gordon said matches could go ahead if there were no cameras present but the football authorities said there would be cameras at every game. They had reached an impasse.

I felt it was all appallingly organized by the PFA. They never gave us any advice about what was going on. There was no real leadership. We found out most of what was happening through the press. I organized a meeting with Dave Richards, the Premier League chairman, so that I could try and understand the issues a bit more because the Chelsea lads, especially the foreign lads, didn't really grasp what they were putting themselves on the line for. They weren't interested in the finer details. They supported all the players the PFA represented but eventually they began to realize that they were the ones that had everything to lose. I began to see that whatever the result of the ballot, if it came to the crunch, most Premiership footballers were not going to risk their livelihood to go out on strike. They were not going to refuse to play.

I went to see Ken Bates. He was livid about the whole thing. I told him he had to take my word that I wasn't agitating for the strike and that I was just telling the boys what was going on and giving them information. Then he started getting aggressive, talking about players breaching their contract and saying there was no way we could go through with it. At that stage, I had to point out that that wasn't really up to him. He got more and more angry with me. The demise of our relationship was another symbol of the breakdown between the two sides.

I spoke to Gary Neville, too. The media had started calling him Red Nev by now but I got the impression that he felt the same as me about the prospect of a strike. Gary's a bright enough bloke and he relishes standing up for his responsibilities which is what his team-mates admire about him, but we were both worried about the prospect of letting down the supporters by not playing. In the end, I called the PFA chairman, Barry Horne, and told him the situation was going to backfire on the union, that whatever negotiations Gordon was having with the Premier League should be conducted on the basis that there was not going to be any strike action. Barry was wobbling, too. I told him we would not do it based on the information we had. I told him that we would walk out onto the pitch at Old Trafford on 1 December, strike or no strike. We may well have been vilified as strikebusters but there was no appetite for a strike at Chelsea. The foreign players were bemused by the idea. I don't know whether what I told Barry had any impact on the negotiations they were having but the two sides reached a compromise agreement not long after that.

Thank God the strike never happened. Even though we got more money than they had originally been offering us and even though it was a worthwhile cause, I felt damaged. I got a lot of stick from the media. One of the papers even mocked up a picture of me marching along with a placard. I was club captain of Chelsea for a couple of years and in that role I had a responsibility to the players and to the club. Sometimes, those two things conflict and then you can be perceived as a catalyst for a problem or as someone who is trying to solve the problem by making the club aware of it. I hoped that in my case the latter applied but I'm not sure Ken Bates saw it that way.

What happened between me and the chairman was a shame. There was friction between us from then on. The following season, we became embroiled in a row over our bonuses for qualifying for the UEFA Cup. There was a clause that guaranteed a £20,000 bonus for each player if we got into the competition and we duly made it by way of making it to the 2002 FA Cup Final. Even though we lost to Arsenal, they were in the Champions League so we received the UEFA Cup spot. But Bates didn't want to pay us. He said there was fine print which said that to qualify for the bonus, we had to get into the UEFA Cup via our Premiership position. By the letter of the law, he was probably right but we all felt his stance violated the spirit of our agreement. Again, he went public about me in a very scathing, dismissive way. By now, I expected that type of treatment.

I haven't spoken properly to Ken since I left which is something I regret. I still have a great fondness for him and Susannah and I am sure it will only be a matter of time until we speak socially. I had some great times with him. In some ways, he liked people who stood up to him, which is why he had such a lot of respect for Wisey. He liked the banter and relationship with people. Ken was always hard work but you felt you had achieved something if you came out with anything close to what you had been hoping for in bonus negotiations with him.

He must have been feeling the heat by then. We kept hearing that Chelsea's debts were piling up and that time was running out. Ironically, the example of the financial collapse of Leeds United was mentioned all the time. Chelsea were supposed to be the next domino to fall and things weren't going brilliantly on the pitch. We finished sixth in the league for the second year running in 2001/02 and even though we got to the FA Cup Final, my only appearance in our knock-out showpiece, we were well beaten in Cardiff by Double winners Arsenal.

I was still loving my football but not quite as much as I had under Luca and certainly not as much as I did under Ruud. Ranieri may have been a lovable eccentric in the public mind but he stripped some of the comforting rhythm out of training and preparing for games. It sometimes felt to some players as if it didn't matter how well they had played or trained because that would not have any effect on whether you were in the team for the next game. Normally, your form is the mechanism that decides whether you stay in the team or not. But that wasn't the way it worked with Ranieri. I found his methods difficult to take seriously. He would have us train in one formation for five days and then change to another for the game on Saturday. You thought you were in the first XI all week and then on match day he would drop you. The thing with a footballer is that as soon as he has finished one game, he starts mentally preparing for the next one. Everything he does in a week is about building up to playing and going in on the morning of the game expecting to play. The uncertainty didn't do anyone any good.

Ranieri seemed to be obsessed with keeping the squad fresh but when I have played in successful teams, the side has more or less picked itself every week. You need a nucleus in a side and if you keep that in tact, then you can afford to mix and match some of the others. Rotation can work but I consider that the particular reward of football is to be selected consistently. I found it hard to build up relationships with players if they were constantly being changed. One of my best seasons at Chelsea was when I played regularly with Celestine Babayaro on the left side and neither of us were injured or dropped. If there is a tactical reason for a change, that's fine, but there's no point dropping it on you at the last minute because that doesn't do anyone any good, surely. How can you go from being involved in all the drills about defending set-pieces on a Friday to not playing on the Saturday. At times under Ranieri, the situation became incredibly unpredictable and unsettling.

When Ranieri first turned up, he couldn't speak English which was obviously a fundamental problem. His main method of getting round it appeared to be to smile a lot – which was nice on one level but slightly disconcerting on many others. On his first day in charge of training, his fitness coach, Roberto Sassi, did this session that was all about quick feet with little hurdles to jump over. It was really sprightly and immediately I noticed that Ranieri had these idiosyncrasies. He stood there by the side of the pitch shouting 'One, one, one, one, one', clapping his hands as he shouted. He was learning his numbers, I think. He didn't seem to get beyond 'one' for a while.

Gary Staker did a lot of the translation but Gary wasn't there on the training pitch. Gus Poyet spoke Spanish and Ranieri had been the coach at Valencia so Gus became his translator. They communicated in Spanish. Gus would be in his kit at half-time, standing by the manager next to the board explaining what Ranieri was saying. When Ranieri started leaving him out of the team, Gus told him he could stick his translating service up his backside. He was sold to Spurs soon afterwards.

The first few days were unconventional. You could sense it was going to be a very different regime. Ranieri brought a goalkeeping coach and an assistant manager called Angelo who didn't appear to have any real footballing pedigree. We said to him one day 'What do you do?' and he said 'I'm a liar'. We thought that figured because he knew nothing about football. Then Franco said he meant he was a lawyer. The lads compared Sassi to a little rat because we'd be talking and he'd suddenly pop up from nowhere. He wasn't very popular at all. Generally, the chemistry under Ranieri was all wrong. The rotation system was excessive. The regime was flawed.

We got another taste of it before the start of the 2001/02 season when we made our first visit to the new summer training camp at Rocca Porena in Italy. It was Ranieri's idea. He loved it there. As the birthplace of St Rita of Cascia it had religious significance and a great attraction for ailing, ageing pilgrims, but very little to capture the imagination of bored, tired footballers; a place indeed so unpopular that during our time there the younger players would sing – to the tune of 'Copacabana' – 'Rocca, Rocca Porena/So shit we all went insane-er'.

This was Ranieri's way: two training sessions a day under Sassi which were tough and we carried on the hard running into the season, so much so that I dread to recall how tired we often were towards the end of games. More than anything, I distrusted the medical regime we were forced to endure under Ranieri. We had blood tests quite regularly and

233

they checked it over exhaustively. Gus was told he was low on iron and they wanted him to have intravenous iron. That's a very delicate thing to do. He told them he had been playing for fifteen years and didn't have a fitness problem so he refused. That didn't go down well at all.

Much as I disliked the physical side of things under Ranieri(probably because I was getting older), I can see how it must have helped an emerging player like Frank Lampard, who remains Ranieri's great success story and his greatest legacy to the club. Not only did Frank's fitness improve immeasurably but, with all that tinkering Ranieri went in for, he also learnt to be adaptable. When it came to learning and improving there was no one as determined as Frank.

As I mentioned, we were all astonished when we were told the size of Frank's fee because everyone felt he had yet to prove himself properly at Upton Park. But Ranieri was getting rid of all the senior players he thought might be a threat to his authority and who he may have felt had gone past their peak. Wisey was one of the players most surprised at the scale of the fee paid for Frank, and he was sold to Leicester City eleven days later. Gus had already been sold to Tottenham that month. Robbie di Matteo had suffered a terrible injury in Switzerland and sadly would never play again. A new regime was beginning to assert itself, there was uncertainty about the place and, for ambitious young players like Frank and John Terry (JT), it was an exciting club to be a part of.

Looking back, it's clear to see how Frank began to transform himself into the player he is now, and, although I feel Ranieri failed to move the club forward, he must take some credit for the development of Frank and JT. Frank started to become a very powerful runner over that first season at the club, after he was signed in the summer of 2001, and also a tough defensive player when he needed to be. Training was hard. In the past, Wisey had been the leader in the running, and I wasn't far behind, but it didn't take Frank long before he was motoring past me in the longer runs.

When I compare the greeting I received at the club from the unforgiving Chelsea squad of 1987 to the kind of characters who were there when Frank came in 2001, I can only conclude that there were better people around for him to learn from. Desailly, who had won everything there was to win, was the captain on the pitch and I would like to think that Gianfranco Zola and me also offered a bit of wisdom. We all wanted to see Frank develop and progress and apart from this support, as the squad changed it allowed him to take on more responsibility as senior players left. Just as John Terry flourished when Frank Leboeuf left in July 2001, Frank seemed ready to assert himself within the group. Players like Zola and me, who were coming to the end of our careers, had clear, well-defined roles within the team and there was no way we could take on more responsibility on the pitch. For that, we looked to the younger players and Frank responded brilliantly.

That Chelsea team did not reach the heights they were to scale under Jose Mourinho and yet, in spite of some of Ranieri's eccentricities, we were technically very good. It was a team that passed the ball well, a good football environment, and players like Frank and JT learnt very quickly. JT had been out on loan to Nottingham Forest in April 2000 and when he came back he, too, seemed to benefit from the way the squad worked together.

Frank's natural peer group when he joined Chelsea included JT, Eidur and Jody Morris and the group of them got into a few scrapes when they were younger. After the incident following 9/11, Frank didn't get into any more trouble and you could see that, even as a young player, he was determined not to compromise his career. That takes some willpower when there is such a strong temptation for young players really to cut loose and enjoy their money and fame. He knew that playing for a bigger club than West Ham meant that he would be under greater scrutiny and he reacted by focusing purely on his football.

I'm surprised at how good JT and Frank have become and that's not a criticism of them but rather a compliment. Their status in the game is beyond anything I would have expected. Mainly it's because I knew them so well and saw them develop. I saw them when they were the unfinished article. In fact, I saw them as the barely started article. I put someone like Tony Adams on a pedestal because he was England captain but JT is JT to me – and now he's England captain, too.

With John, his will is the key. Tony was his hero and he has always set his targets on the next goal. When he was a young player at Chelsea, he used to ask loads of questions. He had a real thirst for your experience. He would ask for footballing help about his positioning. He was always first out on the training pitch. He just loved the game and had this hunger to succeed. John has an incredibly high pain threshold and he has always had the courage of his convictions. Even when

Frank Leboeuf and Marcel Desailly were there, he was confident he could displace one of them in time. Then, when he broke into the Chelsea team, he began to talk about how one day he would love to play for England and be like Tony Adams, and of course he became an England player. As a young player, I thought he had limitations in terms of his size, pace and mobility, to a certain extent. It doesn't exactly sound like a blueprint for a future England captain, does it? Yet he has overcome all of those issues. Furthermore, he has always had great technical ability and is a fantastic passer of the ball, something he has worked so hard on. He's also got two good feet and fabulous control.

Another key factor with John is his commitment. He is like Adams in that respect: he will not be beaten; he will not be overcome. For someone who isn't that tall, he is incredibly strong in the air. As a young player, he was formidably brave. He just sees the ball, nothing else; just keeps his eyes on the ball and commits to it. What befell him in the 2007 Carling Cup Final, when he was knocked out putting his head among flying boots, was a prime example of that. John scored a few goals from my corners. He scored against West Ham and ran into the post at the same time because he was concentrating so hard on the ball; he didn't let himself be distracted by anything else. He is always going to make that ball his. There are a lot of good players who don't have that.

As a young player, JT was at risk of falling into the trap of living the life. He has said himself many times that he made mistakes and that he suffered from that bizarre outlook many young English footballers seem to have of thinking he could ignore the normal rules of everyday life. He was always a great young person, a really good guy but he had this default setting when he was with his mates that got him into trouble now and then. JT had to learn the hard way but it is evidence of his character that he has overcome that problem. People around him made him think about whether he wanted to be one of the lads or the best he could be at his profession and he has made the responsible choice. The power these young players have, the social power, is huge. They can buy what they want, get in where they want. It's corrupting and can be very hard to control.

I never got sucked into that. I have always had a sensible (some would say dull) part of me where I suddenly see things getting a bit out of control. If I was out with mates and it got to the stage of the night where you either got more drunk or backed off, I would always back off. I knew when to stop. That's not to say I wasn't sick in a car park anywhere but I always managed to keep in control of myself – there was always something that kept me in check. I was always quite happy if I'd had a drink. Alcohol can reveal the characters of people and if you look at young footballers, they have to have confidence and that confidence is often accentuated when they have had a drink and can easily take the form of aggression. I never really got stick from fans or anything like that. No one ever tried to wind me up in a pub or anything like that. If they did, I used to put myself down and laugh it off.

But my ability to laugh off what was happening at Chelsea was wearing thin. It didn't help that when Ranieri limped into his third season at Stamford Bridge, I was keenly aware that my contract was running down. I was thirty-three going into the 2002/03 season and my contract had only two years left to run. I didn't want to get to thirty-five and have nowhere to go. I wanted to end my career with Chelsea but I wanted a deal that kept me at the club for three more seasons and then I'd retire. So at Christmas I went to the new chief executive, Trevor Birch, a highly regarded administrator when he arrived, and broached the subject with him.

It was then that Birch told me quite how serious the club's financial problems were. He begged me to be patient and said that everything was riding on whether we qualified for the Champions League at the end of the season. If we did, then he gave me the impression that a contract extension would be no problem. If we didn't, all bets were off. He said that Zola was in the same position as me. When he put it like that, I didn't really feel I was in any position to stamp my feet. Even though I wasn't particularly enamoured of Ranieri, I was happy at the club and still enjoying my football. So I kept my head down and got on with it.

Ranieri had nothing to do with contracts and he showed no interest in even having an influence on my future. He stood back from everything that didn't involve the actual football. He never supported us over the Hapoel Tel Aviv affair and stayed resolutely neutral when it came to the prospect of the players' strike. Maybe he didn't want me to stay but he gave me the impression that he did. The longer the season went on, the clearer it became that Chelsea and Liverpool were going to be involved in a desperate battle for the fourth and last Champions League spot. In the end, it went right down to the wire. Going into the final game of the season, we were locked together on sixty-four points and our last game was against each other at Stamford Bridge.

It was billed as the most high-stakes game in the history of English football. It was estimated that £20 million was on offer for the winners because of the prize money and the attendance benefits the Champions League now brought. In fact, we now know that the stakes were a whole lot higher even than that for Chelsea. Roman Abramovich was waiting in the wings, looking for an English club to buy, and if we hadn't qualified for the Champions League, it may not have been Chelsea. It turns out that the club's entire future rested on that game. Knowing what we know now about the level of debt the club had accrued, there might not even be a Chelsea now if we hadn't drawn with or beaten Liverpool on 11 May 2003.

The night before the game, Birch arranged for the team to stay at the Royal Lancaster Hotel on the northern edge of Hyde Park. That was the opposite to our usual routine where we would have been at home the night before a game. That night, they sat us down for a motivational speech from an American contact of his who was a Vietnam vet. After an hour of stories about night patrols and seeing your buddies being shot, I wasn't sure whether it was Michael Owen I should be concerning myself with or abseiling out of the hotel window and searching the park for rogue members of the Vietcong. Playing in a football match wasn't going to do it for me after that. I wanted to kill someone. I felt like I'd drunk about eight espressos. I was so wired I couldn't sleep.

We all went for a walk in Hyde Park the next morning. Most people were looking bleary-eyed. I strolled along with

Franco for a bit. I felt for him because he'd been left out of the starting eleven. Ranieri had decided to go with Hasselbaink and Gudjohnsen up front. I was trying to sympathize with him about how tough it must be to be missing out but he told me not to worry. He said he honestly didn't mind as long as Chelsea won. He knew what an important game it was for the club and all he cared about was that they were successful. Franco was such a genuine, generous man. He didn't think about himself, just the team. That's why he'll always be a Chelsea hero.

Once we were at the stadium, Birch came up to me in the tunnel half an hour or so before the game. He was incredibly nervous. He told me how much he was relying on me. He said I had to exert all my influence and use all my experience in the game to help the other lads out. He was on the verge of open panic. We went out and played superbly. Liverpool took the lead early on but Marcel equalized almost immediately and then Jesper Gronkjaer got what proved to be the winner in the twenty-seventh minute when he cut inside from the right and curled a left foot shot past Jerzy Dudek. That gave us a cushion because we knew we only needed a draw so we went out and played with more freedom. Liverpool got more and more frustrated and in the final few minutes Steven Gerrard was sent off for a flying tackle on me that actually looked a lot worse than it was. He caught me but I managed to get my weight off the floor so he didn't hurt me as badly as he might have done. By then, it had already been announced that I had been chosen as man of the match.

There were wild celebrations afterwards. I took Georgina and Lucas onto the pitch with me, and all the players did a lap of honour. I didn't know it then but it was my last game for the club. Franco didn't know it then, either, but it was his last game, too. I'd always thought the contract issue would be resolved, particularly if we reached the Champions League. That's what Birch had been telling both me and Franco: if we reached the Champions League, the money would be available to give us a decent contract.

Well, they offered me my year's extension but it was derisory. I hadn't had particularly high expectations about what might be on the table but I didn't think they'd sink that low. When I saw what they were offering I realized that I was entering the end-game at Chelsea. It's part of life in football. I should have realized that earlier – it shouldn't have come as a shock to me. When you start your football career and when you finish it, the club always has the upper hand. You are not in control – other people have the monopoly of power. It's that bit in the middle when you are at your peak and you are established and in the ascendancy – that's when you are in control. At the beginning and the end, you are marginalized by your circumstances, whether it's your age or your injury history. It's exactly the same. That sums up loyalty in football: use and abuse them as much as you can when they are young and when they are older – they are one step away from the football grave; they're expendable. As Roy Keane said, 'pieces of meat'.

I knew I was a senior player now but the offer Birch put on the table was only about half of what I was on. I spoke to him and told him it was a joke. He kept banging on about how they hadn't got any money. I reminded him I'd been voted man of the match in the game against Liverpool that got us into the Champions League. What about the benefits we would reap from that the following season, I said. He didn't have an answer.

In June, Bates sold the club to Abramovich for £60 million which wiped out Chelsea's debts and gave Ken a £17 million payout. I went back to Birch and said that surely now the money was available to improve my contract offer. He said they still felt that what they had offered me was the right deal for the club. I told him I couldn't sign it. I was annoyed for myself but I also felt disgusted about the way they were treating Franco. He was one of the club's greatest players of all time and the offer they had made to him was an insult.

I told Birch that I would never play for the club again if they tried to hold me to the final year of my contract without making me a better offer for another year. How was I going to get a contract somewhere else for the remainder of my career? I had to use what leverage I had to secure a contract at another club and stop Chelsea just running my contract down. It was sad because I certainly didn't want to leave but I did want to play another two years before I retired and they wouldn't give me that commitment. They had made a gesture, but it couldn't be classed as a serious offer.

I suppose I could look back now and think about what I missed out in the Abramovich era, but I probably wouldn't have survived quite long enough to play in the championship-winning side of 2004/05 even if I had stayed at the club in the summer of 2003. Abramovich brought a new level of ambition and because I was becoming more susceptible to injury, I would probably have been overtaken by the raft of new signings that Ranieri and, later, Jose Mourinho made. I don't have any regrets about not being around for that. It simply came a couple of years too late for me.

I left four or five days after Abramovich bought the club. By then, it had become apparent that Chelsea were interested in Wayne Bridge and it soon got to the stage where they made it plain they wanted me to be the makeweight in the deal with Bridge's club, Southampton. So suddenly, the shoe was on the other foot now. The only way the Southampton boss, Gordon Strachan, would let Bridge go was if I was part of the deal.

I enjoyed that. I know it sounds petty but it's the truth. I know that I'd been demanding a move and now I was telling Birch not to force me into one. That may sound like double-speak but I felt I had been treated badly. I'd given a lot of my life to Chelsea, in the same way any employee gives their hours and their effort to any company, and I felt I deserved better. So I suppose when I found myself in a position to get my own back, I took it.

Actually, I wanted to go to Southampton because they had a good reputation and I was an admirer of Strachan. There was a sentimental pull for me, too, because it was the club that was closest to Jersey and I had had links with them when I was a kid. Eventually, I told Chelsea that unless they paid up the final year of my contract, I wasn't going to go anywhere. I ended up negotiating a pay-off from Chelsea as compensation for them driving me out. If you lumped in that pay-off with the wages I was offered at Southampton, it exceeded what I would have earned in the two final years that I had wanted at Chelsea in the first place. That meant that I was in a healthier financial position. Southampton were never going to match

Chelsea's wages but it wasn't about greed for me. It wasn't about the money. It was about my value.

Of course money is important. I heard Steve Coppell say on the television recently that it's 'a universal language'. Football is a short career and you have to make the most of the opportunity. You don't have to be greedy – you just have to be fair and hope that others are fair to you. You know what your value is. I wasn't signing for Southampton to make a fortune. They had a pay structure and I respected that. The fact was that the mess Chelsea had got themselves into and the greed they had shown in coveting Wayne Bridge and deciding I was expendable meant that they ended up paying me to go.

Despite this – and through all the dramas, all the eccentricities, all the weirdness of the training regimes of Vialli and Ranieri – I loved being part of the Chelsea Football Club and I valued the friends I made. I achieved a lot with Blackburn because that was where I won a league title but Chelsea is the club that I feel the most affection towards.

I am as proud to be associated with them now as I ever was. The achievements of the players under Jose Mourinho have brought a great deal of reflected glory for those of us who preceded the Russian revolution at the club. Being an ex-Chelsea player has a great deal more cachet these days than it did a few years ago. They invited me back towards the end of 2006 and I strolled out onto the pitch at half-time. I got a great reception from the crowd – not what Zola would get, maybe, or Ruud perhaps, or Wisey, but a great reception nonetheless. It was enough to reassure me that I have a secure place in their affections and in the history of the club. I applaud the new Chelsea for what they have achieved and I look at JT and Frank Lampard and their progress and their class fills me with pride.

I had some bitterness in my heart when I left Chelsea the second time around but I don't any more – just affection for all the good times I had with some great footballers who became my friends. I know now that when my association with Chelsea came to a close, it marked the beginning of the end of my life in football. I stopped being a contender when I left Stamford Bridge. I didn't know it then, really, but I was entering football's old age. My body started to feel the strain. The days of my prime were behind me.

TEN

Farewell to England

When I missed Euro 2000 with an ankle injury, my England career entered its final days, too. At home, I watched Phil Neville give away the penalty against Romania that was the final straw in our miserable tournament and wondered again what might have been if I could have made a contribution. But I had been out for most of the season until eventually, I went to have the third and final operation on my ankle in Belgium. I was being wheeled into the operating theatre when I heard a great clattering and banging coming from another room. I looked up at the Chelsea physio, Mike Banks, and he explained there was some renovation work going on in the clinic. I found out later that it was somebody having a hip replacement.

My operation was a success so I was back in time for England's last game at the old Wembley, the World Cup qualifier against Germany. I was only thirty-one but it turned out it wasn't just Wembley that was saying goodbye to England that day: it was Kevin Keegan as well, and it was me, too. I wish I'd won more caps than my thirty-six but I

suppose when you look at my ankle injury and the fact that
Sven-Goran Eriksson ignored me when I was still good
enough and young enough to play, it's about right. When I
think about how hard I struggled just to make it as a professional footballer, I'm thankful for what I had.

I was excited about playing for Keegan. Like Hoddle and
Dalglish, he was a superhero for me when he was a player.
He had been an incredibly passionate, heroic kind of foot-
baller and even though he hadn't won anything with
Newcastle, the panache and the verve he brought to St
James' Park was almost worth more than trophies. He hadn't
taken over England at an easy time with the squad in transi-
tion. Stalwarts of the team like Tony Adams, Paul Ince and
Gazza had all faded from international football, Alan
Shearer retired at the end of Euro 2000 and David Seaman
lasted only a few more months. We had very good new players coming through but Keegan struggled to marshal them.

The atmosphere under Kevin was more relaxed than it had
been under Hoddle, but now it was too relaxed. I know that
sounds incredibly picky in a spoilt footballer kind of way but
it was true. It went from one extreme to the other. Kevin let
the players be a bit more responsible for themselves but some
of them were just not responsible people. The laddish culture
in the England squad that Hoddle had squashed flat
reasserted itself and became a problem. I didn't want a
return to Hoddle's suffocating ways but at that level, you
need your players to be more professional than some of them
were. Hoddle had been dictatorial about lack of freedom but
Kevin was very laissez-faire. It created a feel-good factor for
a while but that didn't last.

When we met up with England under Keegan, for instance, we were supposed to be at Burnham Beeches at 6.00 pm on the Sunday before a game. But because they knew they could get away with it, some of the lads wouldn't turn up until really late at night because they had been on a detour somewhere or other to meet up with their mates from London clubs. That kind of thing undermines what the manager is trying to achieve. You need the lads in a group but you have to have people to keep the reins on them, too. Football revolves around the lowest common denominator, which I always found frustrating. I felt I was responsible enough to go for a night out with a few friends without getting into any sort of trouble but because some of the other lads couldn't be trusted to do that, it was made off-limits for all of us once again.

Training wasn't great under Keegan, either. It was good fun but there wasn't a lot of tactical work. We played a lot of sharp, fast football in five-a-sides, which was the routine Kevin had learned under Bill Shankly at Anfield, but we weren't properly co-ordinated in the way we had been under Hoddle. The players didn't really respect Derek Fazakerley, Kevin's coach, and as a player, you have to respect the person who is telling you what to do – you have to have that belief that what he is telling you is right. I never questioned Terry Venables – I presumed he knew what he was doing.

It was the first day of October when we played Germany. It rained incessantly all day and the pitch at the old stadium was like a bog. It wasn't a very auspicious way for any of us to bid farewell to England duty. I never felt we were in control of the game. Kevin played Gareth Southgate in midfield which raised a few eyebrows and there was no cohesion to our play. We never really got going. I had my hands full with their right-midfielder, Sebastian Deisler, who was one of their best players at the time. He has faded from the scene a little bit since then. He was lauded as Germany's next great talent and it got to him. He had a nervous breakdown and when he came back he got some bad injuries. However, that day at Wembley, I felt I had my work cut out to keep him in check.

When we went behind to a quick free-kick from Didi Hamann, it wasn't really a surprise. Nobody stood over the ball, Hamann hit a shot that swerved and skidded off the turf and Seaman got down late to it. By then, he was getting down later for shots. We never really looked like getting back into it and when the final whistle went, we trooped off down the old Wembley tunnel for the last time to a resounding chorus of boos. We all got hammered and Kevin tried to stop and remonstrate with some of the angry fans but it didn't do any good. In fact, it shook him up.

We got back into the dressing room and everyone just felt hollow. You want to have a second chance to play games like that and put things right but you can't. There was absolute silence. Everyone was sitting down with their elbows on their knees, staring at the floor. In the midst of that silence, Kevin suddenly burst in and said he couldn't take us any further and that he was going to resign. I was absolutely stunned. I had never witnessed anything like that before. All the players looked at each other in surprise.

Kevin stormed off towards an area at the back of the changing rooms where the showers were. Fazakerley started arguing with him and trying to persuade him to reconsider. He told Kevin to calm down but Kevin wouldn't listen. They tried to shepherd him away but then the suits from the FA came down to see him and he quit there and then in the toilets at Wembley. What a way to go. He genuinely felt by that stage that he was not the right man for the job. He had already been criticized for England's performance in Euro 2000 and now this was the last straw. He came back in one last time and told us he was going to tell the press he had quit – and that was it.

It created chaos, of course. There was another qualifier against Finland in Helsinki four days later so the lads had to suffer Howard Wilkinson again and a lot of people accused Kevin of leaving England in the lurch. I couldn't play in Finland because I had suffered a tear in my Achilles' tendon. Indeed, I thought my career might be over. I didn't know that my England career already was.

I had been wearing heavy strapping on my ankle and it had begun to affect my Achilles' tendon. I got a small tear in it and it got worse and worse and worse. I missed Finland and then played the following weekend for Chelsea against Manchester United. After the United game, I was in a tremendous amount of pain and it was then that they discovered the tear. That was a career-threatening moment for me because by then I had had three operations on my ankle and it was looking as if my foot was in a degenerative state. The attitude of the doctors was almost as if there was nothing they could do for me.

About that time, I went to the opening of Roberto di Matteo's restaurant off Regents Street. He was there on crutches having had about his twelfth operation. He was discussing severance terms with Chelsea and was about to retire because of injury, and then there was me, with my own career in the balance, up to my calf in plaster. We made a right couple, a real advert for the healthy effects of being a Premiership player. But I was lucky: spending a few weeks in plaster allowed the Achilles to knit back together and I was able to start playing for Chelsea again.

Peter Taylor was in temporary charge of England by then while the FA tried to lure Eriksson away from Lazio. There was a friendly due against Italy in Turin in the middle of November and I assumed I'd be in the squad. Then Taylor left a message on my phone saying he was going to go with youth at the Stadio Delle Alpi. He wanted me to call him back but I didn't see the point. I felt it was a bit of an insult. It was a full England international and he was treating it like it was one of his Under-21 games – I felt it devalued the game. He made David Beckham captain for the first time that night and Gareth Barry played left-back. Actually, he played only part of the game; Seth Johnson played the rest of it – enough said. I admit that was not a particularly generous instinct but you watch games like that and you think 'If Johnson doesn't do well, that proves my point'. You don't want them to lose but you don't want someone who has replaced you out of the blue to have a good game either. It's part of survival. Well, Johnson didn't have a good game, and Barry didn't exactly make a decisive case for inclusion, either. He's hardly played since even though I think he should have been involved much more than he has been. England lost 1–0 as well. None of it, however, made any difference to my fortunes.

I was pleased for Beckham, though. He was England captain for the next five years. That game in Italy was the start of something for him. He and I had some fantastic battles with each other when I was playing against him with Blackburn and Chelsea. Because of our respective positions, we were usually directly opposed. I admired him a lot as a player. He created space for himself really well. When he was out wide at United, you were always struggling as a defender to get there before he delivered. That was Beckham at his best and he has never quite recreated that form because he has never had the luxury of a team that is geared up for him to shine.

He was quick and he was good at running at people and feinting to cross. That would take you off balance and give him time. He didn't have real pace but he was very sharp. He could get past you without having to dribble past you and his work rate was phenomenal. He wasn't a player I feared playing against and I certainly wouldn't worry about him the night before a match but he was still one of United's most effective players. Because United had players like Roy Keane, Paul Scholes and Eric Cantona, they could work the ball to Beckham incredibly quickly and efficiently – one-touch stuff from one side of the pitch to the other – and I often felt I didn't have time to adjust my position to get out to him and block him off. Beckham had a fantastic first touch, too, so he could control a pass and then step back as if it was a dead ball. He'd curl it in and United's forwards would be queuing up for it. That was their perfect scenario.

There was another side to Beckham as well. He developed into a fairly waspish character on the pitch and the better he got, the more of a personality trait that became. Sometimes, players become a victim of their own image and their own success. I did as well. The better you become, the more of a target you become and the more of a target you become, the more you get kicked. It got to a point where David was getting kicked around a lot and his reaction to that was very sharp and pointed. It became disproportionate to the injury that was being visited upon him.

On one occasion, he and I jumped for a high ball together and my elbow caught the side of his head. It was totally unintentional but he went ballistic at me. He and I weren't best friends exactly but I knew him quite well. I'd been out to dinner in a group with him and Victoria a couple of times. I apologized to him but he wasn't listening. He reacted with some choice verbals and I just thought 'Is there really any need?' It was disappointing. His reaction was maybe not that bad in the greater scheme of things but you expect better from people you play with in the national team. I know we all say things in the heat of the moment but there are ways of dealing with that.

Our relationship changed a bit after that – it had more of an edge. Things were never really that confrontational, though, and it didn't change my opinion of him as a footballer. His move to America and his recall to the England team for the 2008 European Championship qualifiers – having originally been discarded by Steve McClaren after the World Cup – showed that he still has a lot to offer on the pitch.

As an international player, you have to accept that you have a limited shelf life and that sooner or later someone is going to discard you, but I wasn't ready for it. I didn't feel it was the right time to retire me but when Eriksson took over, I never heard a word from him – not a jot. All I got was a great big custard pie in the face. There was no contact at all, either formal or informal, no explanation for my demotion. Eriksson just wasn't interested. He picked Arsenal's Ashley Cole and Chris Powell from Charlton as his left-backs. Powell was a good player but there weren't many who thought he was international class. All that mattered, though, was that Eriksson and Tord Grip thought that he was a better bet than me.

Eriksson has told people he did not pick me because I had a suspect temperament. Well, we can argue all day long about my temperament. The fact is that I was only booked once for England in thirty-six games. I'd played in a World Cup and an FA Cup Final and yet he was saying he could not rely on me in a big game. It was a misplaced theory. I had proved I had a lot left to give at that time. I could have played in midfield, as I was doing for Chelsea. If Ashley Cole was going to be the regular left-back, I would have been a good partner for him in midfield. It would have been a pairing of a sprightly younger guy with someone of experience. People went on and on and on about the shortage of naturally left-footed players available to Eriksson and I found that particularly galling. What I didn't like about him, and where I felt his agenda was flawed, was that he based his decision on a personality issue. He did not justify his treatment of me in football terms. Let's face it, he was picking Danny Mills for England and he wasn't exactly 'Mr Calm and Collected'. Neither was Alan Smith. I just couldn't see the logic in what he was doing to me.

One thing that didn't help me was Eriksson coming to watch the FA Cup sixth-round tie between Spurs and Chelsea at White Hart Lane in March 2002. My chances of making the squad were pretty much non-existent by then anyway but Eriksson may have used this game as his final justification. I was sent off for two bookable offences, one of which was a collision with Mauricio Taricco when we were both challenging for a bouncing ball. Nonetheless, I had a fantastic game that day. I scored early in the second half, the fourth goal in a 4–0 romp. But when the sending-off happened, Martin Tyler's comment on Sky TV – 'That's why Le Saux isn't in the England squad' – didn't help my cause. That really annoyed me. However, I guess me getting back into the England squad was one of those things that was just not meant to be. I think Eriksson probably felt I wasn't young enough to be one of his guys. The core of players he picked were a younger group. Maybe he thought I would have seen through him. Whatever the reason, I will never believe that it was a football issue.

If you are a manager who is trying to pick the best players for your team and you have got someone who is playing well but has got a question mark against them, surely you would put them in a squad and see for yourself. What harm could that have done? I guess it got to the point with Eriksson and me where he could not make a U-turn – it would have been a climbdown.

As an international manager, Eriksson was flawed. He made some tactical errors, such as in the Brazil–England semi-final in the 2002 World Cup when he failed to react to a losing situation by bringing on players who could change

256

the game. He also appeared to align himself with certain individuals, like David Beckham, that created resentment in the squad that turned to apathy with a lot of the players. Did Eriksson squander the richest collection of young talent that England have produced in a generation? The results speak for themselves.

About the time when the speculation about me getting back into the squad was at its height, I went to a charity event at the Metropolitan Hotel in London. Tord Grip had donated a prize: it was the chance to take part in a training session with the England team. It was a silent auction and I had a mate with me, Matt, who was doing very well in a job in the City. Matt was adamant that he and I were going to bid for this prize and that I was going to turn up for England training. I got carried away with it and before I knew it, we were in a bidding war with another bloke and the sum we were going to pay had reached £20,000. In the end, the bloke we were bidding against came up and explained that he had two sons who were football crazy and could we just give him a break. You know what, I would have gone to the training session if we'd won the bid. Really, I would. It would have been a huge publicity stunt. It would have been a great story and it would have embarrassed the hell out of Eriksson.

I would have liked that. My only experiences of him were bad. The first time I came across him was when he stitched Blackburn up after Ray Harford had been sacked. The Blackburn chairman, Robert Coar, came into the players' canteen one day and made a pompous speech about how Eriksson would be joining the club from Sampdoria and that he had always been the club's first choice. Eriksson promptly did the dirty on Blackburn and went to Lazio instead. A few days after that, Coar came into the canteen again and made another speech. He said Roy Hodgson would be our new manager and that he had always been the club's first choice.

I only met Eriksson once. He and I were both at the Beckhams' party in Hertfordshire on the eve of the 2002 World Cup, the World Cup I felt I should have been a part of. I was talking to the actor Ray Winstone and he said how surprised he was that I hadn't been included in Eriksson's plans and how it was a liberty I wasn't going to Japan and South Korea. He started getting quite worked up about it and said I should go over and have it out with Eriksson. He said he'd go over and ask him himself. 'If he doesn't answer, I'll chin him,' he joked. I'd had a few drinks by then so I went up to him as he was leaving. I caught his eye and said I knew it wasn't the right time or the right place but that I needed to speak to him about it. 'I just want to know why you've never picked me,' I said. Sven looked very nervous. He said I should call him some time. Not that I would have done – pride wouldn't have let me. Funnily enough, he didn't give me his number anyway.

ELEVEN

Going South Again

I played my last game as a professional footballer on 12 May 2005. By then, I was like a creaking tin man. On Mondays, I would go into the gym by myself because I couldn't take too much impact on my ankle after the weekend's game. I trained as normal on Tuesday. On Wednesday, when everyone else was off, I drove up to London to see a terrific physio called Kevin Lidlow who gave me intensive physiotherapy on my bad ankle just to keep it mobile enough for me to play. I was giving away ten years to most of the players I was up against. To them, I must have seemed like an old man. I'd known for some time that this would be the end but I didn't quite anticipate the manner of my leaving. Southampton, the team I'd joined hoping to accelerate their rise through the top half of the Premiership, were relegated on the last day of the season after twenty-seven years in the top flight. Up in the Midlands, West Brom were pulling off the great escape that we had planned for ourselves. We lost 2–1 at home to Manchester United and went down, and I was part of that. I was helpless to stop it. What a way to go.

It was the first time I had ever experienced relegation and one of the things that hurt most was that there was no time to put it right. There was no shot at redemption for me on the south coast. When the final whistle went that day at St Mary's, I was distraught – not for the end of my own career because I knew it was time to go, but because I hadn't been able to avert what had happened. I was the senior player at the club and I felt I had an extra responsibility to try to drag them out of trouble. We had just about managed to keep that dream alive until the Manchester United game. We'd even taken the lead and if we'd stayed ahead we would have stayed up. But we couldn't hold on.

In those circumstances, I didn't really begin to think about the life change that was sweeping over me until that evening. Mariana had organized a surprise retirement party for me at a hotel in Winchester. Relegation wasn't supposed to be part of the surprise but a few of my best mates and all the Southampton lads turned up anyway and we did our best to have a good time. After we had eaten, they dimmed the lights in the private room where we were sitting and slipped a DVD into the machine. Set to the theme tune from Bergerac and The Beatles song, *In My Life*, it was a highlights reel of my career that the BBC had put together. I know what you're thinking: it didn't last very long.

It went on for about four minutes, actually: eighteen years of my life reduced to four minutes. I looked around the table at some of the other players who were there. They were staring at the images on the screen, engrossed but sad. I looked at them looking at moving pictures of me ageing in front of their eyes: me with long hair and cheeks flushed with effort, me with floppy hair, me with a crew cut, me fresh-faced and impossibly eager, me older and wiser, me approaching the end. I felt as if I had happened upon my own funeral. I looked at my former team-mates and realized that all this must be very sobering for them. There was a truth about themselves as well as about me in that DVD. You watch something like that and you realize how fleeting a football career is, how quickly it passes and how it swallows your youth and takes its leave of you when you are a middle-aged man. Sooner or later, you are going to have to face up to it ending; you are going to have to face up to the ravages of accumulated injury and the finality of retirement.

The riches that footballers earn now haven't changed the enormity of the impact of retirement. In some ways, the money will make it harder for the current generation of players to adapt to life outside the game. Because of their profile and their wealth, today's footballers are shielded from the realities of everyday life much more than I ever was and so the shock of the leaving of the game will be even more stark than it is for older guys like me. Even in football, you don't stay young forever. However much you earn, however many chunky watches you buy with your disposable income, none of it will hold back time.

It was a poignant night but it was positive, too. I felt unbelievably grateful. The montage was almost like receiving an award. I've always been pretty self-deprecating but it made me realize that I wasn't a bad player. It brought some clarity to what I'd been striving to achieve since I became a professional footballer. I scored more and better goals than I thought. I had worse haircuts than I thought. I did what I set out to do and got as far as I could.

My mates Pugsley and Keir made fantastic speeches and Paddy Barclay, my friend from the *Sunday Telegraph*, added his thoughtful views. For the first time in my life, I looked back on my career. I had never done that before; I had never really taken stock. That's part of my make-up – I don't look back. Maybe it has something to do with my mum dying. I used to look back and try and remember the feeling of her being around. After a while, I tried to stop myself doing that because it was too emotionally draining to keep missing something you can't get back. As time went on, I always looked forward. Football encourages you to do that, too. It doesn't give you a chance to look back. Okay, they say, we've just won the league, but we've got pre-season in a fortnight. We've just beaten Arsenal, they say, but it's Liverpool next week. There is no time to celebrate or contemplate: it is always about moving on.

Now, however, there was nothing to move on to, not as a footballer, anyway. That first summer after I retired, I found the freedom quite hard to handle. I would wake up worrying about when pre-season training was due to start. That was always one of the worst parts of the year for a footballer. It felt like it did when you were a kid and you were going back to school after the long summer holiday. Okay, so you were going back to a life of playing football – it wasn't exactly a hardship – but those first few days back in training were always brutally tough work. It was always a jolt to the system.

Even though I'd retired, I couldn't quite shake the routine. It reminded me of what Steve Redgrave had said about the need to 'untrain' himself once his rowing career had finished. Soon, though, the freedom was wonderful rather than unsettling. I went to America with the BBC that summer to be an analyst for them during England's tour of the USA and that was an exciting new step on what I thought was going to be my new career. Mariana and I and the kids had ten days in New York and then we had a family holiday in Argentina. We then went to Majorca. It was great just to revel in having time with my wife and children and not have to steel myself for going back to the grind.

In a way, that's what it had become in my last two years of playing: a grind. I didn't realize it when I left Chelsea but the move to Southampton marked the slow death of ambition in my career. I enjoyed it at St Mary's to begin with, mainly because of the manager, Gordon Strachan. I had great respect for Gordon and I liked what he was doing on the south coast. The season before I signed, he had taken Southampton to the FA Cup Final, where they lost to Arsenal, and lifted them to an eighth-place finish in the Premiership. Because Arsenal took a Champions League spot, Southampton qualified for the UEFA Cup, too. They had a good team, a good blend of players, people like Matt Oakley, James Beattie, Antti Niemi, Paul Telfer and Claus Lundekvam. It was a professional club with good training facilities and a nice new stadium. They looked like they were going places.

Gordon treated me like an elder statesman, which I enjoyed. In a way, he put me on the same level as him. He was my boss but because I was older than my team-mates, he had respect for me. That didn't mean he wouldn't have a go at me if I did something wrong but I felt there was a degree of parity between us. He knew I'd been through a lot and played at the top level for some time and that now and again, it was worth consulting me about things. I'd played against him several times when he was at Leeds and he was a fantastic player and character. He was a great raconteur. He used to tell a lot of stories about Alex Ferguson and the hairdrier. He said you'd walk back into the changing rooms sometimes after a bad performance and you just knew someone was going to get it. He painted a picture of the United players all staring down at their feet, not wanting to catch Fergie's eye. Because Fergie used to wear shiny shoes, Gordon said he always knew he was in trouble if he suddenly saw his reflection staring back up at him in a pair of patent leather shoes.

There was a bit of sentimentality involved in my decision to move to Southampton, too. It felt like a good fit that I would be ending my career there because they were the Premiership club that was closest to Jersey, the club I'd had so much contact with when I was a kid. In a different way from moving back to Chelsea, it felt as if there was something about the club I could relate to. I met up with Matt Le Tissier a lot when I joined and it was nice to renew our friendship. Pulling on the shirt with the badge and that red and white kit took me back to my childhood because everyone had always assumed that if I made it anywhere, it would be there. There was a comforting symmetry about it all, I thought.

However, it didn't take me long to realize that there was a totally different level of expectation and ambition at

Southampton compared to what I had been used to in the previous ten years. I had been accustomed to shooting for the top but the attitude at Southampton was more about scrambling away from the bottom. When that reality hit me, it was like a slap in the face. When I'd signed, I'd spoken to Gordon and the coaching staff about how good I felt about the move and how I felt we had a great chance of doing really well. I had gone into every season I had played from Blackburn onwards thinking I could win the league with the club I was at. But at Southampton, it didn't take long to get the impression that it wasn't ever going to be about winning the league.

Instead it was about getting to forty points and doing as well as you could. I know it sounds naive but I was devastated. I couldn't approach my football like that. Gordon was very pragmatic about the team and about not expecting too much from them. He would say we were going to do our best and we had a great work rate but without the work rate we were nothing. He would talk about how we couldn't compete with a lot of other sides in terms of the quality of our players. Things like that set me back a bit. I thought surely at the start of the season we had to believe we could win the league. If you set your sights on that, you are going to achieve more than if you set your sights on finishing mid-table. I wouldn't accept the alternative.

So I went about it the same as I always had done. I tried to get the people around me to believe we could win the league. We had a great start, too, that first season I was there. We were unbeaten for the first six games. We handed Manchester United their first defeat since Boxing Day and I took a corner that went straight over Tim Howard's head for James Beattie to head in at close range. It was all good. But when we lost at home to Middlesbrough in September and then lost on aggregate to Steuea Bucharest in the first round of the UEFA Cup, the bubble burst and mediocrity set in.

It wasn't that the players at Southampton weren't good players. It was just that they weren't as consistently good as the players I'd been with at Chelsea and Blackburn. Their performances wandered from exceptional to poor. I couldn't claim any points for consistency, either. I picked up a series of niggling injuries as Christmas drew near and had to watch for most of the time as we went on a run of one win in eleven matches in the New Year. Sometime towards the end of that run, Gordon decided that he needed a break from football for a while and resigned as manager.

Steve Wigley took over as caretaker manager and then the Southampton chairman, Rupert Lowe, appointed Paul Sturrock, the Plymouth manager, as the new boss. Where that decision came from, God only knows. He hadn't had any Premiership experience but I think the biggest problem was that Gordon had run such a tight, clever regime and had such a powerful personality that it was always going to be really hard for anyone to fill that void. When Steve took over, we didn't do very well. We were on a slide anyway and when Sturrock was given the job, it was a distinctly under-whelming experience. We beat Liverpool 2–0 in his first game in charge in the middle of March but there was never really any fresh momentum. Sturrock's appointment didn't kick-start the club in the way that the appointment of a new manager often does. He didn't have a lot of charisma and he didn't connect with the players in the way Gordon had. It all just continued to fall away.

I went off injured just before half-time in that win over Liverpool. A month later, I returned for a victory over Manchester City in Manchester and then broke down the game after that, coming off after ten minutes of a defeat to Bolton. That was happening to me more and more, staggering from one niggling injury to another. I was picking up little tears here and there, most of which seemed be a knock-on from problems connected with my bad ankle. It destroyed any consistency I tried to achieve and limited my ability to have the kind of influence on the side that I yearned to have. We didn't win any of our last five games of the season.

We seemed to have stopped the rot when we got two victories in the first two games of the 2004/05 season but then we didn't win again for eleven matches. That was enough to do for Sturrock. To everyone's disbelief, Rupert Lowe gave the job back to Steve Wigley, which was always going to be the wrong decision. It was to Steve's credit that he took it on. There was no ego about his decision to accept the job – he just wanted to help the club – and there were many things about him that made him a first class coach, but I don't think he was cut out to be a Premiership number one.

Still, I took the slide down the table really personally. We tried to put the brakes on so many times. We had meetings and chats and the lads were desperately trying. The club was being mismanaged by that time. My relationship with Rupert was very good on a personal level but the longer I spent there, the more I realized that there was a lot of resentment towards him from some of the players. There was a lack of leadership from a management point of view. The club had been through so many managers in such a short space of time that the impact of Gordon's loss was always going to be huge. It proved to be too big for even the great Harry Houdini to fashion an escape.

Harry Redknapp came in at Christmas 2004 and by that point we were in dire, dire straits. We couldn't get out of the rut. Certain players completely lost their confidence. I had made up my mind by then that it would be my last season. I knew at the start of that season. I couldn't announce my retirement because it would have been totally disrespectful given what was going on. I spent those last months of my career dealing with all that baggage, fighting more and more injuries and thinking 'This isn't what I'm playing football for'.

I was missing games every few weeks, my contract was up at the end of the season and I just felt I was running out of time to stay at that standard – I was coming off the level I wanted to play at. Technically, I felt fine but physically it was getting harder and harder. My body had been through a hell of a lot and I was a very physically orientated player. I had a lot of miles on the clock. If I'm remembered for anything, I'd like it to be that I was an early example of a modern, attacking full-back. Stuart Pearce was the generation before and he was an out and out defender really. Tony Dorigo got forward more. Because my style was an all-action one, I was very reliant on my fitness. When my fitness started to go, it affected me more than it might have affected players who didn't feel the need to cover the same amount of ground that I did.

Harry's arrival did give everybody a lift. He has great charisma. However, some of the impact of his arrival was lost in the great wave of controversy over the fact that he had defected from Portsmouth, just down the coast. The rivalry between Southampton and Portsmouth is as intense and bitter as any in English football even if it is on a slightly smaller scale than say Liverpool and Man Utd or Arsenal and Spurs. Nonetheless it was a move that stunned everyone in football because it stirred up so much anger and resentment. The Portsmouth fans regarded Harry as a traitor and the Southampton fans didn't know quite what to make of it at all. It was all very fraught and so messy that it defeated the objective of giving us a fresh start.

Harry did what he does. He created a positive, happy environment. He created team spirit. He got involved in a blizzard of transfer activity. He signed his son, Jamie, from Spurs and bought Olivier Bernard and Henri Camara. He started playing Peter Crouch regularly and helped to make him the player he is. Crouchy was a great lad who had signed that pre-season after a rough time at Aston Villa but wasn't being regularly used. The day he signed, we were in Austria on a pre-season tour. I was sharing a room with Matt Oakley and when we woke up from a pre-match sleep one afternoon, he had a text message on his mobile from a mate. 'Who's going to walk the giraffe,' it said. We knew Crouchy must have signed.

Harry did everything he could but we just couldn't get out of the relegation zone. He did his best to take the pressure off us. Under him, training became fun and enjoyable. He gave us hope. I always had Harry down as some sort of incredible coach, some master tactician, some guru who had a great secret, but he's none of those things, really. He's more like Kevin Keegan. He's more about motivation, more about making the players feel good, making them feel wanted and valued. I'm not denigrating him – far from it. It's just that he wasn't what I expected. I had misinterpreted him.

The kind of thing Harry would do was take us down to Bournemouth to the spa so we could get a change of scenery and spend some time away from the training ground. He promoted the idea that he would do anything for us if we won, a real players' manager. When he was at West Ham, I had him down as a Terry Venables type with a great attention to detail and all sorts of coaching tips. He wasn't that. Again, I am not casting aspersions on him but it did surprise me. It was difficult for him to turn the ship around. Events had taken over by then and the momentum was against us. It was incredibly pressured because it was the first time I had been involved in a relegation battle. I felt the weight of expectation was on me in particular because I was one of the most experienced players there. I wanted to use my experience to make a difference and influence my team-mates. I wanted to help save us but I couldn't and I beat myself up about that.

The last few weeks of the season, the last few weeks of my career, were utter mayhem. The relegation struggle was like a series of bloody battles. It was like nothing I had ever known before. Chelsea won the title comfortably that season. They had it all wrapped up with a few games to spare just as Jose Mourinho had predicted they would. My old club had won its first title for fifty years and here I was trying to stop my new club sliding out of the top flight for the first time in almost thirty years. It was quite a contrast. With the title sewn up, everyone's attention switched to a savage relegation battle that involved four teams still trying to claw their way to safety: Southampton, West Brom, Norwich City and Crystal Palace.

On the first day of May, we had a titanic battle with Norwich. We beat them 4–3 at St Mary's in a game that swung one way and then the other. I got a goal, my first of the season, and it was 3–3 at half-time. Camara got the winner a few minutes from the end and we staggered on towards another six-pointer with Crystal Palace at Selhurst Park. That game wasn't just a fight metaphorically – it was a bruising brawl of a game. Crouchy was sent off thirteen minutes into the second half when he lashed out after Tony Popovich had chopped him down. I went steaming in to try and stop the trouble but it looked as if I was trying to make things worse and everything kicked off. There was a mass fracas involving most of the players and at the end of it the referee showed the red card to Crouchy and Popovich.

It was 1–1 at that stage and soon after the sending-off, Harry substituted me. The game was on the brink of anarchy by then so he probably did me a favour. I was followed to the touchline by a deafening chorus of boos. They're never slow to tell you quite how much they despise you at Selhurst Park and they can get pretty close to you there. I thought Palace had won it when Nicola Ventola put them 2–1 up in the closing stages but then Danny Higginbotham equalized with two minutes to go and we knew that if we defeated Manchester United at St Mary's on the last day of the season, we had a good chance of beating the drop. It was such a tantalizing thought. I didn't want my career to end with a relegation and Jamie Redknapp was equally desperate to avoid it, too. He had an extra stake in striving for our escape because he wanted to help drag his dad out of the mire.

All sorts of conspiracy theories started to do the rounds in the days leading up to the United game. Everyone knew Fergie and Harry were mates and people speculated that maybe United would field a weakened team. They had already lost the title to Chelsea so there was one line of reasoning that suggested they wouldn't be particularly up for a feral scrap at St Mary's. They were also due to play Arsenal in the FA Cup Final the following weekend. We tried not to take too much notice of all the whispers but as that final Sunday of my career beckoned, it was tempting to believe that we would have the edge in desire and that that might help to rescue us at a minute to midnight.

In the end, they rested Cristiano Ronaldo, Gary Neville, Paul Scholes and Roy Keane. That was nice, but it wasn't particularly encouraging to see Wayne Rooney's name on the team-sheet half an hour before the kick-off. Ruud van Nistelrooy's was there, too. We went out and gave it everything, though. The atmosphere was great. The club had even enlisted the Town Crier to try to wind them up before the game began. After ten minutes, with the adrenalin coursing through us, we got a corner. I swung it in with pace, Higginbotham flicked it past Roy Carroll and when it rebounded off Nigel Quashie's chest, it cannoned into John O'Shea's knee and crept into the goal. We were ahead and, at that point, we were safe.

For a few fleeting moments, it seemed as if we might cut loose and give ourselves a two-goal cushion. Jamie ran onto a pass and took the ball round Carroll and his cross only just eluded Brett Ormerod in the middle. It was a brief window of hope, though. Our defence had, after all, conceded twenty-four goals in its previous nine games, and eight minutes after we scored, United drew level when Darren Fletcher headed the ball past Niemi. Now it was all United and I had to clear off the line from O'Shea. It was all we could do to keep them at bay until half-time.

Soon after the interval, West Brom took the lead against Portsmouth at The Hawthorns, a state of affairs that would send us down if things remained the same. The United fans made absolutely sure we knew that their former hero, who was now the West Brom manager, was about to kick us through the trap door. 'There's only one Bryan Robson', they yelled gleefully and we began to sense the end was near. Soon after that, van Nistelrooy ran onto a cross from Alan Smith and stuck another header into our net. We were finished. And I was finished. I had got to the point where I could only really give sixty or seventy minutes and then I was spent. It was the same against United. I lasted seventy-one minutes and then Harry substituted me with Rory Delap. It was all over.

When the final whistle went, I felt devastated. I was confronted with the final realisation that we were down and that there was nothing I could do about it any more. I had an overwhelming sense of failure and of having let down a great bunch of fans. I didn't feel any poignancy for myself, just for the club. Norwich and Palace went down with us. West

Brom stayed up. I saw some of the scenes of celebration from The Hawthorns on the television later and they brought a lump to my throat. I saw the league table, too. We had finished rock bottom. I knew I was lucky to have been able to choose the timing of my retirement rather than have someone else choose it for me but at that moment, staring up at the rest of the Premiership on the last day of my career, I didn't feel very lucky at all.

TWELVE

Into the Mist

I knew it was time to go. I'd known for some time. Emotionally, I wanted to carry on playing but if I'd tried to get another contract somewhere, it wouldn't have been for the right reasons. I would have been doing it just to stay in the environment I had been used to for the previous eighteen years. Given that I'd spent a lot of that time yearning to develop other interests, it would have been an admission of failure if I'd tried to warm myself on the embers of my career at a football outpost – it would have been a signal that I didn't have the courage to confront life outside the football bubble.

The thing is, football was not just about playing a match. That was the easy bit. Playing on Saturday was about enjoyment, the bit I felt very comfortable about. The problem was the rest of the professional package. It was taking longer to recover from games, and the need for medical treatment meant I was having to adapt my training programme, sometimes missing out on training with the rest of the team. My preparation for games was being affected and I realized that this would be ongoing.

There was also the health aspect. Professional sport is not good for you. It's damaging to your body, and inevitably you end up with arthritic joints. I've been fortunate: I've had one very bad ankle injury but otherwise no major problems with my fitness. I've worked hard at it and I've always been fit even compared to other players. That sustains you through various parts of your career, but I was thirty-six at the end of that second season with Southampton and my wife had started to notice me struggling to get downstairs on a Sunday morning. I've two young children and football had been so good to me over the years that I didn't want to spoil it.

Of course, I've missed the game – aspects of it, anyway. I miss the adrenalin rushes, certainly. I miss that feeling of turning to the crowd after I'd scored a goal or put in a decent cross as if to say 'Look what I've done'. I miss the rush when you run out into the stadium. I miss playing big matches that are a real pleasure to be involved in. I have played in massive games where I have been so in control on that pitch and that gives you a real feeling of power and achievement.

I still feel my life is in transition. There's an anxiety I have felt since I stopped playing. I have lost the security that came with being enveloped in the game. As a player, I didn't have to think too much for myself. It was a bit like being in the army, I suppose. I had to work hard but everything was organized for me, nothing was left to chance. I had a regular routine. I knew what I was doing every day, what my schedule would be every week to the hour, often to the minute. I knew what matches were coming up, when my day off would be, when we would be warming down, when we would be travelling out, when we would be travelling back. I loved that as much as I hated it. I used to fight to carve out my own time within that routine but it did give my life structure. I could tell you when I was going to have a day off in December by the beginning of September. I could tell you what I'd be doing at Christmas when the fixtures were announced in July. There is something comforting about that even if it is frustrating.

I still feel anxious because I'm busy some weeks and quiet others. Part of me still wants a steady structure, a regular stream of something to work on – then I wouldn't have to think too much about my finances. It doesn't matter if it's a small amount or a lot as long as you know what you are working with. In football, you get instant gratification from your efforts on the pitch. Life on the outside is a bit different. The work and preparation you do, the ideas you put forward, might lead to something and then they might not. Every few months, I sit down with my adviser, Richard Thompson, and see where we are at. I haven't decided on anything yet. I don't think 'This is what I need to go and be'. I am doing lots of things and I am hoping that they will guide me. I want to create my own niche.

Surprisingly enough, given all the angst that I felt early on in my career in particular, I do miss the team camaraderie and the relationships that you form within a club. You are in it together and you go through the good times and the bad. They are equally benefiting. You rely on other people to help you as they rely on you to help them. I have always liked that even if, in my first spell at Chelsea, I couldn't exactly feel the love around me. I have always wanted to be a support to other people. I felt like I was a motivator within the team. If someone was having a hard time, I would try and lift them up. When I went onto the pitch, I would talk to the people around me and egg them on a bit. I started to get into the roles of club captain and PFA rep and I enjoyed that responsibility.

There are, however, things I haven't missed. In fact, mostly I have felt a great sense of liberation about not being a football player any more. I did feel a release. It was a relief not to be abused by the crowd every time I ran out onto the pitch; a relief to know that every time I drew attention to myself by doing something good or bad that I wouldn't have to pay the penalty of listening to chants about my supposed sexual proclivities. Funnily enough, I don't pine for that. I hated steeling myself for a game and having to get fired up because I knew what I was going to have to deal with from the supporters. I don't miss having to make myself feel really anxious and on edge to get psyched up for a game.

I wouldn't play again. If someone said 'You can play for another couple of years' I would say 'No'. I could have done that and earned more money than I am earning now but it would have stopped me moving on. A lot of people told me I was mad to stop but I knew it was the right decision. I look at the game and I feel it's changed even since I left it. It's like a revolving door and when it's over, you are flipped straight out of it. It doesn't take long at all to feel totally alienated from the dressing room. I experienced that when I had long-term injuries. You feel very isolated during that period: you are not suffering with the team; you are not winning with the team.

I went to Stamford Bridge in September 2006 to do a walkabout on the pitch at half-time of the Champions League match against Werder Bremen and to be introduced to the crowd. It was lovely to be out on the pitch, waving to the fans and trying to show them how much affection I felt towards them but I saw the guys before the game and I found it a bit embarrassing. I worried a bit about what the players were thinking. Sometimes, it feels as if they're looking at you and thinking 'You're not part of this any more'. Maybe, subconsciously, that's the way I felt when I saw ex-players around our dressing room.

When I see the lads that I know – JT and Frank and Carlo – they are all very open-armed about it. When I see Jose Mourinho, he says 'You belong to this club'. But I would never turn up unannounced and watch training, much as I would love to. I was with Steve Clarke in January and he said to me that I should come down, but I think that's when you start to miss the game.

I have always had the ability to move on in my life. I see the past as the past. Playing football is over for me so it would almost make it worse to surround myself with football again. I want to be in control. If I am involved officially, that's a different matter, but I don't want people to think I can't let go of being a footballer.

I don't think I'm really interested in going into coaching or management. I like the idea of being qualified and doing my coaching badges but I don't like the reality of the time that would entail quite as much. At the moment, I do not see myself getting back into football full time. I threw myself into football and now I have come out the other side. As a player, I put certain other aspects of my life on hold and I'm excited about those other parts of my life more than I am about giving myself back to football. There are other things that I have prioritized.

If I wanted to be a successful manager, football would become all-consuming again and that would be to the detriment of my family. I would be totally obsessed with it if I went into management. It would probably ruin other aspects of my life, including my family, and I'm not prepared to do that. I put loads of things on hold as a player which I was more than happy to do but if I got into management seriously, I would be thinking about the psychology of players, how to get the best out of them, who to sign, who to get rid of, all the time. And I still wouldn't have the reward of playing. Ultimately, it's a job that is never finished – there is no rest.

The only thing that nags away at me is the opportunity to apply how you see the game. I have strong opinions about the game and I love the idea of moulding a group of players into a winning unit. I would apply myself. I would work on the details, which I think is a big part of the job. But I would rather work with young players, a group that you know will be together for a period of time. I'd like to mould their mentality as well as their football skills and then see how they progressed. I'd want to grow something from the roots up rather than have the pressure of dealing with established players.

The challenges that football faces in this country both excite me and concern me. We have a top strata of players earning huge amounts of money in the premier division. Even taking a wider sweep of the lower divisions, average players can be on up to £1 million annually. What is the basis of these payments? We have small clubs going into administration and others struggling to survive. The debt that football carries is huge – if the money disappears tomorrow, what happens? The global interest in football has attracted exorbitant amounts of television money. The creation of the Premiership caused more of a divide, an elite set of clubs that abide by their own set of rules. What is their duty of care to the sport? I think it is important to create a more inclusive system of governance where the long-term good of football is the priority.

The FA should manage the sport better – its decision-making has been too traditionally structured in the past. At the top end of the game, we need a more qualified department within the FA to take care of the Premiership and the England team. One-size-fits-all doesn't always work in football. The current FA set-up can't keep up with the changing game; the West Ham situation is a classic example of the failing of the system.

An area where the authorities should be more proactive is in developing our own home-grown young players. Foreign imports have helped change the game for the good in this country. I would always support players coming to this country from abroad. But there comes a point when you question what's happening to our young talent. It is worrying that in the current climate, clubs find it more financially beneficial to scour the European youth academies for the best young players. The likes of Arsene Wenger and Rafa

Benitez do this all the time. I think there should be a monitoring system, perhaps an age limit below which clubs should be restricted from bringing in foreign players.

There must come a point when it is detrimental to the England side. The presence of technically-gifted overseas stars makes our home-grown players better. But are our best English players only great when surrounded by the top foreign players at club level? What happens when they are put into the England setup with less technically accomplished players? Last season Wayne Rooney played some sublime football for Man Utd when surrounded by the likes of Cristiano Ronaldo and Henrik Larsson. And yet on the international stage, he was often invisible for England.

At international level, I came through the Under-21s and played several B internationals before making my full debut. Those B games were important in giving less-experienced players the platform on which to perform. I certainly benefited from the experience. I believe friendlies are also important to provide continuity so shouldn't be devalued. After all, it still means an England cap, something to be proud of. I enjoyed the camaraderie of the England get-togethers, although I found tournaments a long haul, occasionally monotonous and mind-numbing. But it's worse for the fringe players. Then, running and training to keep fit felt like corporal punishment. I'm a great supporter of families being allowed to accompany players to international tournaments to provide some form of normality. In Germany at the last World Cup, the so-called WAGS were in my opinion unfairly targeted by the media; the reality is they were harmless and didn't distract the players, but became a huge news item when the team itself underperformed.

I'm often asked who I think would be a natural successor to the England job after Steve McClaren. If it's a young British manager, then Martin O'Neill would be my favourite. For the best foreign manager, someone of Scolari's stature would do a good job. Above all, it needs to be someone who excites the players – like Terry Venables in his day – and a motivator who has charisma and refined man-management skills.

I certainly found playing at international level very different from club football. International football is more measured, but when England play they tend to fall into the trap of trying to mimic the European style of play. Instead, they should stick to their strengths, play an English-style pressing game and get stuck in man-for-man, especially against the weaker teams, and be more thoughtful and disciplined against better sides. Our problem is we change our mindset when playing international football. It's interesting to look at another aspect of the England team and its lack of recent success. Footballers from the likes of France and the Scandinavian countries such as Sweden and Denmark spend a lot of their careers playing abroad. When they return home to play for their national teams there's a natural team spirit and a camaraderie at those get-togethers. That togetherness is often missing from the English players, most of whom play for English club sides, kick lumps out of each other week-in week-out, then have to play alongside each other in the international team. The England situation is not unlike that of Spain – most of their international squad ply their trade at home, but they have also underperformed in World Cups and European Championships.

I've always said that football acts as a mirror to society. Thatcher's Britain of the 1980s, the rise of the City, Britpop, Europeanisation, the celebrity culture thing – all these facets of British society came to be reflected on the pitch, with the game acting as a microcosm of the world outside. I was proud to be part of that changing culture in the game. The things I learned from my playing days are as relevant today, and I find can be put to good use, as when I first started out as a professional footballer.

At first, I thought life after football would be a career in punditry and commentary with the BBC. Maybe subconsciously I thought that would soften the fall, that it would be a kind of halfway house – that I'd be involved without being involved. I worked hard at it. I was keen to learn a new trade. I was co-presenting a Sunday afternoon show on Five Live and then appearing that evening on *Match of the Day 2*. Sometimes, I'd do *Football Focus* on Saturday morning and *Match of the Day* on Saturday night as well, which meant being in the studio all day Saturday. On the international scene, I was trialled as a television co-commentator for the Northern Ireland–Poland match, and the feedback from the BBC on my performance was very positive. As a result of that, I had to scale down my radio commitments and began taking on televised games involving England.

I enjoyed it all – up to a point. I was looking forward to going to the World Cup in the summer of 2006 and I had been promised that I would be working on England games as an analyst with John Motson. There was no written contract as such, just a verbal agreement and schedule between myself and Niall Sloane, the BBC's head of football. I found this lack of a contract somewhat surprising, but their commitment to me was crystal clear. At least that's what I thought.

A couple of months before the tournament was due to begin, I got my travel schedule through and the itinerary confirmed that I would be following England around in Germany. Then four days later, Niall rang me and asked me to come in for a meeting. When I got there, he told me things had changed. He said he had decided they needed the experience of Mark Lawrenson on the England broadcasts and that I would be assigned to other matches. I was absolutely stunned. I pointed out that he was reneging on a promise. He was unmoved.

When Niall had first approached me to be the BBC's main analyst on England games, he gave me a long list of reasons why he was picking me. He said I was English, I was young, I'd played against all the players I would be talking about and I'd played in a World Cup. Mark Lawrenson hadn't done any of those things. His main reason now for picking Lawrenson was that he was more experienced than me but he'd always been more experienced than me – nothing had changed there. More to the point, Lawro didn't fit any of the criteria they had given me for the role in the first place. I have nothing against Lawro, but the whole thing felt to me as if it was about more than going back on his word. How could I be sure something else wasn't going to change in the weeks leading up to the tournament?

I told Niall that I didn't feel comfortable working in an environment where someone was so cavalier with their decisions and I walked out. I felt there was no alternative but to leave. As far as I was concerned, it was a total breakdown of trust.

It came as a complete shock when I discovered that news of my exit had found its way to the *Daily Mirror* within hours. Apparently I had stormed out of the meeting in a huff and walked out on the BBC. How I could have 'stormed out' when I was taking the lift down to the ground floor (stamping my feet on the way down, perhaps?) stretches credulity beyond belief.

I did some work with Eurosport instead during the World Cup and was based in Paris. In a way, the BBC situation did me a favour because it forced me to diversify and move into other areas of broadcasting away from football. I went back to Jersey to film an item about life on the island for BBC2's *Working Lunch* series and I presented the programme myself some time later when Adrian Chiles was away. I've really enjoyed working on the programme and have had tremendous support from the *Working Lunch* team. I also do some corporate work and motivational speeches for the international bank ABN AMRO.

Then, in November 2006, I got involved in a project that was about as far removed from the sheltered life of a pampered footballer as it was possible to be – in Rwanda. ITV approached me about taking part in their show *Extinct*. Its aim was to highlight the fight to protect some of the most endangered species in the world. Eight celebrities were approached to explain why eight particular species were in danger and what could be done to help save them. I was chosen to represent the mountain gorilla.

I was very enthusiastic about the project, partly because as a teenager I had worked at the Durrell Wildlife Trust in Jersey. One of my friends is Head of Primates so I was able to spend time with the West Lowland gorillas that live in the park. Durrell have a very successful captive breeding programme as well as training programmes for foreign students who live in countries that provide the habitat for the most endangered species. When I was working there in my teens, I was studying A-level biology. Later on, I started a degree in environmental studies. So, if you took football out of the equation, my other interests were leading me towards conservation.

So I jumped at ITV's offer which meant spending ten days in Rwanda where the world's 720 remaining mountain gorillas live in their natural habitat. I was apprehensive about the trip because of the perceptions I held about the country and the possibility that the genocide might still be close to the surface in people's minds, there was also the idea that the place was somehow anti-Western.

As it happens there was nothing to be nervous about. In fact, it was an amazing place with amazing people. For the first two days, I spent every minute looking at people acknowledging they had been touched by the genocide. I had a heavy heart for them but I soon realized that they don't want you to feel sorry for them – they just want to move on and get on with their lives. Although there are museums and areas where there are mass graves that have been made into official memorials there is so much energy and so much beauty there.

The gorillas live in a national park in a volcanic mountain range called the Virunga Massive on the border with the

Democratic Republic of Congo and Uganda. The scenery was spectacular. It was comparable to the scenery in the Lake District. It was the rainy season so everything was very lush and suddenly I felt I was doing something I really wanted to do.

The first time I saw the gorillas, I sensed I was completing this journey I had begun in Jersey when I was sixteen. Seeing animals in captivity and then seeing them in their own habitat with no barriers separating you and no protection. The first time I saw them, I wasn't scared but deeply emotional. Apparently, that kind of reaction is not uncommon. It is overwhelming seeing the majesty of nature so close.

The trip opened my eyes to other things, too. The poverty was shocking. I knew it would be. But I was struck by the interaction between the people and the environment, something that we have largely lost in developed countries. Every piece of land in Rwanda seemed to be used for agriculture of some kind, right to the peaks of the tallest hills.

We spent a day with a local family, trying to live as they do. We provided them with a small amount of money to buy potatoes, firewood and water. There's a temptation to give them money. If I had given the family we stayed with £100, it would have changed their lives but it would also have isolated them from the rest of their community and left them feeling very awkward. This direct generosity creates more problems than it solves.

In the village, there was a troublemaker who accused the family we were staying with of accepting money from us. It wasn't true but our family got into trouble locally because they hadn't given this imaginary money to the community.

Eventually, we sent representatives to assure everyone that that was nonsense. So the troublemaker got into trouble himself.

Rwanda made me appreciate how important the basic necessities are in life – food, water and shelter – and what lengths people have to go to just to get them. Every step I took made me think about how complicated our lives are in the west because our concerns revolve around the material side of life and how we take the essentials for granted.

Rwanda was a fantastic example of the interaction between people and animals and their inter-dependence. The gorillas rely on the people to protect them but the people rely on the gorillas, too, because they bring tourists to the country. Their experiences help to spread the word that the country is safe again and in turn more people will come and bring income with them.

If the quality of life for the local population is better, there is less pressure on them to go into the park in search of wood, bushmeat or water.

On my return, I gave a presentation at my children's school to raise money to support the Rwanda project. We live a very privileged life and a lot of children aren't aware of how other people live in the world. Conservation will become a much bigger issue for our children. In fact, I expect it will appear on the National Curriculum before too long. Maybe that means they'll pursue it a little earlier than I did. Maybe they won't let their interest get interrupted for eighteen years.

As a result of that trip, I have recently been working with the World Wildlife Fund as a spokesperson for the Amazon

Keystone Initiative to help bring together the nine countries that make up Amazonia, in order to protect it from further destruction. It's a huge privilege for me to be involved in such a large-scale conservation project, and it gives me the chance to contribute to something that I wholeheartedly believe in.

I don't know exactly what I'll end up doing but it feels good to be branching out. It feels good to be thinking about other people and other issues. A footballer's life can be a selfish, introspective life, totally subservient to preparing for and playing the game. Now, even if there's uncertainty in my life, even if I've lost that rhythm that dominated my existence for so long, I've got time to breathe again.

I've got time to think about my mum and analyse properly for the first time the effect her death has had on me. I've got time to look around me, time to branch out, time for my family, time for new challenges. There is little I would change. Even if it was a hard road, football was unbelievably good to me. It continues to bring opportunities I would never have had if I had lived another life. But now that it's over, I feel free again. I feel in the midst of an awakening.

Acknowledgements

I am eternally grateful to my family: Mariana, who has constantly re-read the manuscript, and Georgina and Lucas for their patience when Daddy couldn't play because he was 'working' on the book.

My father, Pierre, and sisters Jeanette and Alison were extremely supportive in helping me feel comfortable enough to write about mum. Mariana's parents Eduardo and Elba were unstinting in their advice and help with the book.

Susie Griffin, a dear friend, spent many hours reading and commenting on the original draft, while Jamie Jarvis came up with the original concept for the title. Chelsea historian Rick Glanvill shared his encyclopaedic knowledge of the club with me and checked the details of some of my early appearances. Richard Thompson, my friend and agent, turned the idea of writing a book into a reality.

Thanks to the HarperCollins publishing team, and Tom Whiting in particular, for giving me the platform to share my story.

To Yoda and the council, thanks for keeping me away from the dark side of the force.

Finally, and by no means an afterthought, a huge thanks to Oliver Holt who I've known since my career first began and whose skill has helped put the book together. I hope it was as enjoyable for you as it was for me.

Index

Index

Index